Forgotten
ORIGIN
OUT OF AUSTRALIA THEORY

Between a Rock and
a Hard Place:

THE OUT OF AUSTRALIA THEORY

By Steven and Evan Strong

D1615284

Published by Steven & Evan Strong, 2016, Australia

Website: http://forgottenorigin.com/
Email: stevenevanstrong@gmail.com
Phone: 61 026281749
Face book: https://www.facebook.com/Steven-and-Evan-Strong-198880073472926/
YouTube: https://www.youtube.com/channel/UCJP-0DDjOa9hsE2-bC_VZBA

ISBN: 978-0-9945268-0-9

ISBN EBOOK: 978-0-9945268-1-6

A CiP record for this title is available from the National Library of Australia.
Dewey Number: 299.9215

First edition, 2016

Author: Steven & Evan Strong
Title: Between a Rock and a Hard Place
Subjects: history/cultural studies/archaeology/anthropology/geology/genetics

Also by Steven & Evan Strong:

Shunned: The Hidden History Of Australia's Originals

Ancient Aliens in Australia:
Pleiadian Origins of Humanity (With Bruce & Daniella Fenton)

Forgotten Origin

Mary Magdalene's Dreaming:
A Comparison of Aboriginal wisdom & Gnostic Scriptures

Constructing a New World Map

Typesetting and design: Erica Schmerbeck

PRAISE AND REVIEWS:

"I thoroughly enjoyed reading this manuscript and I feel so proud that I am a part of the Aboriginal people in our country. I have travelled pretty widely in Europe and I know I shouldn't, but I compare them to our Aboriginal people and culture and while they have technology and all the trappings, I couldn't wait to get home again. They say that home is where the heart is and mine is well and truly in my Nyoongar land. The more I read your books, the more I want to thank you both for the research you carried out. It is spot on and just reading about Professor Slater and his willingness to accept that The Original ancients through his research, were the first human sapiens sapiens is mind boggling. It is also sad that the Australian government and academia cannot accept Aboriginal people but continue to have that conspiracy of silence surrounding ancient Original history. But that's typical of this country. They want to believe that this is a white country but they're mistaken. This can never be a white country. The ancients spirits and the spirits of our old people are with us all the time. Anyway thank you for letting me read it."

Associate Professor
Rosemary Van Den Berg

"Original people of Australia, since the arrival of the Europeans, have been thought of as a backward primitive culture, long forgotten by the passage of time. They did not live in cities or build stone monuments – the true sign of a civilized society. Steven and Evan Strong in their eye-opening book, *Between A Rock And A Hard Place*, bring new light to this first culture. They expose secrets that have long been suppressed regarding this mysterious indigenous nation and bring forward a controversial, yet thrilling new look at the progression of civilization on the Earth."

Rita Louise, PhD
Author of ET Chronicles: What Myth And Legend Tell Us About Humanity

---

"When I first uncovered the lost Slater documents from Brunswick Valley's Historical Society's museum in Mullumbimby, I was astounded that such a momentous discovery had lain dormant nigh over 70 years. A little searching brought me to Steven and Even Strong. Having seen their proven dedication and painstaking work in recovering the true lost history of Australia, I knew that I had found the rightful people to hand over the bright torch of truth. My hope then was that this duo would continue Slater's work. 'Between a Rock and a Hard Place' is the brilliant outcome. It is filled with insights of the first people, unrelenting honest portrayals of the political and cultural difficulties we face. It is a testament to good archeology and scientific accuracy. I am certain in this volume the Strong's have not only produced the most concise and accurate history of the mounds, they themselves have made history. They have brought us one step closer to understanding the origins of humanity."

Richard Patterson
Historian and Author

"Wow what an amazing testimony. Such an absorbing blend of historical, geological and archaeological evidence supported by Original spirituality and knowledge! Slater's fervour and intelligence in researching this amazing site is very clear, even from what little remains of his documentation. (I often scour through the archives at the RRHS/ museum just in case I am lucky enough to come across any more random pages of his notes). Your examination of the anomalies within conventional history are certainly compelling, and your passion for knowledge and truth is extremely contagious!!! I was so happy to see mention of Prof. Mike Morwood in your research. He was my lecturer at uni many moons ago when I studied Archaeology and Palaeoanthropology. He and I spent a lot of time together on many engraving sites in Sydney and other areas of Central Qld ... Thank you for mentioning his research, he was an amazing man!! Thank you also for the honour of reading your book before publication, I am very humbled. Good luck with it all, and keep me in mind if you ever need any assistance with anything! Cheers "

Belinda Rich
BA Archaeology/ Palaeoanthropology & MA History

"As I came to the last words in this book I had a picture in my mind of a thousand scattered bricks and blocks from where the child had swept the original creation aside in play. But then comes the gathering, and just like the coming together of evidence in this book, the shape of the creation begins to emerge again. In this case, the gathering is a compelling vision of how our earliest history is embedded to the continent of Australia. The studious examination of the scattered pieces as they are brought together gives strength to some words used herein: *"how far we have fallen."*

Evan and Steve take the reader through a learned dissection of factual evidence which has proved all too inconvenient for the establishment as they continue to pretend it is not there. Comprehensive descriptions emerge from many 'sacred' iron stones that have been discovered and from their potential meanings. Between this and the preceding research it is clear that the weight of validation can only build and build. Our discipline relates to the sophisticated ancient illustrations on their surfaces which are denied to normal vision. These have been identified at Kariong and even more spectacularly elsewhere on the continent, and their generic style has been carried far afield to other continents.

A big well done for this valuable addition."

Richard Gabriel & Judith Ann
Author Echoes from The Chamber and researchers

"This book is very well written and as riveting as "Shunned"... the Bosnian Rock connection to Australia is very interesting."

Cecilia Hall
Researcher USOKS

"Between the Rock and the hard spot there is an explosive amount of information that absolutely blows holes in the Out of Africa theory..."

Bob Newton
Author, Researcher and USOKS Founder

"A Facinating and well researched piece of work. My admiration and respect to all involved."

Anne Newton
Co-Founder of USOKS, Author and independent researcher

For The Reader:

- As previously stated on cover - *WARNING: To peoples of Australia (Ab)Original and Torres Strait Island descent this book contains the names and images of deceased people*

- The word Aboriginal / (Ab)Original is replaced with the word Original to describe the Indigenous Peoples of Australia.

- Surnames of deceased Australia Original Elders, Custodians and peoples are with-held to observe protocols of respect and culture.

- Other names have been changed to ensure the security and safety of some of our sources.

Dedication:

The Sign of Times

For I must thank my Ramindjeri Spirit
For my Mother the earth and I love her soul

My Father the wind was born free
Just like the air that we still breath

My Sister the moon who can guide me through

And my Brother the sun who shines upon me

And my loved one the water
Who shall always be there
When needed the most

We live together as if we are one

You fellas out there
You still can learn
The secrets from the Old Ones

Karno Walker

Photo credits: Courtesy of Christine Walker and the Ramindjeri People, Photo by Olivia Olley, Graphics by Brett Waller

THE SIGN OF TIMES

For I must thank my Ramindjera Spirit
For my Mother earth and I love her soul
My Father the wind was born free
Just like the air that we breath
My Sister the moon who can guide me through
And my Brother the sun who shines upon me
And my loved one the water
Who shall always be there
When needed the most
We live together as if we are one
You fellas out there
You still can learn
The secrets from the old ones

Acknowledgements:

Dellene Strong: for being awesome, supportive and putting up with us.

Juanita Otto, Rosemary van den Berg and Ildi Budai: for proof reading and editing.

Erica Schmerbeck: for cover and book design and type-setting.

Ros Mulder: for her tireless generosity, collecting and research of the Marked Rocks.

Richard Patterson and Samarah Wood: for cover images.

Samarah Wood: for fantastic photos of the marked rocks.
(Figures: 33, 36, 37, 38, 40, 41, 42, 45, 46, 47)

Erik Bower and Richard Patterson: for their incredibly essential research.

Natalie Jacqueline Paez (Figures: 60, 61, 63, 64, 66), **Richard Patterson** (Figures: 9, 10, 11, 15, 21): for fabulous photos, images and graphics.

Jan Scherpenhuizen: thanks for being the editor of our previous books Shunned (and Publisher), Constructing a New World Map and Mary Magdalene's Dreaming.

John Gionni Di Gravo: kind thanks for the use of the Photo (Figure 76). **Maxwell Museum of Anthropology archives:** many thanks for the use of the photo (figure 79).

Karno, Aunty Beve, Uncle Marbuck and Uncle Gerry: Our Elders & Custodians of Lore who have passed. **Christine Walker, Daren McElroy, Uncle Reg, Brendan Murray, Aunty Minnie , David Fitzgerald, Rob and Gloria Williams, Kevin Boota, Jarmbi'je, Iris Nunn:** our Original custodians, guides and friends. **Richard Clarke & Robyn Brown:** our patrons.

Binnah Pownall, Dermot Kelly, Duncan Roads (Nexus), Kosta Srbinoff, Mark Funda, Darrin Cooper, Mark Pearce, Dylan Wood and Valentino: for touring organisation and help. **Bruce Fenton:** for online/website, indie publishing help, design and advice. **Professor X & Dr Derek Cunningham:** for technical analysis, consultation, advice and support concerning the Marked Rocks. **Trina Barnes, Bob and Anne Newton and the USOKS team, Klaus Dona, Nina Angelo, Sean Vandenberg, Shane Curl and Lavinia Smith Lewis:** for general help, support and being sounding boards.

Rosemary van den Berg, Dr Rita Louise, Cecilia Hall, Richard Patterson, Belinda Rich, Richard Gabriel and Judith Ann, Bob and Anne Newton: Our reviewers, thanks for your time and feedback. **Our donators and supporters:** we can't thank you all enough. To the scores of friends, supporters, readers and audience members from our talks we are grateful and humbled by your interest in our work.

Contents:

Introduction

This books picks up where *Shunned* [1] left off. With a solid theoretical base in science, archaeology, history and religious texts established in our previous book, now is the time to move out into the local countryside and focus upon one sacred site and an ever-expanding collection of exceptionally unique marked rocks.

Before doing so there are a few loose genetic ends to finalise so that there can be absolutely no residual doubt that the Original people of Australia are indeed the very first *Homo sapiens sapiens*, and it was from Australia, never Africa, that the first ocean-going boats set sail to locations throughout the globe.

With that task completed the time is right to set out into the field and begin our examination of a small sampling from the fifty odd sites/artefacts of which we are familiar. First amongst equals has to be the Standing Stones site (Australia's Stonehenge), which in our opinion is not only the most important site in Australia, but the world! That is a huge call to make and we have no doubt many would find such a declaration a touch outrageous, but they have neither been on site nor had the privilege of reading the notes of the eminent archaeologist who investigated this amazing site.

According to Frederic Slater, who at the time of investigation was the President of the Australian Archaeological Research and Education Society, this was the first temple [2] which contained within "the basis of all knowledge in the beginning, now and to come."[3] It chronicles the First Language[4] ever spoken and provides guidelines for humanity that to this very day have still not been met or understood. In what only adds to the intrigue, the technology used in the construction of the site is supposedly well beyond the embrace of any Original rock, stick and bone tool-kit, and has only been equalled in the last century.

In the same highly advanced technological tradition, the ever-increasing collection of Original marked rocks (that we are custodians of today), was made with the assistance of tools and devices that only now have modern-day equivalents. The ever-present problem is that many of these sacred rocks are thousands of years old. The tools required, the massive temperatures applied, adhesives used and sundry techniques on display, are as ancient as they are without parallel until the last half of the 20th century.

Together, this site and these marked rocks just don't fit into any approved version of the ancient past. Nor do they stand alone, all of the fifty odd sites/artefacts we have investigated fall into the same 'doesn't fit' category. In essence, all the books we have written and the many more patiently sitting on the 'reserve's bench' stand in complete contradiction with mainstream historical accounts. It is our belief that virtually everything written and sanctioned in relation to pre-Cook history in Australia is wrong. From the time the very first British boat sailed up the east coast of Australia, the Original truth was the first casualty of the invasion and all that followed.

So ingrained was the need to deny and belittle, that hours before the Union Jack was illegally raised, the truth was ignored even when it was formally recorded. Cook made note in his diary (Wednesday 22nd August, 1770) that he and the crew saw, "one man who had a bow and a bundle of arrows, the first we have seen on this coast." 5 If so, why is it that such an observation has not been taught or discussed in any text, curriculum or university lecture on Australian history? If Cook's observations of the unexpected appearance of a bow and arrows cannot be officially acknowledged or taught in one primary school classroom, what else has been overlooked, ignored or dismissed? Sadly, the answer is the whole truth and nothing but the Original truth, simply because it is just too sophisticated and inconvenient. With a precedent set and a variety of excuses for an illegal theft of continent concocted, anything that does not conform to an unworthy, primitive stereotype is immediately dismissed. The distortions and omissions have become par for this course and deserve to be acknowledged for what they were and still are, outright lies.

The inevitable double-edged sword that accompanies our attempts to present the Original account of the pre-Cook history, is that even when people begrudgingly concede our evidence is sound and a case for revision has been made, they qualify this admission by asking what is the point of crying over spilt milk? The past is gone and what difference does yesterday's news make today. It just doesn't matter anymore.

At first glance this critique has legs. We are surrounded by modern machines designed to produce goods and services for the marketplace, kill and surveil. All of this is solely there to serve the needs and insecurities of a rapidly escalating population. These gifts are wrapped around layers of fear and competition that is so unlike anything previous and seems to demand new thinking and strategies. But there, past the modern-day trappings, resonates a mantra that all are familiar with, but few fully appreciate: the truth will set you free. We are assured that this current state of mistrust and suspicion is merely the natural state of order. It is an inherent trait of our nature to harbour a competitiveness that often has an aggressive undercurrent.

After all, are we not the outcome of the survival of the fittest? Is it not our destiny to conquer those perceived to be inferior? Such a human template excuses all wars and atrocities and justifies the outlay of over half the global income being spent on warfare and security devices. It appears our fate is to behave like angry global vandals constantly squabbling with each other over inconsequential incidents.

But what if the sky is not the limit and we are more than that? Could it be it was always our destiny to be galactic citizens, but this ancestry was stolen by those who have lost their bearings and contact with the spirit within and Original Sky-Heroes [6] above?

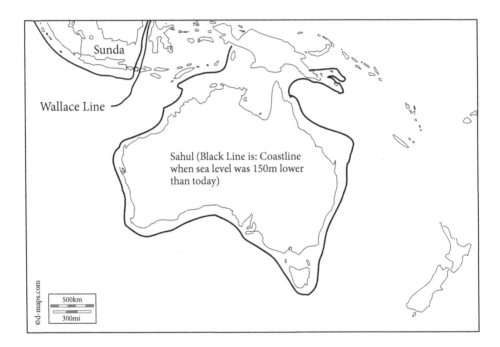

Figure 1: Australia as Sahul (Map) [7]

The archaeology and Original Lore of Australia tell a different story. Spiritual concerns are paramount, and earlier civilisations exhibiting a technology that are considered modern by today's standards, were an integral part of very ancient times in Australia (Sahul[8]). As to whether the Original people saw the inherent flaws in using such devices and made a continental decision to abandon such a lifestyle long ago, or allowed others who came to this land in ancient times to travel down this path is still a question we are unable to definitively answer. It is our suspicion that the choice was made to abandon clothes, buildings and high technology, thus reconnecting with the land and spirits within. But this is as much an intuitive response as it is directed and until authoritative Original guidance on such matters is given, it is still a question yet to be resolved.

What is patently clear is that this blessing from the Original people created a society primarily devoted to spiritual concerns which was underpinned by a co-operative lifestyle steeped in protocol. Clashes between men were restricted to neutral ground and did not involve women, children or the theft of another's land. Each tribal estate remained intact and unpillaged, nothing was stolen and each group had absolute security of tenure. No weapons were made solely to kill humans, and once the battle was complete and grievances resolved, the people went back to daily life without fear of further repercussions. The Shaman, Clever-fella [9] or Wee-un [10] were the mentors; initiation into the secret arts and magic was the mainstay of the tribe and the role they aspired towards.

The secret knowledge that was so treasured in these societies began with the arrival of the Sky-Heroes from the stars. Those truths and testimonials were memorised in Dreaming Stories and set into stone at the Standing Stones site and engraved into a variety of marked rocks we've had the privilege to examine. The problem we face is that the code and language found on these rocks was created at a time when humans were far more intelligent and insightful than the motley rabble which remains today.

The ultimate question, as yet unanswered by either hominid or visitors from many constellations, relates to the reason why the Sky-Heroes came to this distant outpost and felt the need to alter the genetic code of one type of hominid. What made this place of such a pressing concern with so much time, energy and technology spent in creating a semi-improved, but significantly flawed hominid, referred to as *Homo sapiens sapiens*? The answer we believe can be found at the Standing Stones site and engraved into the marked rocks. Regrettably interpreting this arrangement and the engravings is beyond our capacities, to glean anything more than a crude understanding and make a few vague generalisations is the best we can muster on this exceptionally daunting occasion. Be it ever so humble that it's the best we can do, and as meagre as that is, at least it can set the wheels in motion and point in the right direction.

However, do not despair for all is not lost. We know of Original Elders and Keepers of Lore who understand so much more, and it is our hope some meaning and wisdom will be revealed over the next few months.

We feel that there is just enough on offer to set off in the right direction and reach first base. It is our hope that the books that follow will take us further down a path that without question, began in the stars, and in Australia's case is inextricably linked to one constellation: the Pleiades.

Chapter 1

AUSTRALIAN ABORIGINAL HAIR TELLS TWO STORIES OF HUMAN MIGRATION, BUT ONLY ONE IS CORRECT

First up it is time to update and tidy up a few genetic loose ends and examine the results of the most recent scientific research that keeps returning to the same people and geography. The next two chapters follow on from an extensive overview of research in the sciences from our previous books, which all point to humanity beginning in Australia at a time far more ancient than is proposed by the current acceptable theories on human evolution.

Off The Bottom Rung Of The Ladder

Finally the Australian Aboriginal people have been allowed to drag themselves off the bottom rung of the evolutionary pecking order. An article appearing in the *New York Times* (September 22nd, 2012) written by Nicholas Wade, stated that "a lock of hair, collected by a British anthropologist a century ago, has yielded the first genome of an Australian Aborigine."[1] The content within his report seems to summarise both the unexpected findings of this genetic analysis, and equally, a series of unresolved questions, which the researchers openly concede that it does contradict with their central hypothesis.

In the simplest terms, with the genomes of all four races now fully recorded and the numbers crunched, some basic observations can be tendered and the timeline reshuffled. The two youngest races are European and Asian, both believed to be about 40,000 years old, from that point backwards it gets awkward. It may surprise many, but most scientific research is an amalgam of verifiable facts and a sizeable portion of supposition, and it is no different here. In determining whether the Africans or Original race deserves first place on the rostrum, the researchers opted for the current titleholders, but this decision was based on the assumptions of others, not through any personal investigation on site. The researchers suggested that the ancestors of the Original race separated from their African kin 75,000 years ago. Once leaving home base (Africa) they spent considerable time in transit before permanently settling in Australia.

Before examining their incomplete understanding of Original ancestry and the accompanying timeline, there are some glaring ambiguities that demand to be resolved. When reading this report what becomes immediately apparent is a liberal use of qualifiers, "best guesses,"[2] "series of puzzles,"[3] "enigma,"[4] "we can't really put geography in there."[5]

We are of the belief that the second and third sentence of Wade's opening paragraph is pivotal in repositioning the Australian Aboriginal race, and it also highlights two popular assumptions which contain flaws that seriously undermine any attempt to supply "best guesses." [6] It must be pointed out this is not meant to be a critique of either Wade or the scientists involved, as they are merely relying upon the information readily available, which is accepted by nearly all authorities as fact.

Nevertheless, Wade states that, "the Aboriginal genome bolsters genetic evidence showing that once the Aborigine's ancestors arrived in Australia some 50,000 years ago, they somehow kept the whole continent to themselves without admitting any outsiders. The Aborigines are thus direct descendants of the first modern humans to leave Africa without any genetic mixture from other races so far as can be seen at present." [7] Within these two sentences, are what we believe to be two fundamental errors. The first relates to the missing 25,000 years. Once leaving Africa around 75,000 years ago, which is what the researchers claimed did occur, what happened next? The Asians and Europeans are not even on the genetic drawing board for another 35,000 years, so what did these Africans abroad do for so long before sailing to Australia? Where was this time in sightseeing spent? Even less logical is the notion of entry into Australia occurring 50,000 years ago.

One out of Eleven is all we Need

We are aware of eleven sites/artefacts which are all claimed to be much older than the 50,000 years proposed by the Danish researchers. For this conventional entry date into Australia to stand firm, all eleven dates must be wrong, ten out of eleven errors is not enough. Each of these more challenging dates has the backing of highly qualified authorities/Elders, and of course in many instances, but not all, has attracted criticism from equally respected academics. The sites/relics include:

LOCATION	ACTIVITY	DATE
Great Barrier Reef	Fire-Stick Farming	185,000
Jinmium	Tools	175,000
Lake Eyre	Skullcap	135,000
Lake George	Fire-Stick Farming	120,000
Devonport	Rock-engraving	<115,000
Jinmium	Art	75-116,000
Point Richie	Shell Middens	80,000
Panaramittee	Rock-engraving of saltwater Crocodile	75,000
Rottnest Island	Tools	70,000
Lake Mungo	WHL 3 Complete Skeleton	61-65,000
Lake Mungo	WHL 1 Cremated Bones	61,000

Figure 2: Table 1: Eleven Sites with Anomalous Dates [8]

Figure 3:
Site Locations of Anomalous Dates
(Map) [9]

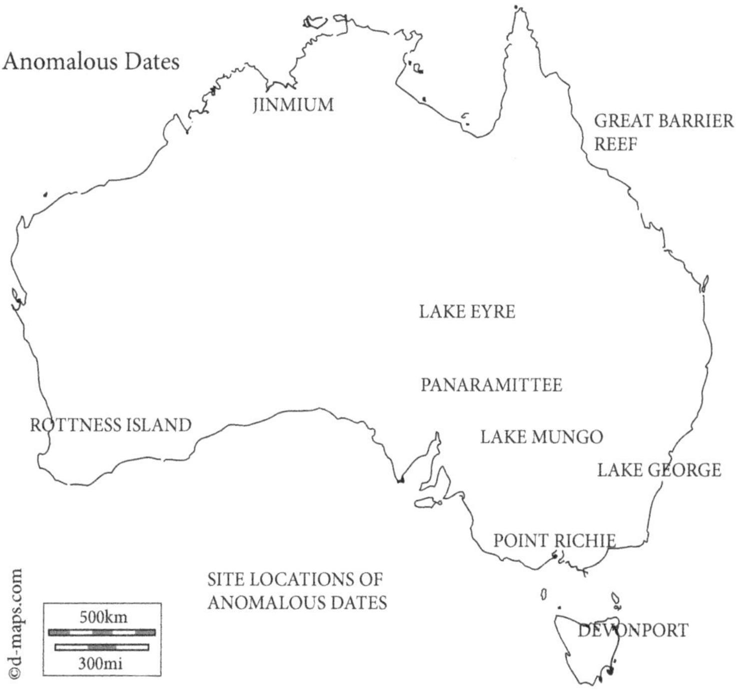

JINMIUM

GREAT BARRIER
REEF

LAKE EYRE

PANARAMITTEE

ROTTNESS ISLAND

LAKE MUNGO

LAKE GEORGE

POINT RICHIE

©d-maps.com

SITE LOCATIONS OF
ANOMALOUS DATES

500km

300mi

DEVONPORT

Rummaging around Home Base

From our perspective the dates attributed to a midden at Moyjil /Point Richie, Victoria, is sufficient in itself to dismiss a fundamental tenet of the Out-of-Africa theory, as it has been mistakenly applied to Australia. Conventional academic wisdom has it that somewhere between 50-60,000 years ago a few adventurous African modern humans, hoisted their sails in the very first boat capable of crossing oceans and soon after set foot in northern Australian. Once settled, being sailors and reliant upon the sea and coast, they kept close to the shore as they sought out new locations in this foreign land. It took close to 20,000 years before reaching the southern sections of Australia, and even longer before making their way inland. So say the accredited academic books and scholars. This means southern extremes like Point Richie, were unoccupied until 40,000 years ago, but the minimum human occupation date in this region is 80,000 years, which is at least double what was assumed to be absolutely set in stone.

The chief researcher (Jim Bowler[10]) of this site is adamant that a date of 80,000 years is valid and we suspect that there is a real possibility it could be older. He conceded that "we have come up with an age of 70,000 to 80,000 for the shells with a preference for the 80,000."[11] We are not sure that his choice of the word "preference"[12] is either genuine or appropriate. Bowler is a staunch advocate of the entry into Australia by Africans, and primarily dismissed Alan Thorne's[13] dates of >60,000 years for Mungo Man 3 simply because it contradicted his expectations of how and when Australia was colonised by Africans.

The problem he now faces is that for African settlers to be ensconced in the far southern reaches of Australia at least 80,000 years ago; the so called entry date has to be recalibrated and extended back to no less than 100,000 years.

What to do? Start again and accept the most recent science or set up the drawbridges and hold fast to the status quo? Bowler chose a popular third option, one many in Australia have opted for previously whenever inconvenient archaeology manages to bubble to the surface and, as before, it seemed to work. Make a very quiet public announcement, downplay the implications and throw in a large dose of caution with a vague promise to do something somewhere in the future, but never be specific as to when this would happen, or supply any plan of action. Knowing that this research is at least two years old, but did not come to our notice until a fortnight ago, made this tactical obfuscation an effective short-term ploy. Bowler advised against making any hasty assumptions, urging all that the "dates and evidence of human activity need to be validated through sustained research." [14]

It all sounds so calm and measured, advising a circumspect approach, but there is a fatal flaw in the recommended protracted time in carefully weighing options seems to span decades. Bowler and the Australian specialist in core extraction, Gurdup Singh [15], along with Peter Ouwendyk, co-wrote a paper in 1983 declaring their unanimous conclusion of the analysis of a core sample taken from the Great Barrier Reef. They were in agreement that the dramatic increase in charcoal in the core extracted from the reef was due to the fire-stick farming initiated by the Original people and that this began 180,000 years ago.

If there was a genuine intention to follow up, is this site not a worthy candidate to compare against? Knowing that there are at least nine other sites in Australia standing in direct opposition to the Out-of-Africa theory, of which eight are dated to be more than sixty thousand years old, Bowler has all but a cricket team full of sites to compare against. The only fact that remains uncontested is that in the two years since this announcement to ruminate and reflect, Bowler has not made any attempt to heed his own advice. But we shouldn't be too harsh on Bowler, as this is the standard practice in Australia and in our experience we would expect no less than a fanatical need to conform.

If still defending the current time of entry and slow spread around the coast, means these Africans arrived at the northern top end of Australia no less than 100,000 years ago. That number is double the arrival date the Danish team took as a fact and 25,000 years before the Original ancestors supposedly first set foot outside of Africa. With no critic of Bowler's science or paper the only conclusion that can be drawn is that the Out-of-Africa theory has been disproven with no room to negotiate.

Obviously many, but not all of these sites/relics have critics, but again our goal is not perfection just anything above 9% is sufficient for our purposes.

Sailing From, Never to, Australia

Another fundamental error in the founding assumptions is the belief that such a boat journey across open water, with enough people aboard to counter in-breeding in subsequent generations if making landfall in an unpopulated location, first took place some 50-60,000 years ago. We believe that this date is far too conservative and proven to be false.

"In 1998 Dr Michael Morwood of the University of New England published the first evidence that some 800 000 years ago *Homo erectus*—our upright but smaller-brained ancestor—had reached the island of Flores, east of Bali, in what is now Indonesia. The new evidence was published in the international scientific journal *Nature*. . . . The dating is reliable - volcanic tuff deposits from above and below indisputable stone artefacts and associated extinct fauna were securely dated by the well-tried and trusted fission-track method."[16]

All theories, until this juncture, awarded the momentous crossing of any part of the ocean separating Australia and Indonesia, to an unidentified group of Africans stationed in Asia who supposedly sailed to Australia. Morwood [17] found that at around 800,000 years ago a far less intelligent species of hominid assumed to be Homo erectus, suddenly appeared on an island that is separated by nineteen kilometres of open water. It seems certain they must have constructed a boat capable of carrying close to twenty people to negate in-breeding. If seaworthy enough to cross nineteen kilometres of sea 800,000 years ago, what if a few alterations and extensions were made to this proto-type over the proceeding hundreds of thousands of years? Could improved versions of this vessel, which would require very few modifications, be capable of carrying the same number of people a little further over the proceeding hundreds of thousands of years? If coming from the north, and future generations were inclined to continue past Flores Island, they would discover the uninhabited island of Timor. Beyond that, if this adventurous tradition was to continue, there are no more Indonesian islands to colonise, but there is one large continent to the south, Antarctica and lots of water. Admittedly this requires these supposedly less intelligent hominids making even more sophisticated alterations and using complex language to inspire, advise and co-operate. Despite the academic angst this may cause, once they set sail to and successfully colonised Flores Island, there is no other viable alternative.

When one considers no academic authority has challenged Morwood's rigour or his dating techniques used, and virtually no publicity or discussion has ensued, it becomes difficult to try and assess the impact of Morwood's announcement. There has been virtually no response from anyone past a deafening indifference. Josephine Flood [18] noted that the greatest problem for all interested in pre-history is that the archaeology at Flores Island is so sound and unchallenged. There is no other alternative but to accept Morwood's finding and then ruminate over the vacuum this acceptance creates.

Owing to the considerable antiquity, Morwood assumed that the hominid responsible could not be any form of *Homo sapiens* and had to be a strand of erectus. The immediate problem this creates relates to the intellect needed to build such a vessel, and more importantly mount a convincing case for others to join him or her in an adventure without parallel. It is assumed all types of erectus were barely able to grunt let alone assemble a cogent argument to persuade and convince without a language or precedent to rely upon.

The Rapidly Evolving Genetic Models

What weakens the credentials of any proposition that the Original people are merely an earlier ancient group of adventurous Africans who set sail to exotic locales, is a variety of mtDNA[19] studies that relegate the African emergence of Homo sapiens sapiens to a time well after the Original people first came into existence. This subject, supplemented by an array of genetic experts, has been canvassed extensively in our earlier book *Shunned* [20]. However, on more than one occasion we have been criticised for supposedly preferring one or two rogue radical geneticists to suit our case and ignore the majority. They are wrong, and to that end we felt it fitting to cite three more prominent Australian archaeologists/historians, of which none have made any public statement challenging the Out-of-Africa theory. Irrespective of their reticence to attack this mistaken theory of an external migration, what they have actually stated in the public arena leaves no other alternative but to dismiss this theory in its entirety.

Josephine Flood is still comfortable with the concept of Africans sailing to Australia, nevertheless, she has no hesitation in observing that the Australian Aboriginal's mtDNA is "most different from Black Africans." [21] Keith Windschuttle, with the exception of a massacre at Myall Creek, denies the reality of the hundreds of instances of wholesale slaughter of Original tribes throughout Australia. In fact, he claims the peaceful British 'settlement' of Australia was the best thing that ever happened to the Original nation and is an advocate of a highly sanitised version of Original history. Windschuttle was even more expansive in delineating the African 'no-go' zone, insisting that "fifty years of blood genetic research ... has failed to provide any clue to Aboriginal origins ... May I state here and now that our extensive blood grouping survey ... over three decades have produced no genetic evidence that the Negro ever entered the Pacific."[22] And so the list of academics who admit that the whole Original genetic equation is far too complex grow by the day. Tressa Jamieson highlighted the two major problems all genetic research encounters, in that the variation in Australian Original mtDNA is "remarkably high,"[23] which then logically leads to a situation where if this hypothetical migration of Africans into Australia did actually take place, they migrated "earlier in human history than first suspected." [24]

If there are any that still feel the Out-of-Africa theory perhaps can be discarded in the Australian area, but holds fast throughout the rest of the globe, the most recent and quite extensive comparison of Y Chromosomes [25] compiled by Anatole Klyosov [26] and Igor Rozhanskii (The Academy of DNA Genealogy, Newton, USA) must surely call into question any African exodus anywhere, at any time. Their research determined that, "a more plausible interpretation might have been that both current Africans and non-Africans descended separately from a more common ancestor, thus forming a proverbial fork. A region where this downstream ancestor arose would not necessarily be in Africa. In fact, it was never proven that he lived in Africa."[27] They are actually saying the same thing as we are, nothing has ever been proven and as the research and techniques used in genetics has become more refined, Africa's prominence has gradually eroded.

The final cut in the death through a thousand incisions of this outdated theory of human existence and movement, surely has to be "the data obtained from the 'Walk Through the Y' (chromosome) international project conducted by Family Tree DNA (Texas and Arizona)."[28] What they found was that "not one non-African participant out of more than 400 individuals of the Project tested positive to any of the thirteen "African" sub-clades[29] of haplogroup A."[30] Out of a possible 5,200 matches between African and non-African participants, the score obtained was an empathetic zero, not one solitary 'hit.' With not one solitary African Chromosome found abroad, not just missing in inaction in Australia but throughout the globe, all that can be stated with confidence is that Africa is the first place to cross off the list. The researchers and science stand united when seeking out humanity's origin through the male genetics, they are adamant "Adam"[31] cannot be African.

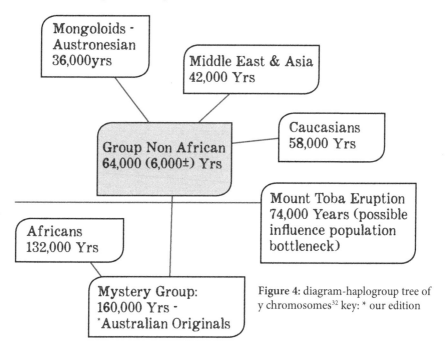

Figure 4: diagram-haplogroup tree of y chromosomes[32] key: * our edition

Elsewhere the Danish team tracing our female lineage are very confident that the European and Asian race are much younger than the African and Original races. Put this all together, knowing Eve cannot be Asian or European, and that "Adam"[33] is not African yet his ancestor is at least 160,000 years old and "remains unknown"[34] to the researchers, we are left with one candidate standing on the blocks in both cases. The Original people alone tick both the female and male boxes.

The first and only Australian study (1999) surveying Original Y Chromosomes, was no less Africa-unfriendly. Containing "two haplotypes[35] unique to Australian Aboriginals,"[36] the comparison made to populations outside Australia provided the same "unique"[37] pattern. It was noted that the people measured outside Australia produced 41 haplotypes, whereas "most (78%) of Aboriginal haplotypes fell into two clusters, possibly indicating two original separate lineages of Aboriginal Australians."[38]

What does become obvious is the repeated use of the term unique, which contradicts Wade's expectation that the hypothetical first African settlers were indeed sealed off, thus remaining "without any genetic mixture"[39] in steadfastly refusing to admit "any outsiders."[40] If so, why is it that Original mtDNA and Y Chromosomes bear no relationship to the African people from which they supposedly descended? The Original genetic coding should be saturated with African mtDNA and Y Chromosomes, but that certainly isn't the case.

Consistent to that non-African theme is an analysis of over 10,000 vials of Aboriginal blood that was originally collected during the early to mid-20th century, to be used for transfusions. Josephine Flood's investigation begins where many others left off. "Uniquely, full-descent Aboriginals lacked A2 and B of the ABO group system, S of the MNSs system and Rh negative genes r, r' and r" … Western Desert people show a distinctive genetic pattern with the world's largest value in the N gene of the MNSs system … possibly the world's only racial group lacking in the S blood antigen." [41] If compelled to use terms such as "uniquely,"[42] "distinctive" [43] "world's highest"[44] and "only racial group lacking"[45] when describing a race that should be almost genetically identical/similar to Africans, there is nothing in this report that will provide comfort for those championing the Out-of-Africa theory.

With mtDNA, Y Chromosomes and all three blood groupings yielding no similarities to African people, it should come as no surprise that a comparison of the skull morphology of Australian Aboriginals was consistent in denying access to the African people. Professor Lanarch (Sydney University) was unequivocal in stating that "we therefore have no hesitation in omitting the Negritos as the ancestors of the Australian Aborigines."[46]

When Wade makes claim to when and where the "Aboriginals split"[47] from their African ancestors, he wisely prefaces this theoretical division with a series of provisos.

Wade openly concedes that "the genetic data offers no information as to where these populations splits may have occurred."[48] One of the other team members of the Danish Natural History Museum, Morten Rasmussen, only reinforced the inability to cement any relationship between genealogy and any specific location in declaring that, "we can't really put the geography in there."[49] So often this reality has been lost. Wilson[50] and Cann's[51] original paper, which they recanted, acknowledges that genealogy can never supply geography when stating Eve was "probably"[52], never definitely, born in Africa. As Wade correctly pointed out, "genetic dates are based on a mixture of statistics and best guesses,"[53] and in what must cast even more doubt in assuming that "the earliest known human presence in Australia was at 44,000 years ago,"[54] he also concedes that "the Aboriginal occupation of Australia presents a series of puzzles." [55]

One of the apparent contradictions the researchers observed relates to the style of tool technology that seems to be present throughout Australia, they were aware it is totally unlike that found elsewhere in the world. Their description of "primitive"[56] again is subjective, but it does serve to illustrate that the differences were dramatic and seems to infer they either regressed once stepping ashore, or it was always different simply because this style of technology began in Australia and continued separate to what was occurring outside the continent.

Blowing up the Past

To that expanding "series of puzzles"[57] we would like to add another fact that is always missing in action whenever the Out-of-Africa theory is discussed. Let us assume all eleven sites/artefact are indeed 50,000 years old or younger, and the collection of mtDNA, Y Chromosomes, blood analysis and morphology studies are also in error. There is still one remaining event that contradicts common sense and runs in direct opposition to the notion of Africans migrating from their homeland, irrespective of whether this occurred 75,000 years or even 60,000 years ago: the eruption of Mount Toba, in what is now Indonesia.

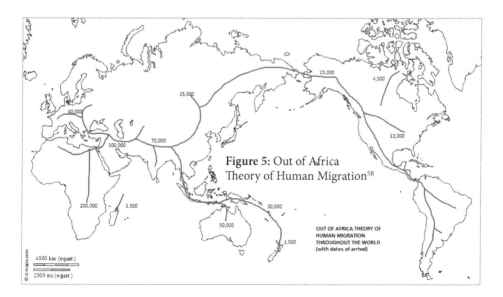

Figure 5: Out of Africa
Theory of Human Migration[58]

OUT OF AFRICA THEORY OF
HUMAN MIGRATION
THROUGHOUT THE WORLD
(with dates of arrival)

4000 km (equat.)

2000 mi (equat.)

Irrespective of whether these Africans ever made their way to Australia, any such exodus must first be assessed after factoring in the impact that the Mount Toba[59] eruption had upon the world's population. According to Josephine Flood, the "global population was reduced even more when the Toba volcano in Sumatra erupted 74,000 years ago-the world's biggest disaster of the last 2 million years. This enormous eruption spewed ash to the north-west, covering India, Pakistan and the Gulf Region in a blanket 1-3 metres deep ... and spread as far as Greenland ... this catastrophe reduced the world's population to between two to ten thousand."[60] The expectation being that two isolated pockets of humanity, one in the southern extremes of Africa, survived the holocaust, and secondly that Australia, which escaped the cloud of thick ash, was unpopulated.

Our problem is, as this eruption decimated the world population (except Australia) so severely, what inspired the very few Africans still standing to abandon the only safe haven they knew of and seek out unknown locations? Such a scenario runs counter to human nature, surely after this eruption the fortunate few would first carefully re-establish their tribal estates, then slowly edge outwards. With so much of central and northern Africa now vacant, why were these unoccupied estates ignored. Apparently breeding like rabbits, the entire continent was restocked as they surged out of Africa. Ignoring thousands of kilometres of Asian land now vacant. They sped onwards until reaching the southern coast of Indonesia, then set sail towards a continent completely unsighted.

Alternately, with most of the world virtually unpopulated, and Australia untouched by the global catastrophe due to prevailing winds, this was an ideal opportunity to set sail from, never to, Australia. As to which option makes more sense, as always it's all a matter of "best guesses." [61]

In deciding which of the "best guesses" [62] to nominate as most likely, before making a decision it is always advisable to check up on the latest science. If anything, the most recent science is even more unequivocal in extending Homo sapiens tenure on this planet. The three reports/updates we will examine in the next chapter are compiled by academics of the highest pedigree and on each occasion their conclusions resonate to the same initial inspiration and location: Australia.

There is some Original archaeology in the form of shaped and marked rocks which will now take centre stage, and certainly add considerable weight to an Original Elder's declaration that "all peoples of the world come from us." [63]

Chapter 2

CHAPTER 2: THE FINAL NAIL IN THE COFFIN

The extensive genetic research in America just completed in mid-2015, along with the two very recent comments made by eminent scholars, is as unequivocal as it is inconvenient. No one was expecting the conclusion, timing or increase in types of hominids. In fact the academics comparing genes confided that they did everything possible to find an alternative, simply because any other place in the world outside Australia would have been a far more palatable departure point. Despite their best efforts in spending "a really long time trying to make this result go away,"[1] it was to no avail. The science was indisputable, Australia was the focal point of their research.

So too, did neither expert's recent musings have any apparent link to Australian history or archaeology, but it soon becomes obvious that both the map of ancient pre-Clovis occupation sites in America and an admission of defeat are very much Australian-centred and solely due to Original genes.

We will begin our brief overview at humanity's first point of departure, Australia, then examine the findings of two experts, one from America and the other from England, who are both advocating the wholesale reconstruction of large segments of ancient history and human evolution.

Stepping Outside the Shackles

Unlike the current archaeological inertia and intransigence in Australia, in America there are a few more adventurous academics and a marginally more tolerant climate for those predisposed to reconsidering, no matter how uncomfortable the consequences. Undeniably, the team of geneticists working in Brazil were equally aware of the need to conform and did their utmost to run with the current flow, but when all else failed they held fast to their scientific principles. David Reich[2] is the senior author of the paper and a Professor of Genetics at Harvard Medical School, and he openly admitted that the final result was "incredibly surprising."[3] He had no reason to doubt the current theories that account for a migration into America of one racial group beginning "about 15,000 years ago."[4] He agreed that "there's a strong working model in archaeology and genetics, of which I have been a proponent, that most Native Americans today extend from a single pulse of expansion south of the ice sheets-and that's wrong. We missed something very important in the original data."[5]

The"Tupi-speaking Surui and Karitana and the Ge-speaking Xavante of the Amazon had a genetic ancestor more closely related to indigenous Australasians than to any present day population."[6] The comparison was extensive and included "the genomes of people from about 200 non-American populations."[7] They conceded that they "don't know the order, the time separation or the geographical patterns,"[8] and that "a more diverse set of founding populations of the Americas than previously accepted"[9] should be considered.

The three locations they identified (Australia, New Guinea and the Andaman Islands) need a little clarification as they are tainted by today's geography and politics which certainly did not apply in ancient times. Until 8,000 years ago Papua New Guinea was part of the Australian mainland (Sahul) and had been for millions of years. So if the "unknown wave of migration"[10] occurred further back than 8,000 years ago which is extremely likely, then they are one homogenous genetic group and do not need to be divided by today's geography.

To classify the Andaman Islands as part of Asia at any time is a huge stretch, the people, culture and technology, even to this very day, are dramatically different from any other part of Asia. Although politically affiliated to India, the Indigenous people of these islands are very hostile to any off-islander presence. No tourism is allowed, government officials rarely visit the island and are under constant armed-guard whenever they do, and it is patently clear that no-one who isn't local is welcome. They maintain their tribal lifestyle, keep apart and have shown every intention to maintain that isolation. It has been long known that the genetic make-up of these people has striking similarities to the Original populations of Australia.

The methodology and rigour of this genetic study is beyond reproach and cannot be challenged. "Genome-wide data, with its hundreds of thousands of independent characters that evolve effectively neutrally, should be a statistically powerful and robust way to test whether a distinct lineage contributed to Native Americans."[11] It must also be stated that the idea of the Original people living in America in ancient times was already known in archaeological circles through the comparison by Dr. Walter Neves[12] of 55 skulls found in Brazil. The researchers noted that, "this discovery is striking in light of interpretations of the morphology of some early Native American skeletons, which some authors suggested have affinities to Australasian groups."[13]

Another member of the team, Pontus Skogland[14], had the vision (which seems to be in short supply in Australia) to highlight the three areas of research that were now on the horizon, yet outside the reach of any genetic study of blood. "We don't know the order, the time separation or the geographical patterns."[15]

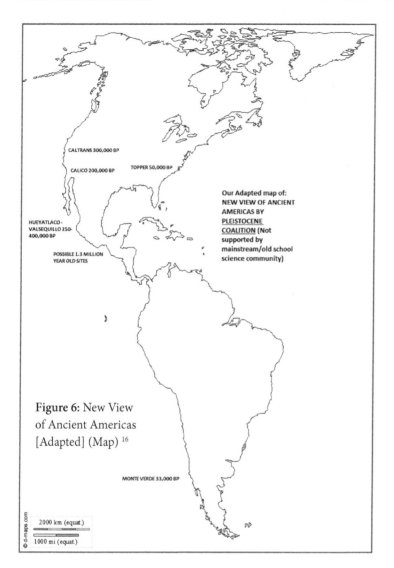

Figure 6: New View of Ancient Americas [Adapted] (Map) [16]

Who Came First?

In solving such problems in sequencing and location, different techniques, fields of science and archaeological sites are required, and, in what may surprise many, this is in ample abundance throughout both North and South America. A map detailing a compendium of sites considered to be pre-Clovis [17] (>15,000 years old), was recently published by an American archaeologist for whom we have the highest regard. Dr Virginia Steen-McIntyre [18] identified six different locations where human occupation is claimed to have occurred between 33,000 to 1.3 Million years ago.

One site in particular that is replete with an amazingly diverse and sophisticated battery of geological dating techniques, all producing six figures, is as complex as it is duplicitous in the repercussions that have persisted to this very day. It has polarised opinions, seen friendships lost and careers destroyed. The only two points of consensus remaining are that it is considered to be a perfect archaeological site to investigate and was inspected by the most talented academics in America. Past that point everything written and said about the huge array of archaeology that came out of Lake Valsequillo[19] is open to question, rancour and much worse.

Bought to the site to Lake Valsequillo was an abundance of impressive dating techniques, providing unchallengeable proof that *Homo sapiens sapiens* were in America at least 250,000 years ago, or there has been a monumental stuff-up and nearly every expert on site got it horribly wrong. This archaeological impasse is covered in *Shunned*[20] ; what has changed since we wrote that chapter is the new genetic research now on the table confirming our belief that there was an Original presence in America. This new evidence supplemented by proof that humanity is far older than assumed, and that the Out-of-Africa and into Australia 60,000 years ago theory is also wrong, presents a powerful case that in very ancient times Australian mariners set sail to America and then settled in this new distant land.

If the Australians did sail to America hundreds of thousands of years ago, as has been proven through Original genetics, ancient bones and archaeology, why stop there? If they did it once, why not twice, or as many times as was needed to reach each and every part of the globe?

"It's not all Good News." [21]

The very recent announcement at the 5th Annual Meeting of the European Society of Human Evolution by Professor Chris Stringer [22], on the officially gazetted existence of a cruder and older form of Neanderthal/Neandertal has shaken the hominid family tree to its very core. There is a universally accepted pivotal separation between all Hominids and *Homo sapiens* from a common older ancestor some time ago. Once dividing genes, the *sapiens* off-shoot continued down a different path as did the Neanderthals, Denisovans [23], Red Deer Cave People[24] and many other strands. The earlier archaeological evidence of this separation occurring about 180,000-200,000 years ago in Africa was a perfect fit a decade ago, but not anymore.

The DNA extracted "from fossils in Spain are about 300,000 to 400,000 years old,"[25] is of massive concern simply because the hominid sampled was an "ancestor-or close relative-of Neandertals."[26] This means that no less than 300,000 years ago this historic genetic parting of the ways between sapiens and non-*sapiens* had not taken place, with the real chance the date of separation is much older as this is the minimum estimate.

The presence of that one semi-Neanderthal in Spain automatically disqualifies the credentials of the accepted genesis of modern humanity in Africa beginning up to 200,000 years ago. It didn't happen then, this date makes that clear. If the timing is unclear, logically the place "where"[27] modern humans first appeared is no less uncertain and warrants "new debate."[28] The supposed exodus of *Homo sapiens sapiens* some 75,000 years ago en route to Australia after 25,000 years wandering around the neighbouring countryside, is no less tenuous and open to reconsideration. In fact, according to Stringer, both the timing and location of the "origin of H. sapiens"[29] is now open to "new debate."[30]

There is no doubt that Stringer lamented that he was the bearer of bad news and had some trouble factoring in this unexpected upward revision. There was no certainty for him or his peers beyond the inability of every accepted theory to accommodate this increase in numbers. "That means that the ancestors of modern humans also had to split earlier than expected from the population that gave rise to Neandertals and Denisovans, who were more closely related to each other than they were to modern humans ... This would mean that the ancestors of humans were already wandering down a solitary path, apart from other archaic humans on the planet, 100,000 to 400,000 years earlier than expected."[31]

The science is incontestable as is the severe collateral damage to the current historical models; a regression in years of this magnitude is a difficult number to assimilate for all assembled at this conference. "It resolves one controversy-that they're in the Neandertal clade," says paleoanthropologist Chris Stringer of the Natural History Museum of London. "But it's not all good news: From my point of view, it pushes back the origin of H. *sapiens* from the Neandertals and Denisovans." [32]

Stringer has, on behalf of mainstream science and academia, conceded that the agreed historical narrative of the emergence, timing and location of the first *Homo sapiens sapiens* is now proven to be wrong. With genetic science passing the final verdict and a fundamental error identified, new ways of thinking and analysis are required. As Stringer warned those seated, there is no alternative but to engage in a "new debate about when and where the branches belong."[33]

We are more than willing to respond to Stringer's call to "debate"[34] and can go further in offering an Original perspective which will assist in filling in some gaps and reposition some flawed assumptions about "where."[35] Our first recommendation, if genuine about the need to recover the lost history, is to start this process very simply in changing one word, then branch out. It was never Out-of-Africa, but always Out-of-Australia. That admission is an excellent first step forward on an Original road that inevitably leads off into the stars above.

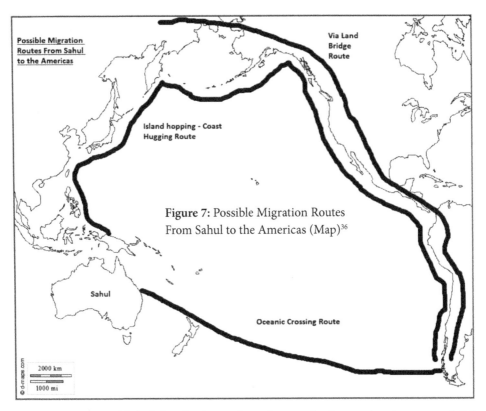

Figure 7: Possible Migration Routes From Sahul to the Americas (Map)[36]

Having established that the Original people were the first modern humans and did sail to many countries, what next? Apart from the spreading of Original genes was any other useful contribution made while abroad? When the British first came to this country and dropped anchor, they saw nothing of worth so took the land, destroyed the culture, dismissed Original tenure and proclaimed the entire Original nation to be under the jurisdiction of Terra Nullius. Deemed legally undeserving and sub-human, these people did not farm, fence, build and were bereft of wheel, building or guns. If this is the case, what was exported outside of a pointy stick, sharpened stone and no wardrobe?

Everything! It is our belief that not only *Homo sapiens sapiens* genes, but culture, art, sailing, astronomy, spirituality, democracy, gender equality, dance, music, surgery, philosophy, language and technology began in Australia. Without doubt, these are bold claims to make and demand to be substantiated. And to that end there is one sacred site and an ever-increasing collection of marked rocks that provide the scope, breadth and magnificence of what the Original people bequeathed to humanity. We are of the belief that the guidelines, technology applied and language chronicled into these rocks and the Standing Stones site, has no equal on this planet.

Top of the Class by a Margin of 0.000001%

As a classroom teacher I was often forced to scale student's work into numbers and positions in the class/year. It was an onerous task that I found a real burden because it was so difficult, subjective and always led to someone in the class coming last. No chore was more frustrating than assigning top rung on the ladder, there were always many close deserving candidates with so little separating them. We face the same problem here in selecting the top two pieces of archaeology from over fifty. Picking the top two was not too difficult, but there is so much on offer in both areas of investigation and so little to separate between the site and the set of rocks.

Despite the faultless credentials of both candidates, we will lead off with the Standing Stones site, if for no other reasons than it is more communal in complexion and there is a good chance it can be restored to its former glory.

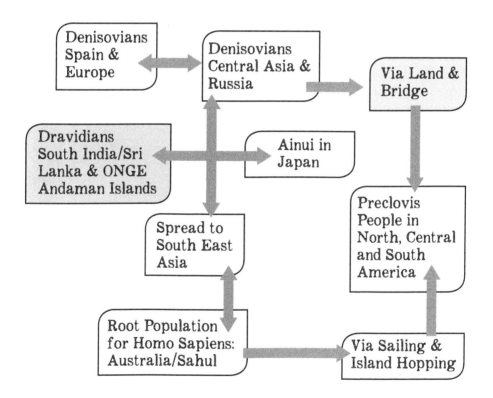

Figure 8: Diagram: Out of Australia Theory - spread in the pacific[37]

Chapter 3

THE STANDING STONES- THE MOST IMPORTANT
ORIGINAL SITE IN AUSTRALIA, PERHAPS THE WORLD

(This chapter is dedicated to recently deceased Ramindjeri Elder,
Custodian of Southern Law and the First Sacred Language, Karno
[last name withheld due to Original protocol]).

The resurrection of a complex that is without equal in Australia, perhaps the world, began about two years ago in the backroom of a local historical society. Richard Patterson (historian and author) had just joined the local community organisation and inspired by a whim, decided to wander out to the backroom and have a look around for something out of the ordinary. And there it was, an old disused filing cabinet with an unmarked box inside. It was what lay within that is so brilliant or ridiculous, because there is no other option on this planet available, that so astounded Richard. And equally, not long after, led to our involvement.

Figure 9: Computer Image of Standing Stones by Richard Patterson[1]

Inside that black box were sixteen letters written by Frederic Slater (President of Australian Archaeological Education and Research Society) to the person working on site. Slater's record of this amazing site contained archaeological explanations, maps and diagrams that describe a huge Original rock complex that had no equal in this country. The largest boomerang-shaped mound is close to three hundred metres across and had a permanent arrangement of 184 Standing Stones, of which most were shaped, and some marked in formal symbols used in the First Language. The smaller mound is seventy metres long and it has been examined over the years by quite a few geologists and geographers from the local high school, who all agreed that the sandstone rocks and sand used in this construction is not local.

What is certainly not part of the geology of the general area, positioned as it is in the middle of a caldera, are the hundreds upon hundreds of shaped sandstone rocks spread throughout the site. But there is so much more to this sacred complex than two mounds. There were many stone arrangements, some of humans, others of animals and no doubt many of constellations. Very close to the larger mound, no less than two hundred rocks were used in creating a very representational portrayal of two adult emus, each guarding eleven eggs stacked in two rows of four and one of three. According to Slater they represent the "Gateway of eternity." [2]

Richard contacted us and arranged the first of many meetings we had with the elderly gentleman who was the present owner of this farm, and the son of the farmer who wanted him to destroy this complex in 1940. This desperate act came about due to pressure from all quarters, including a government threat to confiscate their land. Over the next six months we met close to half a dozen times and began to piece together the scope and immense significance of this site. The reason we spent so much time and research on this site is simply because the contents of the 16 letters Frederic Slater wrote to his colleague, who was living nearby and spent eight months meticulously recording and drawing what was spread over a huge area, literally rewrote world history and had to be examined.

Before addressing the sensational claims Slater made about what he regarded as the "oldest ... temple in the world,"[3] which he believed to be at least "40,000 years old"[4] and contained "the basis of all knowledge in the beginning, now and to come,"[5] we need to assess his credentials and standing amongst his peers. According to an article on Slater's work found in the *Adelaide Mail* (Saturday 23, October 1937, page 6), "Mr. Slater has been a student of the Australian aboriginal (sic) all his life, and is an authority on his (sic) language. By request he has supplied native names for hundreds of Australian homes."[6] Another newspaper report in 1937 makes note of the pleasing "publicity that has been given to the paper read before the Science Congress" [7]. Slater was also acknowledged as one of nation's foremost Egyptologists and we suspect the breadth of his expertise was the reason he was chosen by his peers to act as their representative.

The esteem in which he was held was acknowledged openly in many media reports throughout the 1930's and voted upon, that is the reason why descendants of Mrs. David Dunlop (Eliza Hamilton Dunlop [8]) approached him. She was the wife of the first magistrate of the Wollombi and won the trust of Original people who decided to share with her a "vocabulary known as 'Murrigiwalda' (sacred language)."[9] Slater had exclusive access to a unique handbook that acted like an Original dictionary which provided the "key to many avenues of investigation" [10] to decode the rock arrangements and engraved symbols found at the Standing Stones site.

Reading Between the Lines

Contrary to all linguistic expectations the Sacred First Language is very complex, numerous in forms of communication and word count. By Slater's estimation there are more than "28,000 words"[11] in this language, and if that isn't impressive enough, the itemised account of the mechanics of this language only emphasises its sophistication. Slater noted that there are:

- ten elements, [12]
- "sixteen letters of the alphabet," [13]
- "seven sensory symbols," [14]
- "21 parts of the body used as symbols," [15]
- "38 symbols of the hand," [16]
- "20 different forms of suffixes," [17]
- "and a hundred or more other symbols in which animals, birds ..." [18]

I am sure that during this breakdown of the separate elements of this language more than a few readers paused and perhaps winced when the mention of an alphabet was made, and thought surely not. We have a very clean, precise figure A on Ros' Rock 2, and that letter is on at least half a dozen others. But don't just take our word for it, as we don't have the manual, only Slater had that luxury.

Slater provided meanings for quite a few of the letters his on-site colleague found and since the letter A is the one letter we have identified we felt it would be interesting to trace this letter's ancestry. According to Slater this letter's principle meaning (every symbol can have up to four different meanings) is "immortality of the soul with a light coming in," [19] and in what only adds to this mystical imprint Slater added that if the A has an "open space at the top of the V tells the direction of light." [20]

All of the letters in the First Language take on a completely different persona. The whole language is saturated in spiritual inspirations. The three other vowels Slater supplied meanings for are consistent in the same esoteric overtones:

- E represents "a light going out," [21]
- I the "inner self," [22] and

- O "God and man" [23] or alternately, "towards." [24]

Even though more numerous, it would be unwise to expect that the far more common consonants were delegated to more pragmatic interests. The whole language resonates to the same central principle (the Dreaming):

- K is the "seed, germ of life," [25]
- Y "the young tree going forth," [26]
- C means the "four divisions of life" [27] and
- Li "holds within the Light of Lights from the Maker." [28]

Down on the Farm

So much of this stone complex has been destroyed when the disc plough and tractor tore the site apart. All that remains are the two main mounds and hundreds of shaped sandstone rocks scattered around the immediate area. The presence of these artificially marked rocks immediately creates three unresolved problems.

* **Figure 10:** Smaller mound 29

This area sits inside the largest caldera in Australia and is very igneous in geological complexion. In fact the closest outcrop of sandstone is over twenty kilometres away. The larger sandstone rocks weigh tonnes and the smaller mound has 3,500 cubic metres of sandstone and exotic material, all of which is not local. The experts who have inspected this site over the last 76 years agree that the smaller 70 metre long by 5 metre high mound is not natural, of that simple truth there is no room for debate. Then to extend the distances involved in the importation of sandstone, we have found both fine and coarse-grained sandstone rocks on this site. The coarser grains are the first to be deposited upstream further inland and usually at a higher elevation.

If the transportation of sandstone and fill is one issue to deal with, then the manner of cut and implied technology required, is a much bigger concern. Some edges are still sharp enough to cut skin, perfectly straight and without a hint of a percussion bulb left behind when rock hits rock. To make these rocks needs nothing less than a metal blade.

Written testimonies provide absolute proof that the mound was came upon initially by first settlers, with Original people standing on the mound, in 1840. There is no doubt this is an Original construction that is incredibly ancient, but the technology is so modern. Juxtapose the obvious use of a metal blade against an Original hunter-gatherer society that is reputed to use stick, bone and bone technology before the British Invasion, and we immediately run into a huge impasse.

Once on site it only gets more difficult to reconcile with any conventional account of pre-Cook history. Slater was reading this ancient rock-script with the 'dictionary' from which to decipher what was left long ago, which is both an ancient testimonial and completely different view of ancient world affairs. He had absolutely no doubt that this site stood alone in global significance, and it was for this reason he advised his colleague who was working on the complex, to "just place yourself in the position of Petrie or Carter exploring the Egyptian tomb. Your work is of more importance for it relates to the existence of the first men on Earth, their history and their philosophy. They believed in an Invisible God and the immortality of the soul. They set up no craven image; but within this temple you will find the seven elements which are the basis of all knowledge, all science, all history and all forms of writing, which began in numeration." [30]

These are monumental claims made by a highly respected archaeologist, one of the best in the country. According to his translation of this site humanity, culture, wisdom and even language began in Australia. This is the dominant theme of his research. Slater's intensive study of the First Sacred Language left him in no doubt that Australia is the place where humans first spoke and recorded this tongue in a formal script. Irrespective of geography, whether "Phoenicians, Romans, Jutes, Danes, or Anglo-Saxons, the language which we speak is not Anglo-Saxon but just aboriginal (sic) … Gaul or Gwal (Goual) which is in the language of our aborigines (sic) means "speech." [31]

Many may assume that this influence was solely oral, as the Original people never had a formal set of symbols and numbers. They are manifestly mistaken and underestimate how widespread Original language, mathematics, philosophy and spirituality was throughout the ancient world. As Slater correctly observed "the Egyptian numbers - in their hieroglyphic writing are exactly the same as our aborigines (sic). Yet when we examine their teachings closely and their hieroglyphs we find that the ancient cult of the blackfellow prevailed among the Kings, Princes, Priests, Learned men and rich relations were all instructed in the ancient religion and knowledge of the elements." [32]

Frederic Slater was a very measured man not given to wild fancy, as every word spoken can be taken as being representative of his colleagues. That being the case, to make a declaration of the gravity given in 1939, where he stated that the Standing Stones site contains "the basis of all knowledge in the beginning, now and to come,"[33] deserves more than a blanket denial and over 75 years of silence.

Reaching for the Stars

Slater's admiration of Original lore and Culture is boundless, simply because he was able to interpret what was incised, engraved and shaped and then stand back in awe at what was laid out at the 184 Standing Stones site. This small sampling taken from Slater's hand-written notes is sufficient to give a general feel for the first conversation and language, but once again runs counter to prevailing linguistic models.

Every theory related to the first time humans spoke and recorded their comments and thoughts, is predicated upon a rudimentary vocal range, palette and range of interests. Food, weapons, fire, people sharing space in the cave and the most basic concerns, are the proposed topics of interest, while loftier mystical concerns are missing from every suggested list of what was said. That being the accepted case, what are we to make of what Slater claims to be a human construction detailing a formal language that is at least 40,000 years old? Especially so when considering what was placed on this sacred mound was meant to be read for an eternity.

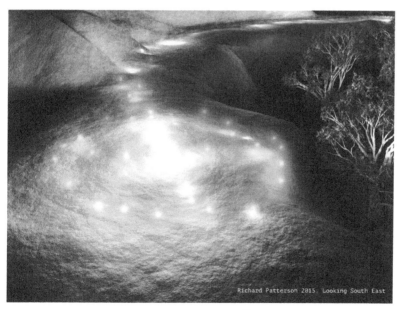

* **Figure 11:** Richard star map computer image [34]

- "Enter and Learn the Truth of the Divine Light." [35]
- "The Breath of God is the Divine Light of the Soul." [36]
- "The light of Truth flows like a river of fire from God to the soul of man and woman united." [37]
- "Guided by Truth man came to earth through darkness from the light of life that shines far off." [38]
- "The soul of man came from the immortal light to drink the water of life from God." [39]
- "Man (life) came to Earth as man with his senses (seven of them) and was established in truth." [40]
- "God came in with light from Darkness and gave man a soul and the sons of man brought in with light became the pillars of heaven." [41]
- "He who brought life into the world set down man and woman and gave them the sacred means of propagating life." [42]

These Original insights and many others not supplied are stunning pieces of wisdom and intriguing snippets of history, and the reasons why Slater was convinced that this mound is the beginning of everything. In the brief selection above there are hints of genetic splicing, constant references to coming to Earth through space (darkness) from another distant celestial location (light far off), the promise that this mound is the pathway to enlightenment and many other avenues to consider.

Of paramount importance in assessing the accuracy of Slater's translation is the existence of solid proof that substantiates that there was, and still is, an ancient mother-tongue. Even if the Original language did begin in Australia, that is no guarantee as to the validity of Slater's interpretations. So with two boxes still to tick, what evidence is there that can validate Slater's sensational claims?

A Message "From Afar"[43] Delivered Through the Mail

Very early on in proceedings, when I first alerted Karno to my rudimentary understanding of what Slater was researching, I went through all his letters and put together a basic compendium of major symbols, letters and meanings. Within this compilation were elemental icons and markings that form the foundation of the First Language. It was my intention to send this down to Karno, but he pre-empted that delivery through the post by first sending his statement of position and familiarity.

The one page sent has thirty symbols Karno insists are part of the First Language. He had no access to Slater's diagrams, in fact no-one but ourselves and Richard Patterson had seen them, yet every icon he chose that isn't coloured red and thus sourced from Tasmania, is in Slater's notes and on the second page of my crude dictionary.

Of the nineteen symbols Karno claims to be Githubal [44], all nineteen are also in Slater's notes. The Githubal Tribal Estate borders this region and present-day representatives of that tribe are currently involved in determining what happens next at this site.

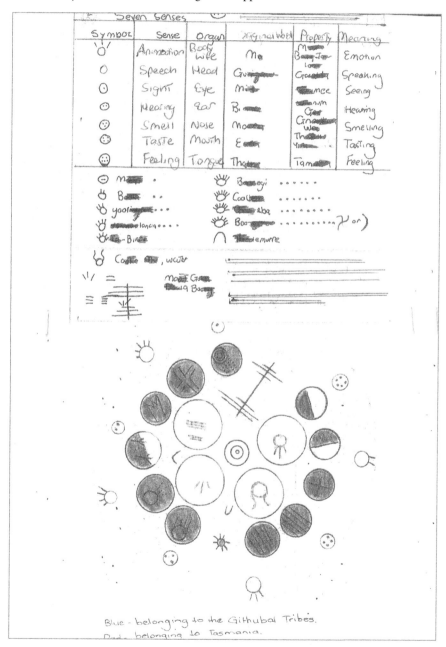

* **Figure 12:** Mix of Karno's and Slater's Symbols [45]

We are for the first time putting on public display the sheet Karno sent so long ago totally lacking in any direction from Slater or his drawings. Alongside is the second page of my rough dictionary with all sacred words covered. Every symbol Karno drew has a meaning in Slater's dictionary of the First Language. With a comparative match of nineteen out of nineteen, the chances that this came about through pure chance are not worth considering. This Ramindjeri [46] Elder and Culture Man absolutely knew the first language ever spoken, and it was never lost.

Karno's sheet encompasses and binds three geographic regions to the Southern Law Confederation[47] , which he spoke of often. Karta (Kangaroo Island, South Australia), Tasmania and the Githubal Tribal Estate (Far North Coast, NSW) are linked together through a shared language and long-term alliances. He was insistent that this confederation included most of the bottom half of Australia and the East Coast.

One of a Kind

We know that Original Elders from Cape York came to the property soon after the site was bulldozed ready to carry out sacred ceremonies that belonged to their tribal estate. We have read in the national newspapers of Elders coming from Broome and Stradbroke Island to this site hoping to enact their songs, dances and rituals. This is the only place we know of where ceremonies from outside country were permitted, and moreover this was openly conceded in the press.

Slater often referred to this complex as "Australia's Stonehenge,"[48] and this is the only occasion where he actually makes a serious lapse in judgment. The stone pillars in England were repositioned without the assistance of a map, nor did they know the name of each stone and the narrative attached to the site. Stonehenge marks out where the path of the sun and moon extend, the Standing Stones site is the first temple and records "the Mystery Track of Life and Death." [49] The Australian site chronicles the first language, the wisdom of the ages and the meaning of life. There is no reason to compare the two, as the English site serves astronomical purposes while the Original site serves every purpose.

We have the notes, diagrams and maps of Slater; the mounds are intact, and many of the rocks were disc-ploughed into the ground, or lay on the slope or down at the bottom flatter sections. Karno gave the song of the rocks and hand signs to local Original custodians and with the map in hand nearly everything can be put back together again. Many rocks are still on site but some rocks, primarily the marked rocks and three very heavy tall rocks, are no longer there. The three largest missing rocks were stored in the dairy but were taken/ disappeared soon after the cessation of global hostilities in 1946. As sizeable a hole these three rocks are, they can be replaced. All around the region dozens of similar sandstone rocks weighing up to two tonnes were stolen and used for all manner of projects. Some were repositioned without permission in council parks and private residences, but can be traced or replaced. Of far greater loss are the rocks that were marked with symbols and letters.

These rocks are essential to the integrity behind any attempt to resurrect this ancient rock arrangement.

Attempts are underway for all tribes concerned to join together and begin the process of rebuilding. As important as this step is, the loss of those crucial marked rocks is an obstacle that must be overcome if we are to rekindle the fire of the distant past and perhaps begin to understand the hidden truths found within a stone complex that contains "the basis of all knowledge in the beginning, now and to come."[50]

The investigation, reconstruction and renaissance of the Standing Stones complex will continue for decades. What has been found and recovered so far is merely the first tentative step on a journey that spreads throughout the globe and spirals into distant constellations. There is so much to take in, especially when Slater has declared that knowledge and culture begins on this mound, and it has become increasingly obvious our understanding of this site is far from complete and we still have a long way to go.

The Way Forward

We have decided that the best approach in sharing what we have learnt, which has been very much an evolving process, is to start at the beginning and follow through as we did at the time. The next six chapters appear in the same sequence when first released as individual articles, on occasions issues will be repeated in a different way as our understanding evolves we will refer back to areas previously raised. Within that framework, extensive editing and merging of articles has occurred, but the chronology and general integrity in the order in which new insights and discoveries were made has been maintained.

As with all our archaeology, this account begins in the presence of Original Elders and Custodians of Original Lore on a site that is without equal in Australia. But this time around it was not only the Elders who were on site, the Guardian Spirits of this sacred location were also in the air and ready to take flight.

Chapter 4

AUSTRALIA'S STONEHENGE RESURRECTED:
ORIGINAL ELDERS & CUSTODIANS ON SITE

This Original complex of terraces, mounds and stone arrangements,[1] according to Frederic Slater, contained "the basis of all knowledge in the beginning, now and to come."[2] Going onto site knowing such phenomenal claims were made by an expert of considerable standing, was a mixture of relief and apprehension. Nothing was certain and until our entry was sanctioned by the Guardian Spirits and deemed in accord with Original protocol, nothing was going to happen and no archaeology could take place.

Before offering any commentary on logistics, measurements, the massive quantity of sandstone found in an area that denies any geology that isn't igneous, or the thousands of cubic metres of exotic material that makes up one mound, we must first acknowledge the wisdom and guidance of the Original Elders and Custodians of Lore (Uncle Harry, Jarmbi'je, Rob, Kevin, Iris, Karno, Adam, Mark, Scott and Darren) who joined us on site. Invariably we begin every investigation after consulting with those who speak on behalf of the people who were here first. Only then, with a clear and present understanding of who, what, where, and to a lesser extent why, is it appropriate to walk on site and begin any archaeology.

We always work as a collective under the banner of Southern Law and Wirritjin[3] (Black-fella White-fella Dreaming). No one speaks for any individual, but with, and on behalf of the entire group. That being the only path taken, we will present what the Original Elders and Custodians said and did without specifying who. This was always the only way, no egos, all as one, therefore, no names just outcomes and possibilities.

DAY 1.

From the moment we stepped onto the outer edge of this isolated site, nearly everyone sensed the presence of the "Old Ones".[4] After all the appropriate ceremonies were given and sensitive matters negotiated, the Elders and Custodians needed to go ahead first to have time to examine the site and be alone with the Guardians. Our team of close to twenty volunteers had to wait and bide their time and hope permission would be granted to enter this sacred place.

The closer we got the more the original men called aloud to the "Old Ones,"[5] stating both our intentions and deep respect. They sensed their presence and power within and without. While most of the Original men were standing on the largest ridge, one of the Elders, a man of immense stature and knowledge of the Old Ways and Language, called on the Spirits of this sacred site for a sign.

What they got was so much more. They just kept on spiralling in, ever increasing in numbers. Three hawks came as summoned, appreciative as the Elder was, he called for more. A fourth, then fifth bird joined the procession. With five hawks directly above them, the Elder was mightily pleased, but the tally was incomplete. He asked for six, then seven, but it was still one short of the number that most resembled the stone configuration on the mound and symbolised Wirritjin: eight. And so the last bird came, eight hawks circled above their heads as they stood gazing upwards on this most sacred mound.

The omens from above were Heaven-sent, and approval was given, so I was directed to go back and bring all those waiting some distance away. Since we had been on site for close to half an hour, I decided to run down the hill at a solid pace and keep that speed until my lungs gave out. As soon as I hit the flats a shadow appeared barely a metre in front of me, it was one of the eight hawks. Always just a few steps in front, I kept running mindful that my feathered escort was setting the pace and urging me to hurry. My breathing was becoming more laboured and shallow, and sweat was trickling down my face, but I had no other choice than to keep up with my feathered pace-setter. It was only at the last gate, some 200 metres from our assembly point, that the hawk peeled off and resumed normal duties.

With everyone gathered in one spot on a flat area between the mounds, tasks were negotiated and all were reminded before setting forth that this was a place where Clever-fellas and Kadaitcha[6] men sang and danced ceremonies of the highest order, communicating directly with the Spirits and the "Old Ones."[7] Originally it was my intention that we dig two small pits, the first of between 0.5 to 1 metre in width at a depth of 1-2 metres and the second was to be much smaller. My expectation was that one pit was to be dug near the smaller mound and another on the very edge in the damaged section.

This mound was the burial site dedicated to the most revered men of high degree. Spanning thousands of years, and possibly much longer, from all who attended only the wisest and most spiritually advanced were chosen to lay in rest inside this 70 metre almost perfectly symmetrical burial mound. Slater warmly praised his dedicated colleague for his discovery of Original bones on site, referring to the mound as a "burial ground,"[8] claiming it to be a "feather in your cap."[9]

During our first break, I felt the timing was right to introduce an extremely unusual and obviously artificially shaped igneous rock of seven sides and messages.

It was found by one of the Original people on site that day and was fashioned by tools and technology supposedly absent in this continent before Cook. One of the Original Elders, a man steeped in ancient Lore, took some of the men to the top section of the southern mound and asked us to decide which position we thought marked the centre-point of the southern circle. Our advisor then carefully placed the rock on the ground and shared with us six of the seven different messages/meanings. Alas, I was without pen or paper, and due to the overload of information, stories, hand signs and archaeology, I only remember the four that related to the six seasons, a solstice, one important direction and the exact position of the northern circle.

That night I kept sensing there was a need for speed, that the next day had to be quick and brief as we could, and that no spade or shovel was to be part of this day.

DAY 2.

On the second day a spokeswoman of Original sensibilities who held a powerful connection to this site, joined our party and took the non-Original woman away to assess motivations, clarify purpose and strengthen contact to this sacred land. They then returned to continue counting rocks, a task they had a good chance of completing in the remaining time available.

The men in our party were broken into groups of two and three. A party of two was sent out to range along the ridges in search of sandstone, and found nothing that wasn't igneous. Another group went out in search of a rumoured much smaller mound and found nothing, while the rest of us continued the count of stones on the higher sections and plateau of the main ridge. The number of stones on the smaller mound was into the hundreds and nowhere near complete, but our time on site was.

The team left and it was time for the Elders and Custodians to sit on country in a circle and set future directions. A spokeswoman for Aunty Millie Boyd spoke first, setting the tone and direction of what followed. She was relaying the wishes of one local female Spirit that all seated held in the highest regard. She spoke of sharing culture or perishing, and that news of this place and its significance must be shared freely. An incredibly ancient and holy site of the highest order, from this point on every step taken and word uttered while on and near site has to be in accord with a sacred complex where the First Sacred Language was gifted to humanity, and men of the very highest calibre were interred.

We talked for hours and came to a consensus on all issues. All agreed these hallowed grounds and arrangements sat on extremely sacred land which was part of a massive Southern Law confederation that covers close to half the continent, and that future actions must be in accord with the principles of Wirritjin (Black-fella White-fella Dreaming). We also agreed that the sites' location and identity of the present owners will be kept secret, and that no one must even consider approaching this site unless given proper ceremony. It would be too offensive and dangerous to do otherwise.

With an Original foundation set into stone, hand signs, hawks above and the Spirits' consent, our next chapter is the actual archaeological paper that came out of our two days on site. What we have compiled is an account of the archaeology and measurements, angles, tally of sandstone rocks and foreign technology on site, that contradicts so much written about not only Original, but the world's pre-history.

Chapter 5

AUSTRALIA'S STONEHENGE MAY RE-WRITE WORLD HISTORY

During 1939 two extremely open-minded and dedicated men spent a great deal of time trying to come to grips with what one of those men, Frederic Slater, President of the Australian Archaeological and Education Research Society, claimed to be Australia's "Stonehenge."[1] Countless hours were spent measuring and drawing a huge variety of stone arrangements, alignments and engravings placed above and beside a series of "terraces"[2] and "mounds."[3] This ancient complex, according to Slater, formed "the basis of all knowledge, all science, all history and all forms of writing, which began in numeration."[4]

Our tasks are simple: examine and assess the work and notes of Slater and his colleague and compare this to available archaeology and geography, oral testimonies of Original and non-Original people past and present, and as always, consult with Original Elders and Custodians before embarking upon such a daunting investigation. We also intend to pick up from where they left off. First and foremost it would seem Slater's recommended next target, the smaller 70 metre mound, is deserving of discreet investigations. Consisting of material foreign to the region, Slater claimed that the nearest site able to cater for the sandstone tonnage on site is "14 miles"[5] away. If he is correct, questions relating to extraction, metal blades and transportation in a land of stick and stone technology need to be addressed.

What is a little more problematic is proving or refuting in absolute terms whether Slater was correct in proposing that "the mound is one of the oldest; I should say the oldest, forms of temples in the world and dates back to the Palaeolithic age with the advent of first man."[6] Equally, and possibly even a touch more sensational, is Slater's belief that the most ancient of all tongues on Earth, the "Sacred Language,"[7] was first chronicled at this complex.

Just before anything could be resolved or formally investigated, the Second World War began. Government agencies pressured the landholder and the site was destroyed soon after. All discussion came to a close until mid 2013 when Slater's correspondence was found amongst unmarked files in the local Historical Society by Richard Patterson.

Site Description.

Very little, in terms of general location, specific soil types and geology, can be shared for fear that such information would betray either the position of this complex of "terraces,"[8] "mounds,"[9] "circles"[10] and "stone rings,"[11] or the landholders' identity. All that can be said is that the site is quite remote and can be found within 40 kilometres of Mullumbimby.

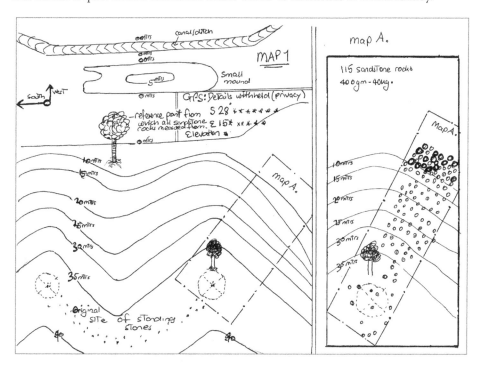

Figure 13: (Map 1) of western slope of bigger mound [12]

The bigger mound is on a westerly slope and the smaller mound was built on top of a level swampy plain of black/grey loam. On parts of this flat wide plain sugar cane is grown and the slopes that have been cleared are grazing beef cattle. The alignment and distance from the ocean is known, but again sharing such information achieves nothing bar narrowing down possibilities and geography. What can be stated with absolute certainty is that this area contains no natural deposit of sandstone, while igneous rocks, some weighing hundreds of kilograms, can be found across all slopes and gullies and throughout the level paddocks.

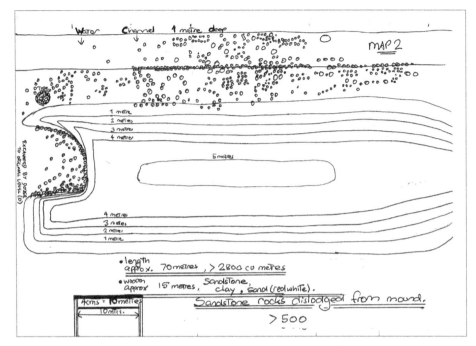

Figure 14: (Map 2) Smaller mound and scatter of sandstone rocks [13]

Of particular interest, on the two days permitted to conduct archaeology, are the two mounds (see Maps 1 and 2). The smaller mound, which is approximately 70 metres long and 5 metres high, seems in opposition with the surrounding landscape. There are hundreds of hectares of flat land all around, and this mound is at least 50 metres from any natural slope. A variety of commentators had made note of the obvious artificial nature of this construction. A teacher from a nearby school, Xxxxxx Xxxxxx, who was following up on the scant details still available in 1964, made reference to "the presence of a single mound of this type in an entire swampy flood plain, the locals say imported. So far I have not had time to carry out a profile examination, but again our geographers on staff cannot understand its presence." [14] Even though he maintained a degree of scepticism, he posed a rhetorical question that we must attempt to answer. "How can a natural line of small sandstone pieces suddenly appear in a line and on a mound in a swamp when all surrounding rocks are igneous?" [15]

The much larger mound, which spans well over two hundred metres, was originally the place where the Standing Stones were carefully positioned and realigned throughout the year. Not only were all the stones of this construction and the many other inter-connected arrangements nearby bulldozed and disc ploughed, it seems the actual mound itself was 'de-terraced.' In one of Slater's first letters to his on-site colleague, he not only asks "how many terraces on the mound," [16] but reminds him if he can "ascertain the number of terraces on the hillside" [17] it would solve one of the many riddles associated with this site.

He privately hoped that there were "six terraces."[18] Further on, he requests that more investigation into the terracing be done, suggesting that if the terraces have "wavy lines" [19] it may "indicate something flowing or moving onwards." [20]

Even though all signs of the terraces are gone, not so the displaced rocks that were on the mound, they are spread all over the slopes of the larger mound and some can be found down on the flats, over 50 metres from their original position. A large proportion of the sandstone rocks that are easily seen, seem to have worked edges, flat sides and straight lines, but bear no impact or percussion marks as would be expected if fashioned by rock tools. Apart from the two mounds and hundreds of sandstone rocks, no other stone arrangements or unusual formations are apparent.

* Figure 15: Sandstone "shaped stones" [21]
* Figure 16: Sandstone "shaped stones" [22]
* Figure 17: Sandstone "shaped stones" [23]

Methodology

Slater's work was nowhere near complete, and when first establishing a working relationship with his colleague on site, he set out 15 points to look for in searching for facts connected with the XXXXXXX circles, terraces and mounds. [24] Due to the phenomenal overload of sites and stone arrangements not all of these points were addressed, particularly when it came to conducting any archaeology on either mound, except charting the positions of each rock and determining its meaning.

It was our intention to dig two small pits, one near the edge, and the third 15 metres away from the smaller mound. The off-site trench is important in establishing what the natural soil is, and whether there are deeper deposits of sand and sandstone similar to the material inside the mound. One small trench needs to be dug at a location where the mound finishes and the natural soil is re-established, we will be searching for the layer of original soil (grey/black loam) which we believe sits under the mound, thus proving this material was placed above the natural topsoil.

We also needed, in the most approximate terms, an estimate of the amount of exotic material found within the smaller mound and record the length, width and height, but we also have to factor into our calculations the gradual slope on the eastern side and much steeper rise on the western side.

Any thought of excavating one thimble of soil from any mound was always dependent on what took place once the Elders and Custodians stood on the bigger mound. From the time the eight hawks circled above, the prospect of turning over one sod of earth from these mounds was never going to be part of our two days on site.

Even though Slater's colleague surveyed the area for sandstone deposits of any size, and made claim that the nearest deposit was at least "14 miles away," [25] one group was sent out to check every ridge and the flat area for any sign of sandstone (and any other formations or anomalies).

After considerable negotiation, all women were restricted to the lower parts of the slope, which was more clustered and intense in sandstone rocks and their brief was to count, observe and GPS all visible rocks. They were not allowed to touch or move any rock, just record. Further up the rise on the plateau was the place where men danced and sung ceremonies in the Sacred First Language, and because of this the top of the mound was taboo to all women as we entered the site. The future, as always, is an unknown commodity.

To begin with, excavating two trenches near the smallest mound was our highest priority. Apart from the chance of establishing its age through organic matter, lack of exposure to sunlight and decay of rocks, we had to determine whether the mound is a combination of soil, sandstone, clay and sand and how different this exotic mixture is to the surrounding geology.

The southern section of the smaller mound has been extensively damaged through excavating the sandstone and sand to use as road-fill. Unlike the natural soil, the material in the mound is very porous and an excellent road base to use on soggy flat plains. Behind the mound is a level flat section of 2 metres then a drainage ditch used to divert the build-up of stagnate water. The area (3 metres by 70 metres) is strewn with sandstone pieces of various sizes and numbers at least 500. Unlike our count of all sandstone rocks that tumbled down the southern section of the bigger mound, of which every rock will be assigned elevation and GPS co-ordinates, it is my expectation the sandstone behind this mound was fill, and will not show indications of a human hand, tools or a message. As such, a mud map, although still to scale and fairly exact in positioning, is sufficient for our purposes as long as the count is careful.

Results

Of the two trenches, only one was excavated as expected, another was hastily convened and barely scratched the surface.

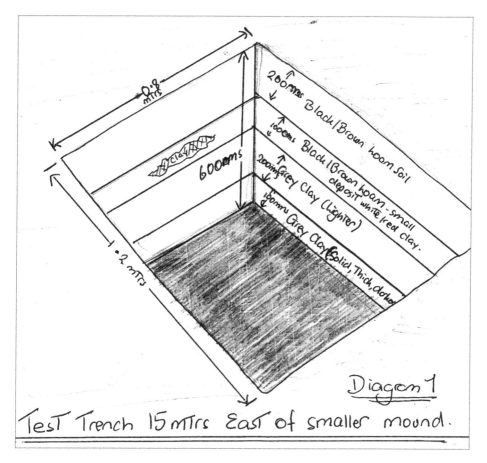

Figure 18: (DIAGRAM) Test Trench [26]

To begin with, we will lead off with the only successful task completed with a spade- the test trench which was situated 15 metres east of the smaller mound (see Figure 18 Diagram). The trench is 1.2 meters by 0.8 metres and 60cms deep. There are 4 distinct layers of soil evident, the first and most recent is a 20cm layer of black/grey loam. Beneath that layer there is a smaller 10cm layer of the same type of soil, but with a browner tinge and one small isolated deposit of a clump of white and red clay. There is no other clay like this on any of the four sides of this rectangular trench. The third layer is a 20cm mixture of lighter grey clay and loam, while the last layer (which could run much deeper) of 10cms is also grey clay, but is more dense and darker with less loam.

* **Figure 19:** Test trench [27]

Unlike the bulldozed far southern section of the smaller mound, which is entirely made up of sandstone, white and red sand, and clay, the black loam and grey clay that makes up the surrounding soil is present and accounted for at every location except the small mound.

This mound was and still is one of the most sacred of sacred burial grounds reserved for only the most advanced and revered. It was only after we came off-site and reviewed Slater's notes that the confirmation needed was found, which had been carefully underlined then forgotten. Not only did Slater's co-worker verify it was a burial site, but that the complex and elaborate methods of internment are indicative of someone of the highest standing. "The finding of the burial ground is another feather in your cap ... the "thrice bent man" appears to have had a place; but the sorting out of the bones and placing of the skull above two perpendicular ... leg bones indicates a symbol which is worth examining."[28]

The explanation continues through constant reference to the actual words used in the Sacred Language, which we are not at liberty to share, but we can assure you the meaning is extremely sacred and includes "the place where life was breathed." [29]

At our time on-site the significance of the mound was there but misplaced. Due to an overload of information none of this was mentioned at the time. From an archaeological stance, digging into an area so obviously destroyed by the bulldozer during the excavation of material to form a road base, is a lottery. It is badly damaged and the floor was open to the elements, but as all other intact locations were out of bounds, all we had to choose from was a site where the side shelf of sandstone ran vertically down to what was close to level ground. Beside the vertical outcrop of sandstone, we dug a narrow ditch of 50 cms and 20 cms in lengths. It is comprised of dense clay, sand and an occasional piece of sandstone, and very tough to pierce. A great deal of effort, shared among two, saw the ditch finally deepen some 20 cm. What was obvious was the trench off-mound was 20 times bigger, but both required the same effort. As small as it was, we did identify and film one thin 3 cm layer of black/grey loam. There was more clay/sand underneath, but due to the upheaval and removal of soil this is to be expected.

Most importantly, and despite all the rearrangements, the same soil found everywhere except this mound, can also be found at ground level inside this artificial construction.

After spending three hours scouring the countryside, high and low, our survey team could not find one sandstone rock let alone a quarry of the proportions needed. Igneous rock was found all over, in one gully very close to the bigger mound, there were at least three hundred sizable boulders and all were igneous.

The smaller mound was measured. It is 70 metres in length, 10 metres in width and stands close to 5 metres at its highest point. There are sandstone rocks strewn all over and some very intriguing rock arrangements on the mound. One that was examined and recovered on departure was of a circle of small rocks with agate and crystals placed inside. There is one massive tree growing near the crest, which we believe is much more than one hundred years old, and was intentionally meant to be part of the mound and funerary rituals, as it represents in the First Sacred Language one of the "pillars of heaven." [30]

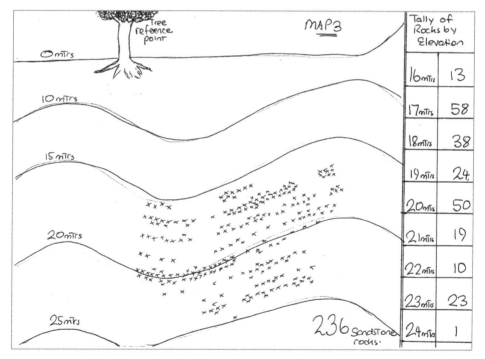

Figure 20: (Map 3) GPS placement of sandstone rocks [31]

Our search for sandstone rocks falls into three categories. On the southern edge of the bigger mound, from an elevation of 24 metres down to zero, the women used one large tree as their common reference point and charted every rock visible on the ground (see Figure 21). As directed, no rock was touched by women but was counted, given elevation and GPS co-ordinates.

Less precise in positioning, but hopefully exact in tally, was the method adopted when counting the number of sandstone rocks/pieces found behind the smaller mound (see Figure 15). Such was the number of rocks and short amount of time available, and the real chance it was merely sandstone fill for the mound, we chose to quickly count and scan the surrounds then attend to other tasks. What was quite notable was the exactness of the spread of sandstone, the irrigation/drainage ditch continued in both directions for hundreds of metres, but past either flank beyond the mound, there was not one sandstone rock to be seen, anywhere.

What did become apparent was that my assumption that all of the sandstone rocks on the smaller mound were fill was wrong, some were obviously worked, and this then made me question whether the stones that lay on the flats between the mounds were all from the larger mound.

Our third approach was the least precise and most rushed. This tally was taken on the second day when it was made clear the Spirits wanted haste. Taken from the northern edge/circle (see Figure14: Map 1, map A), we walked down the slope towards the flat and drew a circle every time a sandstone rock was sighted. Positioning was rough at best, and most likely a margin of error of up to 10% should be factored in, as we were less than vigilant in both looking and recording. Nevertheless, although incomplete, the final count of 115 is useful as an absolute minimum, and point of further investigation. What did surprise was the size and weight of sandstone rocks and boulders lodged in the flat soggy area at the bottom of this ridge. Some weighed close to 50 kilograms and had straight lines, edges and 90 degree angles.

Not only were there two types of sandstone rocks, one was worked into the desired shape and edging, while the others were un-worked and used as fill or was part of an arrangement. There also seems to exist a real chance more than one quarry or source of sandstone was accessed. Virtually every sandstone rock, regardless of whether natural or exhibiting evidence of shaping and chiselling, is fine grained and deposited when the turbulence in the water depositing the sand had subsided. At the time of writing we have identified one sandstone rock that breaks that mould (see figure 22). It is coarse grained: an agate or some form of crystal is embedded into the rock. The grains and pieces of rock that formed this rock were deposited when the flow of water was fast, and much further upstream than the overwhelming majority of sandstone found on site.

* **Figure 21:** Coarse grain sandstone rock[32]

Once permission is gained we intend to take one sandstone rock off-site to be examined by geological experts of the highest order. We'll also take one piece of sandstone from the location Slater and his colleague thought to be the most likely quarry. Any comments in relation to make, origin and similarities or differences should assist greatly.

Of course, the tally of 851 sandstone rocks seen and counted is literally the 'tip of the iceberg.' The farmer who ploughed these arrangements and terraces, understandably so as his fathers' land was under threat of government seizure, was still alive until 2015 and remembers using a disc plough. Which means wherever there is a cluster of sandstone, a common occurrence, the chances are even more rocks lay just below the surface. What is unfortunate was that some of the most substantial rocks were carefully placed inside the farmer's barn, but alas, within a decade someone snuck onto their property and stole the rocks. We can only hope that person was not stealing, but safeguarding until the day the rocks can be returned, which is nearly upon us.

Another issue under consideration is Slater's belief an actual Original alphabet of 16 letters existed and that some of those symbols were engraved onto rocks on the bigger mound. We do know that some symbols were engraved into some of the larger rocks that were stolen or kept under safe keeping, and there are markings on rocks on-site that require much closer scrutiny. There is also talk of a later inspection and unsanctioned collection of marked rocks, but at this stage we can offer nothing conclusive.

A Cross-over Between Methodology/Conclusion

Confirming whether this is indeed the first formal piece of human communication, called the Sacred Language, and that the 'Standing Stones' detail the history of humanity and the "Mystic Track of Life" [33] seems an almost impossible task. Slater's claim, that the first language is a seamless blend of hand signs, stone arrangements and alignments, body parts, symbols and numbers, and was first spoken in Australia, contradicts elemental assumptions that underpin our understanding of human evolution. What appears to be even more puzzling is the content. The expectation is that first language would be the least sophisticated and most basic in expressing emotions, the need to survive, food and sundry concerns when, trying to come to grips with just staying alive. Passages such as "The Breath of God is the Divine Light of the Soul," [34] or "the light of Truth flows like a river of fire from God to the soul of man and woman united," [35] stand united in utter contradiction to the accepted scenarios. Instead of 'what's for dinner,' or 'Barry was here,' we get statements of Divine Purpose and mystical insights.

Conclusion/Hypothesis

As radical the notion of the first language beginning in Australia may appear to be, we have already heard an Elder of the highest repute state that the first Original Language began in Australia (see You Tube, Egyptians in Australia Part 2 [36]), and read of an interesting academic ruse that led the mischievous academic responsible (who is one of Australia's leading experts in Original rock engravings) to admit that there is no less than a 50% chance that all written language began in Australia.

What began as a ploy devised by Australian rock art expert, Professor Bednarik [37], to counter the criticisms that archaeologist Lesley Maynard was subjected to, who claimed that an ancient form of Original art, referred to as Panaramitee art, which is characterised by a style referred to as "Tracks and Lines genre," [38] was the precursor to all forms of language and written communication. Such was the intensity of critiques, which had been levelled at her for many years, Maynard stated she "was happy to bury it." [39]

Bednarik, aware that "some of the art of other continents resembled the Panaramitee," [40] devised a simple questionnaire in defence of Maynard's stance, with a twist in the tail. "He sent out copies of seven unlabelled diagrams of engravings .... and asked eight rock art specialists to identify whether they were Panaramitee style or not. In fact, they were all from North and South America, Africa and Europe. The score of wrong answers was an abysmal 98%," [41] in that nearly every response nominated Australia as the country in which this art was created. Bednarik was left with two alternatives, either that it's "not possible to identify a Panaramitee style, or ... this is a world-wide style." [42] We, of course, subscribe to this world-wide style originating in Australia then spreading throughout the globe.

Frederic Slater, the President of the Archaeological and Educational Research Society, was adamant not only did the First Language begin in Australia, but that he had access to accurate records compiled from Original people who still knew the Old Ways and Tongue. However, in that respect, Slater made one of his very few errors. To begin with he displayed an acute appreciation for the depth and intricacies of the Sacred Language, but underestimated its resilience. "You are working in a much higher cult which I doubt is understood by present day Aborigines ... The teachers have all gone."[43] We beg to differ, the "teachers"[44] are not gone, just out of sight until the time is ripe, and most assuredly one of those Elders, who spoke on behalf of others with similar knowledge of Lore and Sacred Language, was on-site with us when counting rocks and chipping at the edges.

* **Figure 22:** Pyramid rock capstone used southern circle [45]

* **Figure 23:** Pyramid rock capstone used southern circle (note accompanying rock) [46]

That small error aside, a man of his standing and knowledge, particularly in Egyptology, would only venture to make such challenging statements once fully armed with archaeological evidence of the highest calibre. The confirmation of his notes and interpretations along with a summary of some of the "28,000"[47] words Slater had assembled, by an Original Elder fully versed in these matters, appears to be sufficient in every respect.

When what we had always called the six-sided rock was brought onto country, the way it was used, along with the accompanying hand signs and gestures as the Elder shared the six, and at a later date seven, meanings that this one rock subscribes, was just as Slater had described in his letters. That rock belonged to this sacred mound, and has since been placed under care by appropriate people. What we did see was exactly how it was positioned and understood in the past. Both President and Elder were in accord. With each word from the sacred Language having four meanings, there are "20 different forms of suffixes"[48] along with accompanying hand signs. This is, without a doubt, the most difficult and mystical language ever spoken. If this is indeed the very first time humans expressed their inner thoughts and inspirations, how far have we fallen?

The smaller mound promised so much, and from an archaeological viewpoint delivered very little. Fortunately, the little time that was allowed was ample for our purposes. With the exception of the small mound, all soil on the flats is a black/grey loam. The thousands of tonnes of exotic fill, sandstone and clay is a perfect road base simply because it bears no resemblance to the local swampy terrain. It was transported to this site, and equally, there are sandstone rocks on-site that weigh close to 50 kilograms.

There are records of Europeans, who were busy felling and burning trees disturbing Original people on the mound in 1840, who fled with a few special rocks in hand. It is not a post-Cook construction, that is a fact, but equally, it has no equal in this country and requires a scale of quarrying and transportation that was supposedly never part of the Australian landscape until the British Invasion.

There are no sandstone deposits in this area, nor should there be. Geological maps and hours searching the surrounding area only confirm what Slater claimed in his correspondence, this sandstone was imported from somewhere far off. Whether it is a site 22.5km (14 Miles) away, or much further as we suspect, it will be resolved soon, but for now the distance is secondary. What can be stated is that it is a massive amount that came from a long way off.

Many of the sandstone rocks found on the northern and southern slope have right angles, smooth faces and lines that seem to be very unnatural. All of these rocks were brought from afar, and leads us to conclude they have been quarried, transported, shaped and in some cases engraved, using technologies which were not supposed to be part of any pre-historic Original tool-kit.

So, in summing up, what was our check-list and were the main questions answered? In the case of the small mound/burial ground, yes. It is definitely an import, made from material brought from some distance. There are sandstone rocks by the thousands within and scattered around the edges, most were used for fill but a few were definitely worked and shaped. We have found quite a few of the stones that originally formed "the Mystic Track of Life," [49] and have a map identifying the position of each rock that was charted about four months before it was reluctantly disc ploughed. The second, much bigger mound was most definitely levelled and terraced before the site was ploughed in 1940, this was also unheard of, but of even more importance was the message written on this boomerang-shaped mound. It breaks every linguistic convention in relation to the content and way humans first spoke. Never the province of esoteric philosophers, the first language was assumed to be basic, few in number and crude in presentation. The Original Sacred Language is a sublime, sophisticated and spiritual merging of symbols, arrangements, hand signs, body parts, animals and numbers into the first spoken and written language.

There are more questions unanswered than resolved, and no doubt some of our explanations are quite radical and not without alternatives. Nevertheless, the smaller mound is totally unique in this country, the materials inside foreign to the surrounding countryside and the sandstone rocks do not belong. Something, whether the participants in attendance or technology applied, was part of a construction and complex, which just doesn't fit into any accepted account of pre-1788 Australia.

If other civilisations were in this country, as both Slater and ourselves are absolutely convinced, it would be remiss to not include Slater's take on not only their presence, but reverence. We are both in agreement in stating the Egyptians came as apprentices to be tutored in the esoteric insights and cultural refinements that were a part and parcel of the Australian landscape and Original philosophy. "There is no mistaking the fact that the aborigines (sic) … gave not only to the Egyptians their knowledge and their foundation of hieroglyphics and their philosophy, but formulated the basis of all knowledge in the beginning, now and to come."[50]

Rocks, dirt and archaeology aside, along with the multitude of questions raised, we believe all of this is secondary to the real gift and ultimate blessing this complex can bestow upon humanity in these uncertain times. It has nothing to do with history or yesterday, but tomorrow. From the time the eight hawks first appeared on request, and even before, the Original Elders and Custodians were united in sensing the power and presence of the "Old Ones."[51] They were back, and they weren't going and that has an impact on all of us irrespective of colour, creed or gender. As bold as Slater's declaration was, in suggesting these mounds and messages "formulated the basis of all knowledge"[52] yet "to come,"[53] the Elders and Custodians are insisting that's exactly the case. Was before, and will be again.

Opinions aside, there are facts and historical irregularities that are, as Slater rightly observes, "of worldwide interest."[54] Amongst all the excellent and sympathetic research, occasionally Slater erred, and one of his very few misunderstandings, his claim that this place is "the Stonehenge of Australia"[55] is simply wrong. The circles of standing stones at Stonehenge chart solstices and important astronomical events. The complex in Australia however, contains the "basis of all knowledge,"[56] astronomical markers, our First Language, solstices, religious tabernacles and humanities' past history-beginning all the way back to Creation and spanning forward to future prophecies.

Maybe, just maybe, we have got everything wrong. It doesn't really matter either way, because as it stands these Standing Stones and all that did surrounds this site, just doesn't fit into any accepted theory of human evolution, development and settlement. That is a fact. The rest of our research is a work in motion totally at the control of Original Elders and Custodians of Lore. As long as this harmonious arrangement and sequence continues, the truth will prevail and more facts will be revealed.

Acknowledgements:

We would like to thank the following Elders and Custodians of Original Lore (as is the case in our second article the Original people act as a collective, we gave first names only then and will do so again). Deepest gratitude to: **Karno, Rob, Kevin, Uncle Harry, Mark, Jarmbi'je, Iris, Darren, Scott and Adam.**

We also wish to thank all the volunteers on-site. Many have spend considerable time and money in helping yet again and did so for all the right reasons. Thank you so much: **Jim Nutter, David Holstein, Erik Bower, Adam Gotllieb, Ryan Mullins, Gavin Bragg, Sarah Newsome, Richard Patterson, Paul and Phoebe Hoogendyke, John Sirigos, April Holloway, Binnah Pownall, Dellene Strong and Cacey Blackburn.**

Chapter 6

THE AUSTRALIAN MOTHER TONGUE

There are two fundamental elements in the research on the Standing Stones site that are not only intertwined, but are the pivotal points upon which the credentials of the site revolves. First and foremost, talk of a very complex and cryptic language recorded into rock that precedes all other tongues has to be examined in more detail. As sensational as the existence of this first global language may be, any translation, with the original source seemingly lost, is totally dependent upon the character and motivations of the archaeologist who investigated the site.

If these two areas of investigation each earn a tick, then the chances that this site is not only the most important archaeological site in Australia, but the world, increase dramatically. In essence, it all comes down to one piece of advice Slater gave his on-site colleague. If he is right then this is the oldest temple[1] in the world and repository of ancient wisdom. If so, it is only logical for Slater to advise his co-worker to "just place yourself in the position of Petrie or Carter exploring an Egyptian tomb. Your work is of more importance for it relates to the existence of the first men on Earth, their history and their philosophy."[2]

Credentials of the First Language

We have already heard from an Elder of the highest pedigree (Aunty Beve) state that the first Original Language began in Australia (see You Tube, Egyptians in Australia Part 2[3]). What began as a ploy devised by Australian rock art expert, Professor Bednarik, to counter the criticisms archaeologist Lesley Maynard was subjected to, created more questions than answers. What it certainly does do is give some credence to Aunty Beve's insistence the first language began in Australia. Maynard claimed that an ancient form of Original art, referred to as Panaramitee art, which is characterized by thousands of small, pecked petroglyphs, was the precursor to all forms of language and written communication. Such was the intensity of critiques, levelled at her "for some years,"[4] Maynard stated she "was happy to bury it."[5] As discussed in the previous chapter Bednarik carried out a clever test that showed that this form of communication may well have been global in its scope.

Frederic Slater was adamant that not only did the First Language begin in Australia, but that he was able to access the records of a non-Original woman who was taught the Old Tongue.

However, in that respect, Slater made one of his very few errors. To begin with he displayed an acute appreciation for the depth and intricacies of the Sacred Language, but underestimated its resilience. "You are working in a much higher cult which I doubt is understood by present day aborigines. (sic) The teachers have all gone."[6] We beg to differ. The "Teachers"[7] are not gone, just out of sight until the time is ripe. Most assuredly one of those Elders, who spoke on behalf of others with similar knowledge of Lore and Sacred Language, was on site with us when counting rocks and chipping at the edges.

That small error aside, a man of his standing and knowledge, particularly in Egyptology, would only venture to make such challenging statements once fully armed with archaeological evidence of the highest calibre. The confirmation of his notes and interpretations along with a summary of some of the "28,000"[8] words Slater had assembled, by an Original Elder of today, who is fully versed in these matters, appears to be sufficient in every respect.

When what we had always called the six-sided rock was brought onto country, the way it was used, along with the accompanying hand signs and gestures as the Elder shared the six, and at a later date seven, the meanings of this one rock records was just as Slater had described in his letters. The rock belonged to this sacred mound, and has since been placed under the care of appropriate people. What we did see was exactly how it was positioned and understood in the past. Both President and Elder were in accord. Each word from the Sacred Language can have up to four meanings, "20 different forms of suffixes"[9] and an entourage of hand signs. This is, without doubt, the most difficult and mystical language ever spoken. If this is indeed the very first time humans expressed their inner thoughts and inspirations, how far have we fallen?

The Immediate Surrounds

There are records of Europeans, who were busy felling and burning trees disturbing Original people on the mound in 1840, who fled with a few special rocks in hand. It's not a post-Cook construction, that is a fact, but equally, it has no equal in this country and requires a scale of quarrying and transportation that was supposedly never part of the Australian landscape until the British Invasion.

There are no sandstone deposits in this area, nor should there be. Geological maps and hours spent searching the surrounding area only confirm what Slater claimed in his correspondence, the sandstone found on this site was imported from somewhere far off. Whether it is a site 22.5 km away, or much further as we suspect, will be resolved soon. For now the distance is secondary. What can be stated is that there is a massive amount of foreign fill and it came from a long way off.

Many of the sandstone rocks found on the northern and southern slope have right angles, smooth faces and lines that seem to be very unnatural. All of these rocks were brought from afar, and leads us to conclude they have been quarried, transported, shaped and in some cases engraved, using technologies that are not supposed to be a part of any pre-historic Original tool-kit.

So, in summing up, what was our check-list of questions to be answered? In the case of the small mound/burial ground, yes. It is definitely an import, made from material brought from some distance. There are sandstone rocks by the hundreds within and scattered around the edges, most were used for fill but a few were definitely worked and shaped. We have found quite a few of the stones that originally formed pieces of "the Mystic Track of Life,"[10] and have a map identifying the position of each rock which was charted about four months before it was reluctantly ploughed. The second, much bigger mound was most definitely levelled and terraced before the site was ploughed in 1940, but of even more importance was the message written on this boomerang-shaped mound. It breaks every linguistic convention in relation to the content and way humans first spoke. Never the province of esoteric philosophers, the first language was assumed to be basic, few in words and crude in presentation. The Original Sacred Language is a sublime, sophisticated and spiritual merging of symbols, arrangements, hand signs, body parts, animals and numbers into the first spoken and written language.

There are more questions unanswered than resolved, and no doubt some of our explanations are quite radical and not without alternatives. Nevertheless, the smaller mound is totally unique in this country, the materials inside foreign to the surrounding countryside and the sandstone rocks do not belong. Something, whether the participants in attendance or technology applied, was part of an equation, which just doesn't fit into any accepted account of pre-1788 Australia.

If other civilisations were in this country, as Slater is absolutely convinced, it would be remiss to not include his take on not only their presence, but reverence. We are both in agreement in stating that the Egyptians came as apprentices to be tutored in the esoteric insights and cultural refinements that were part and parcel of the Australian landscape and Original philosophy. "There is no mistaking the fact that the aborigines (sic) ... gave not only to the Egyptians their knowledge and their foundation of hieroglyphics and their philosophy but formulated the basis of all knowledge in the beginning, now and to come."[11]

Rocks, dirt and archaeology aside, along with the multitude of questions raised, we believe all of this is secondary to the real gift and ultimate blessing this complex can bestow upon humanity in these uncertain times. This sacred site is so much more than a historical relic, and has as much to do with yesterday as it has with tomorrow. From the time the eight hawks first appeared on request, and even before, the Original Elders and Custodians were united in sensing the power and presence of the "Old Ones."[12]

They were back, and they weren't going and that has an impact on all of us irrespective of colour, creed or gender. As bold as Slater's declaration was in suggesting these mounds and messages "formulated the basis of all knowledge"[13] yet "to come,"[14] the Elders and Custodians are insisting that is exactly the case. Was before, and will be again.

Opinions aside, there are facts and historical irregularities that are, as Slater rightly observes, "of worldwide interest."[15] Amongst all the excellent and sympathetic research, occasionally Slater erred, and one of his very few misunderstandings, his claim that this place is "The Stonehenge of Australia"[16] is simply wrong. The circles of standing stones at Stonehenge chart solstices and important astronomical events. The complex in Australia contains the "basis of all knowledge,"[17] astronomical markers, the First Language, solstices, religious tabernacles and humanities' past history. This temple and all the surrounding stone arrangements go all the way back to Creation and spans forward to future prophecies.

Maybe, just maybe, we have got everything wrong. It doesn't really matter either way, because as it is these Standing Stones and its surroundings, just doesn't fit into any accepted theory of human evolution, development and settlement. That is a fact. The rest of our research is a work in motion totally at the control of Original Elders and Custodians of Lore, and as long as this harmonious arrangement and sequence continues, the truth will prevail and more facts will be revealed.

Chapter 7

ON THE BOAT AGAIN

Being a devout life-long non-swimmer, every journey by boat to the site that we've named 'Emu's Nest,' is laced with equal lashings of anticipation and dread.

Surrounded by sand, salt water, dunes and mangroves there is nothing about this site that is natural. The 185 metre spread of rocks, numbering in the tens of thousands, found below, on and just above the shore line, have no relationship to any other part of the creek bank or nearby geology.

Where did the Sandstone come from?

Before attempting any translation of the Standing Stones narrative, we must first address some pragmatic considerations upon which we were originally unable to throw any light.

When first examining the Standing Stones, one fact highlighted in Slater's correspondence was of prime interest. All of the marked and shaped stones found on both the larger and smaller mounds were sandstone, and as observed by Slater, the nearest deposit of sandstone is over 20 kilometres away. This in itself is challenging. But in our examination of the site, we found both fine and coarse grained sandstone, which logically means some of the sandstone brought onto this site came from much further inland than the finer grained rock.

We now believe we know how this exotic geological cargo reached the mounds, and from where the ships carrying these rocks docked and unloaded.

By the Sea-side

It took a little over an hour of paddling along a creek that ran adjacent to a beach. The creek is salty and both banks are lined with mangroves or sand with a few stands of volcanic rock. We could always hear the waves crashing, all that varied was the volume.

It was only when the surf was at its loudest, that I first sighted our target. Positioned at zero elevation within a massive caldera, surrounded by igneous rock and sand, my expected primary focus was to be the exotic nature of these sandstone imports. And there were thousands upon thousands to choose from, and there were many other types of rocks present, which only added to the intrigue. But all of that background fill was overshadowed by the thousands of rocks bearing flat lines, faces so smooth with sharp hardened edges.

Just as it is at, and between, the two mounds some distance away, many of these rocks were also shaped and showed no evidence of the characteristic percussion points associated with any Original rock on rock technology. A more sophisticated tool, at the very least a steel blade, was an essential part of the technology used to shape these rocks.

What was even more remarkable was that unlike the Standing Stones site, which is nearly all sandstone, this site contained an extensive sampling of all manner of sedimentary and igneous rocks, some we have never seen before. Present on-site is sandstone that is coloured white, yellow, grey and red, and a combination thereof. Equally, there is a substantial variation in the hardness of these sandstone rocks. Some rocks can break in the hand, while others require a blade just to scratch the surface. Basalt, igneous rocks of many types, conglomerates, some close to 30 cm in diameter, quartz and other rocks we've had great difficulty in identifying, were spread all over the site. Even if every engraving and shaped rock was the outcome of natural forces, why is it that there is such an incredible array and quantity of rocks in one specific location surrounded by mangroves and sand? Undeniably, under any normal setting this combination of rocks could never be found together, the Laws of Nature will have it no other way. All we can state with certainty is that outside human intervention and transportation from elsewhere, there is no geological explanation available.

We have chosen eight examples from this bounty from times long gone. In each case, and so many others, there are either a variety of features that are examples of the rarest geological events or this is evidence of different ways of shaping and communication through very sophisticated means. We are mindful that nature is capable of creating all manner of irregularities and shapes. But even so, the concentration of so many very unusual rocks that are so dissimilar, complimented by the variation in rock arrangements spread above and around the only elevated land in the area, seems to add credence to the possibility this was all down to human activity. The commentaries are deliberately brief, as we believe the rocks speak for themselves.

* **Figure 24¹** :

This triangular sandstone rock is 35 cm long and has an almost perfectly flat 180 degree side. The two top edges are parallel, with a triangular right edge and flat underside (not shown in photograph). All three faces are very smooth and level.

* **Figure 25²:**

A semi-rectangular sandstone block with one diagonal edge, 32cm high, 12cm long and 5cm wide. The two featured edges are both at 90 degrees, parallel to each other and all four faces are flat and level.

* **Figure 26³:**

A triangular sandstone rock with straight lines, precise angles and a sharp top edge. All three sides are flat and even, and the top edge is 38cm long. To the left is a rock with what looks like an engraved curved cross. Not only are the markings extremely deep and unusual, it corresponds identically with one of Slater's most important symbols of the Sacred Language. As mentioned previously, the words of the first language words can have many meanings, this sign means "B*********-the Guide to Truth,"⁴ and can also represent the number nine.

The full coverage of the shaped rocks would take several books, but three examples is sufficient and in accord with the rocks found near the two mounds. What is interesting as it is intriguing, is that a high proportion of the shaped rocks appear to have a flat base, sometimes quite small, that is capable of balancing the weight of the rock.

What is of even more interest and deserving of extensive research are the rocks exhibiting deep incisions, patterns, engraved lines and symbols.

* Figure 27[5]:

This rock is divided into eight distinct sections, the incisions or fractures are extremely deep, but as with other rocks there is no sign of any cracking on the flat unmarked base. We believe that there was no natural agency responsible.

Figure 28[6]:

This rock has a very flat level unmarked underside, without any marking or fracture, yet has over 40 segmented sections on the curved topside. Each has been separated by deep incisions into what may be an igneous rock, being much harder than sandstone, this only accentuates the need to have access to the hardest and most durable metal tools. It measures 24 cm by 24 cm at its widest, and there seems to be a discreet symbol/Original letter in the bottom right hand sector, and the possibility of another symbol just above the centre.

* Figure 29[7]:

This sandstone rock is also flat underneath and quite smooth, and was engraved into five parts. The most interesting cut is the deepest, it stops at both edges and there is no trace of it continuing on the other side. To engrave so deeply into sandstone and cause no further fracturing takes a real degree of skill complimented by the use of sophisticated metal tools with very fine blades.

* Figure 30[8]:

Another sandstone rock engraved into segments, eight on this occasion. What is particularly interesting is the V shape on the right side, past the point where both carved lines stop, there is no further cracking.

* Figure 31[9]:

An engraving that again looks to signify "B*********."[10] The deep incisions in the sandstone rock show no evidence of fracturing underneath. There are a few fine cracks running off this incision. The depth of engraving again is indicative of a fine touch with a powerful metal blade.

Shaped rocks aside, there is much more to this complex, the quantity and variations of stone arrangements is as massive as it is overwhelming. There was so much going on here, and at this stage anything past the most basic deductions is beyond our present brief. There are rock walls, circles, lines of rocks and arrangements that don't have any academic label. There are rocks weighing hundreds of kilograms that have been moved some distance, others were stacked while some rocks were positioned in single lines.

The Jetty at Emu's Nest

What only cements the connection between the huge variety of rock constructions and deconstructions, is the structure that juts out of the shore-line at Emu's Nest. This arrangement resembles a jetty or a wharf, It's a 9 metre (30 ft) by 5 metre (16.5 ft) sandstone construction that sits higher than the surrounding shore. The jetty is made entirely out of sandstone rocks, both fine and coarse grained, which vary greatly in colouring. With the saltwater at least two metres higher, this is a perfect place for vessels to dock three thousand years ago. This was undoubtedly the location from which the rocks at the Standing Stones site were transported. From here, marked and shaped rocks (along with many other goods and sacred objects) were sent out from the coast to the Standing Stones site and other places of importance.

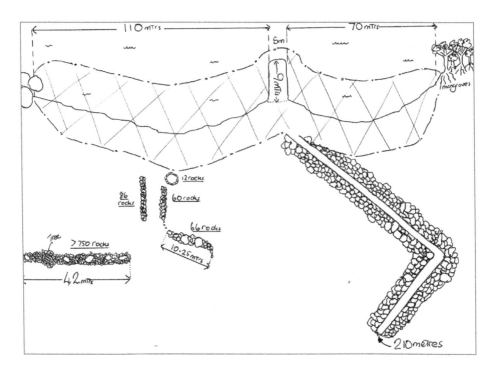

* **Figure 32:** Emu's Nest Jetty Diagram[11]

We believe that the 185 metre spread of tens of thousands of rocks was originally part of a rock wall built along this section of the shore-line, and that the wall collapsed around 500 odd years ago when a tsunami hit this part of the east coast of Australia. The strength and motion of a tsunami is consistent with rocks being spread between 8-10 metres (26-32 ft) into the creek and only 2 metres (6.5 ft) up the slope of the creek bank. We suspect that the wave knocked the wall over and forward just up the bank, then the backwash dragged the fallen stones back into the water.

On a Road to Nowhere

What only adds to the mystery, is what seems to be a massive construction involving the placement of hundreds of tonnes of igneous rock above and below a 'road' which begins five metres to the south of the jetty. Exhibiting a consistent width of 2 metres as it curves up a slope from the jetty to the top of the rise (elevation 35 metres), this section of road measured 210 metres. But we hadn't finished, as there was more road ahead.

All the rocks are igneous, and quite a few weigh hundreds of kilograms and some weigh over half a tonne. There is neither a contemporary nor historical record of such a huge collection of rocks placed below and above a road or any like construction in this area.

The repeated stacking of rocks to maintain the integrity of this road seems in contradiction to the randomness of any bulldozer blade, and more keeping with human hands or tools. Moreover, outside mud- crabbing, the mangroves and sand provide no economical incentive to construct a rudimentary track, let alone a road of such proportions.

NOW IT GETS HEAVIER….

The whole scenario gets very complicated when trying to understand how igneous rocks, weighing over five hundred kilograms, were moved and positioned above and below the road and the two Original rock arrangements at Emu's Nest. I remember recently standing on the road with a colleague, Jim Nutter, who playing the role of 'devil's advocate', suggested this was all the result of an old bulldozer, clearing a track down to the mangroves. Rather than debate possibilities, I pointed out to Jim four rocks, all of considerable weight, all carefully stacked on top of each other, and asked him what blade or bulldozer was capable of that balanced arrangement. He quickly moderated his position, by one degree, agreeing that this was ancient and that people from way back were in involved in placing these particular rocks, but hastened to add that maybe, much later, the dozer came down to repair the older construction.

Standing in nearby Mullumbimby are many numerous sandstone slabs, some weighing tonnes, which came from 'somewhere' nearby and repositioned within the town and parks as features and bearers of plaques. Their origin through official channels is unknown, but not unknown to our research team. We are confident that all rocks imported to the area, whether weighing one kilogram or a tonne, were originally shipped to and unloaded at the jetty, which forms part of Emu's Nest.

One unknown in this equation is the logistics once docked. We have no Dreaming Story or Elder's guidance, nor any account in Frederic Slater's translation to draw upon. The manner of transportation of the heavy rocks to various inland locations and the exotic fill at the smaller mound at the Standing Stones site must at this stage remain hypothetical.

Around the Corners

Complementary to the wharf, walls and road, there is an abundance of all manner of Original stone arrangements which number more than twenty. We decided to begin our research by focusing upon two rather impressive rock arrangements found on the northern side of the jetty.

The Original stone arrangement closest to the jetty seems to be made of three sets of interrelated rock walls/alignments. All have some sections where the rocks are stacked, and together they lead down the slope towards a simple circle of 12 rocks, which is positioned within metres of the creek. The first part of this layout begins with wall/line of rocks measuring 10.25 metres. With the exception of the southern section of the wall, which curls up the hill and points directly towards a striking igneous outcrop of about 4 metres in height and 5 metres across, the main body of rocks are aligned in a straight line 38 degrees to the south west. There are 66 rocks in this first line, and what doesn't seem coincidental is that before finally veering up the hill, if maintaining the line the majority of rocks are pointing directly towards a second igneous boulder of similar dimensions. In our opinion this rock arrangement's primary role was to deliberately highlight both huge boulders, which more than likely are of great significance to Original sensibilities.

There is a gap of about 5 metres between these arrangements with a spread of three rocks which seem to connect the upper rock line to the two lower group of rocks and the circle. Both lines face east 105 degrees, with the arrangement closest to the first wall having 60 rocks, and the northern wall 86 rocks one metre apart. The rock circle is two metres from the smaller rock arrangement.

The two smaller lines of igneous rocks (8 and 10 metres in length) vary in weight from about 1 to ten kilograms. We believe that the higher wall is obviously the centre point, and that there are by our estimation, at least nine rocks weighing over 100 kilograms. In what only adds to the difficulties in logistics and construction, one of the rocks in this arrangement weighs no less than a half a tonne.

The second line of rocks we examined is simpler in design, much longer and far bigger. Such is the quantity and variation in size - an approximate count of 750 is a bare minimum. Measuring 42 metres and only 3 degrees off north, there are 6 rocks weighing over 100 kilograms and one over 500 kilograms.

Pushing the Limits

Of no less interest, but certainly more open to interpretation, is the huge array of rock markings. There are literally thousands of rocks that exhibit all manner of markings, depressions, incisions, lines and 'bulbs' which are spread along the shore-line and further up the slope. Without a doubt some of these markings are due to natural agents, but where do we draw the line, because many are certainly marked by tools? Even if every rock bearing some type of depression or fracturing is indeed natural caused by a large variety of geological forces, why is it that all of these many different marked rocks are found within one concentrated cluster down by the sea surrounded by sand?

The real problem is that if this is all simply down to nature, some of the fractures are extremely deep. Many incisions cut through more than half of the rock and show no evidence of further cracking or fine lines, either on the underside, or past the point where the depression stops. In some cases, we feel with no residual effects, clean cuts of consistent depth with no prospect of fracturing, only a metal tool or something even more sophisticated could be responsible.

What is even more problematic is the huge selection of what seemed to be, as Frederic Slater proposed when dealing with the appearance of so many sandstone rocks with straight lines, edges and flat sides at the Standing Stones site, "shaped stones."[12]

Undeniably some of these rock's features are due to natural forces, but some rocks have so many flat sides, sharp angles and straight lines, that they really do seem to be pushing the limits of natural processes into the stratosphere and well beyond. In every case bar none, not one rock examined displayed any semblance of a percussion point, which is very much a part of the effect that a hammer-stone has on any rock when used in shaping. No indentation was visible, and nor for that matter is there any indication of any chisel marks. Knowing as we do now that shaped stones like these were a device used to convey language, directions and heavenly abodes, etc, it is not that easy to readily dismiss any stone with straight angles and flat sides. None more so than the photograph supplied (Figure 34) of a small rock found on-site.

*Figure 33:
Sharpe angled marked rock[13]

The narrower 'top' section of the rock has broken off some considerable time ago. It would seem this shaped rock tapered off to a peak, with all four faces and lines converging to the same shared point exhibiting a symmetry that is rarely, if ever, part of Nature's plan. The stone artefact has seven sides. Three faces are at (what we assume to be), the thicker back-section, and from that base there are four sides of which three of the edges running forward are still very sharp. It seems logical to assume that the more weathered sides and faces were also just as acute and smooth when first constructed. Neither percussion nor blade point can be seen, and even the concept of a non-iron blade shaping this rock is an extremely difficult proposition to accept.

Another anomaly peculiar to this site is the puzzling diversity of micro eco-systems growing within the 5 acres we have investigated. Flanked by mangroves, there are discreet stands of palms, grass trees, lawyer cane, eucalypts, lamandra, paper barks, salt tolerant rainforest trees along with other rainforest trees and vines that are supposedly extremely sensitive to salt water or air.

A partial explanation can be found within an explanation which an Original custodian made on site. At the shoreline to the south of the jetty he noticed stands of lamandra and lawyer cane on the bank, literally within a metre of the salt water. The constant flow of fresh water seeping underneath and into the creek blocking the entry of saltwater running upstream would certainly explain why these plants are cm's from salt water. The consequent dilution of salt water may explain why the mangroves were absent and the presence of lamandra and lawyer cane were so close to the edge, but many of the diverse stands of vegetation are much higher up the bank and harder to explain.

At this stage of developments there are very few, if any, definites beyond acknowledging a trail of irregularities. In the simplest terms there are far too many rocks which are too varied and marked, the geology on display is too close to the ocean and too much at odds with the immediate geography. As to why, when, who or what was responsible, the jury is still out and most of the evidence is yet to be collected and collated. Until those tasks are completed it would appear passing any definitive commentary or conclusion would be unwise.

Nevertheless, once this site is placed into context and in association with the 184 Standing Stones, an ancient road (probably Egyptian or older) in the Nightcap National Park and other sites in the general vicinity, what is consistent is the evidence of a highly sophisticated technology and activities outside the embrace of any Original rock and stick tool-kit. In our opinion, at the very least there is an ancient Egyptian connection on display, and we are confident that most of the archaeology reaches much further back in time.

Whether these relics and activities are sourced from earlier Homo sapiens or erectus communities, the fabled Lemurian civilisation or outsourced to the Pleiades, is a moot point. The only finding that can be stated with absolute confidence is that wherever the archaeology leads, the answer will not be found in any accepted Australian text-book or curriculum dealing with Original pre-history. The rest is history.

With the point of first arrival identified and a huge variety of rocks, including many more sandstone rocks, numbering in the tens of thousands located at a separate site, the next question to grapple with relates to the shapes and markings engraved into these rocks. What do they mean? Why was this site chosen? And just as important a consideration yet to be fully examined, relates to the man who wrote this account. How can we believe a person who lost his reputation and claimed nearly everything written about the ancient world history is wrong?

Chapter 8

THE SACRED LANGUAGE OF ROCKS

FACT OR FICTION

At this stage of the proceedings, every claim made by Slater and his colleague (whose name we cannot supply as it would give too many clues in relation to location), bar one, has been addressed, and in most cases substantiated beyond reasonable doubt.

The smaller mound is not natural and nor are the materials selected to construct this burial ground. That it was a sacred burial site reserved for the most spiritual and revered, was intuitively sensed by Original and non-Original alike when we were on site, and confirmed by Slater's notes and his co-workers description of "thrice bent man"[1] and another form of elaborate internment of which we are unfamiliar. The sandstone rocks, which will eventually number in the thousands once our investigation is complete, are not part of the local geology, and the obvious shaped and worked edges of many of these rocks was achieved with tools and technology that was not supposed to be a part of any Original tool-kit.

Interpretations aside, these are facts supported by the geology and archaeology on the site. The bona fides references of the many "terraces,"[2] made by both academics and supported by the local farmer, is a little less concrete, but to deny the construction of the terraces, the farmer and both academics have to be lying. I have met the farmer responsible, the other two gentlemen died and I cannot vouch for their character, but I have absolutely no doubt the farmer is desperate for the truth to be unveiled. I know for a fact that he is too honourable a man to deceive or lie, and because of his undoubted integrity, it is with greatest confidence we place the existence of these terraces into the absolute fact category.

Rock Language

So too the existence of carved letters or symbols. Some of our group saw markings on the rocks that looked decidedly artificial, but since the women who were responsible for recording the rocks were denied permission to move or even touch them, more investigation by the men was required. This will take place the next occasion that we are on-site.

In the meantime, as it was with the terraces, both academics and the farmer acknowledged seeing many inscriptions on the rocks. Slater often goes into great detail in both identifying individual letters from the Sacred Language, and supplying definitions that resonate to a repeating esoteric theme.

- "It is the letter K - the 7th letter of the 16 letters alphabet.
  K: Means a seed - the germ of life."[3]
- A: "immortality of the soul with light a coming in."[4]
- "W: from darkness to the earth."[5]

No letter performs a phonetic role or a component sound of a single word as such, but more an esoteric statement of cause and effect.

For exactly the same reason given when discussing the credentials of terraces, we also accept as fact the existence of an Original alphabet and accompanying symbols. It has recently come to our attention that a person invited onto the site in the 1960's to examine the archaeology has been accused of taking marked rocks. We have been told by someone who we are convinced is honest, that these rocks had engraved letters and that another incredibly important artefact was also taken off the mound.

But the last claim attributed to this complex, that this is the first and most Sacred Language created by modern humans, and that Slater was able to correctly translate this ancient mystical script, is a much more difficult assignment. Despite the theft, hints and possibilities, we found nothing on site that validated Slater's hypothesis, but not so off-site.

Six Reasons Why

We intend to present six pieces of evidence, some circumstantial, others have a solid archaeological base and one comes from a place and inspiration that is timeless. Undeniably nothing, in this particular case, can give a definitive answer. Nevertheless, the culmination of so many corroborating divergent sources all leading to the same possible conclusion leaves alternatives, outside of what Slater claims in his notes, in short supply.

First up, upon initially reading Slater's claims that this complex is a testimonial to the First Sacred Language that was spoken and recorded in rock by Original people; this was no surprise to us as we had heard and fully accepted such claims much earlier. Aunty Beve was a Darkinjoong[6] Elder of undeniable pedigree who has recently passed over. Fully initiated according to ancient Original protocol, Aunty Beve was the Keeper of the Women's Dreaming Stories, and the person we always consulted whenever on her country. A woman of impeccable standing, her word on Original Lore should never be challenged. As such, her public declaration over three years ago (You Tube Egyptians in Australia Part 2[7]) when discussing the origin of the 300 hieroglyphs engraved into sandstone walls at Kariong, that there is in the region engraved writings that not only pre-date any Egyptian script, but was created by Original men and women, left us open to this truth well before reading Slater's correspondence.

* **Figure 34** :
Bambara Glyphs[8]

A crucial element of Slater's translation relates to the authenticity and accuracy of the semi-dictionary of the First Language symbols. Slater was given the work of another. The wife of the first Magistrate of Wollombi, Mrs. David Dunlop (Eliza Hamilton Dunlop) was a remarkable woman who not only won the trust of the local Original people during the first contact period in the 1840s, but had a real love of culture and Original causes. She translated many Original writings and poems and penned lyrics for a scathing song about the Myall Creek Massacre. It was for all these reasons, and many others, she won their trust and was allowed to learn the symbols, signs and angles that make up the First Language.

Unfortunately, although Slater had compiled a book *("Australia the Land of Seven Elements"[9])* which was devoted totally to explaining the grammar, inter-disciplinary merging of numbers, 38 hand signs, 21 body parts, 16 letters and numerous other components identified by Dunlop that underpin the First Language, his ego refused to budge and the war intervened. Earlier in his correspondence he explains his intention to publish his book, but only after convincing one troublesome critic[10]. Considering he was espousing a theory that saw the Original people as the intellectual superiors of the ancient Egyptians and that they came in supplication seeking wisdom, he is taking an extremely radical stance. Conventional thinking was that the Original people were the most primitive and backward peoples on the planet, therefore, waiting until all mainstream academic objectors had ceased criticising him seemed a futile exercise. Moreover, once the whole complex was destroyed after months of conflict with Government officials, anthropologists, and representatives from the Australian Museum, Slater withdrew from the fray, said no more in any public arena and died in 1947.

Despite the damage and escalating antagonistic academic climate, Slater was adamant that this was the First language spoken, and it can't be denied his translation and commentaries are quite thorough and well thought out. Until a critic actually examines his written explanations, knowing that he was elected as the leader amongst his peers throughout the country, Slater's assurances and research should be given the respect it deserves.

What is also a serious point of interest are two sites Slater refers to which bear witness to other examples of Aboriginal writing. Being the highest authority on such matters, Slater was often called on by authorities to investigate new, and sometimes extremely old, discoveries. Conversant in ancient Original tongue and script, his investigations were brief and concise. "They had me out at Maroota-beyond Windsor to a ceremonial ground which the anthropologists have been endeavouring to decipher for 25 years. It was deciphered in 25 minutes. The Manly Council asked me to give them a drawing and a translation of aboriginal (sic) writing found on the site of an old house … quite close to where Governor Phillip landed and found the blacks "Manly fellows."[11]

What needs to be appreciated is that two government organisations sought out Slater's expertise on the Original tongue, and that the Manly Council requested a copy of a "translation of aboriginal (sic) writing."[12] If acknowledged as a language, and seeking out Slater's translation, it seems logical to assume he is indeed an expert of the ancient Original written language. If so, his claim that there is a Sacred Language, the first on this planet, must be given even more credence.

Degrees, Alignments and Letters in the Post

To begin with, for us, the most challenging concept of all the elements that make up the first formalised communication entails the language of stone arrangements. Until I stood on the mound with an Original Elder conversant in the Sacred Language of rock angles and edges, I couldn't fathom how this could actually work. Once we chose what we felt to be where the central point of the southern circle originally was, the Elder placed the seven-sided rock on the ground. He supplied more meanings than any remembered and my misgivings were resolved. What we can confirm was that amongst the many meanings the rock also pointed to the location where the northern circle was aligned, and that this Original man was telling a truth that was old as humanity, and some.

The fifth reason why we are so convinced Slater was right in identifying the Sacred Language and "the Mystic Track of Life,"[13] as chronicled on the larger mound, is the most amazing and substantial. What was sent to us recently from a representative of the Elders concerned, could only come about if they also knew of the first tongue. And that is it! At this moment it's too secret and private to be discuss, but the reason we received this concrete proof was to set us on this path. The rest is a matter of faith. Under that banner, we ask the reader to trust us on this matter. What we have been given is the ultimate incentive to stand by Slater, but for now, must remain under wraps. (Since this was written it has been decided to give more details, which appeared in an earlier Chapter 3.)

Cryptic or Literal, it all Reads the Same

In concluding the case on behalf of the Sacred Language we complete a circle that began with Aunty Beve. It is our belief that some of the hieroglyphs at Kariong and the Standing Stones 40 kilometres from Mullumbimby, share the same narrative and inspiration. They are, we believe, essentially telling the same story in rock, but through different script. And this, of course, is the last step in our research, the translation and understanding of what this ancient tabernacle was meant to say is nowhere near complete.

Knowing we will fall short no matter how this is approached, as a first step, the best we can do is compare and contrast between the two narratives and continue our research once establishing four common themes.

- "The Breath of God is the Divine Light of the Soul." [14]
- "The light of Truth flows like a river of fire from God to the soul of man and woman united." [15]
- "The Grand Inspector of Workings." [16]
- "Enter and Learn the Truth of the Divine Light."[17]
- "The soul of man came from the Immortal Light to drink the water of life from God." [18]
- "Life comes in and Life goes out in darkness to the light that holds it forever." [19]

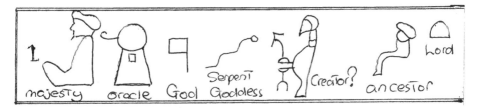

- "From Darkness to Light." [20]
- "Clouds across the sky." [21]
- "Darkness." [22]
- "Man … was not given power to endow man a soul." [23]

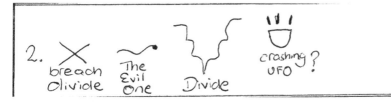

- "Life is brought in a bag." [24]

- God came in with Light from Darkness and gave man a soul and the sons of man brought in with light became the pillars of heaven." [25]
- "He who came from on high brought life into the world." [26]
- "He who brought life into the world set down man and woman and gave them the sacred means of propagating life." [27]
- "Divine light emanating from a rod which tells of the fire that brought life from afar point east to west." [28]

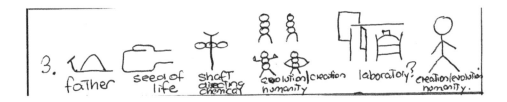

- "The divine light emanating from the rod which tells of the fire that brought life from afar point east to west." [29]
- "Guided by Truth man came to Earth through darkness from the Light of Life that shines far off." [30]
- "Truth brought out on wings to earth from God to man." [31]
- "The divine light of God gives the soul and the fire which brought life from afar." [32]
- "The truth brought in from the fire which brings life from afar." [33]
- "Man (life) came to earth as man with all his senses (seven of them) and was established in Truth." [34]
- "The fire - that brings life from afar off comes through darkness of the clouds which conceal within the divine light directed by God for man to hold." [35]

In concluding this comparison, for now, the only comment we would like to offer relates to the last and largest section. There are seven declarations littered with:

- "came to earth," [36]
- "life from afar," [37]
- "comes through darkness" [38] (quite possibly space),
- "wings to Earth," [39]

- "shines far off," [40]
- and coming "to Earth as man with all his senses." [41]

Outside staring into space for inspiration, we can't see where else this passage could lead.

Admittedly we have taken license in our extra-terrestrial interpretation, and never having ascended upwards further than a domestic jet is allowed, our expertise in space travel is non-existent. But there are others who flew much further and it seems fitting to conclude this comparison with their observations, and that of their Commander-in-Chief.

- "At no time, when the astronauts were in space, were they alone: there was a constant surveillance by UFOs."[42] (Astronaut Commander Scott Carpenter)

- "We all know UFOs are real, all we need to ask is where are they from."[43] (Astronaut Dr. Captain Edgar Mitchell)

- "There's a government inside the government and I don't control it."[44] President Bill Clinton's response to a question asked "by senior White House reporter Sarah McClendon, "[45] about "why he was not doing anything about UFO Disclosure."[46]

- Paul Hellyer "first spoke out about his belief that governments are concealing an alien presence back in 2005, when he said that UFOs are as prevalent as airplanes in our skies" [47] and "has accused world powers of concealing the presence of aliens on earth, is calling on the government to release what he believes is hidden information about UFOs "[48] (Canadian Defence Minister, Engineer, writer and Commentator).

The last words given on Slater's character, motivations and honesty should be left for the man under question to present his side of the argument. It is such a bizarre tale, at one time he was the elected representative of all Australian archaeologists, then within a year he just disappeared and died soon after with nothing said or commemorated in his honour. It is a strange and somewhat tragic story, best told by the person who was censored and reviled for simply telling the Original truth.

Chapter 9

CONSPIRACY: THE MAN WHO WAS
THEN WASN'T

I came ever so close to relenting and using the dreaded 'c-word,' conspiracy, as the heading for this chapter. Slater's stellar career and research started out with so much promise, then fell into a heap and literally disappeared.

What can be stated with complete confidence is that the topic of ancient Egyptian influence in Australia was thoroughly canvassed and received favourably within academic circles and mainstream press. From the period between 1910 and 1937 a variety of eminent scholars and researchers were united in their belief that there had been some sort of interaction between ancient Egyptians and Original people. Sir Grafton Elliot-Smith (Professor, medical Doctor, anatomist and hyper-diffusionist prehistory proponent), Professor A.P. Elkin (anthropologist and writer: Sydney University), Dr. Hermann Klaatsch (anthropologist, writer and introduced field studies into academia) and Slater were but four of the many who proposed that there was an ancient Egyptian contact in Australia.

Then the climate had swung full circle, at sometime between 1937 and 1939 academics, the media and representatives from the Commonwealth of Australia took the matter into their own hands and made sure strife would befall any who objected. As Frederic Slater confided in personal correspondence, "I have shipped a sea of troubles."[1] During these turbulent times of suspicion and threats of confiscation of property, long formed allegiances evaporated and incredible pressure was placed upon Slater and those who tried not to buckle under the lies and the eventual wilful destruction.

Fortunately, as is always the case, when pirates and deniers of truth are at the helm, their lies and actions were never fully concealed. Yes Slater's academic standing plummeted, all his academic records mysteriously vanished, and we cannot find one official reference to him anywhere bar what we have written recently. Nor could we find one visual image of his face or even a stray foot, it is as if he never existed.

This cover-up seemed a resounding success and once again the urge to use that reviled 'c-word' stirs within. So complete was the eradication of one very special site that brought all of this Egyptian talk beyond the 'tipping-point,' Slater and his colleagues towed the line and backed away.

Despite the vacuum and collateral damage, his letters, diagrams and notes, along with all the personal correspondence sent to his on-site colleague escaped the censor's attention. When reading his personal correspondence in chronological order it becomes quite obvious that as the months in 1939 pass, Slater becomes less buoyant and more suspicious. His mistrust for those speaking on behalf of officialdom seems to verge on paranoia, but once reading of the events and approaches that led up to his loathing, I feel he was actually quite justified.

Reading the Lines and in Between

Slater's opening letter was already laced with equal amounts of foreboding and excitement, and alas, ominous in nature when it came to future developments. He was positive that what was found at the Standing Stones site "will be of worldwide interest."[2] As promising as that opinion was, there was a steep price to pay and it was obvious Slater had already identified those whose motives were suspect and devious. In a tragically prophetic warning, Slater advised his co-worker to have nothing to do with one of the many agents-provocateurs.

"Re the invitation of the Anthropological Society to send down some specimens. Don't. They know nothing. They are only making another attempt to steal the brains and property of others." [3]

What is quite illuminating and certainly divides the lines of demarcation, is that the same Anthropological Society was standing behind and beside Slater barely two years earlier when he had received kudos for a job well done. The team whose work in 1937 Slater proudly presented as a joint paper to an enthusiastic audience at the Science Congress, contained two members of the Anthropological Society that he now despised. People he commended as being "proper"[4] "archaeologists"[5] and "explorers,"[6] are now deemed to be unprincipled scoundrels liable to "steal."[7] "Mr. W. J. Enright"[8] was a "former president of the Sydney Anthropological Society of Sydney,"[9] and Mr. Roy H. Goddard was one of the "delegates of the Sydney Anthropological Society;"[10] two years later the whole membership and former colleagues are damned by association. This leads us to believe that this shift away from the Original truth and First Language and towards the academic status quo was already in progress before the Standing Stones site was brought to Slater's attention in early 1939.

In what only widened the scale and complicity of the officially sanctioned agencies now railing against archaeology of the highest order that Slater and others were advocating, he reminded his assistant that "the Anthropological Society is run by the Museum. Nuf sed."[11]

It is not as if Slater was going to roll over and accept the inevitable. He was very pro-active and was constantly trying to find ways to circumvent the actions of the many he knew were now actively conspiring against him, and the Standing Stones site in particular. In his second letter he proposed that this site was so "important to archaeology and must be preserved as a national memorial."[12] It was a theme he would raise throughout his letters, and on occasions provided specific details as to how this could happen. Despite the positive façade, deep down we suspect he knew he was swimming upstream as everyday passed and the currents were accelerating in the opposite direction.

Slater saw this dispute in terms of a battle, in one corner was the rigour of his archaeology and translations of the Standing Stones, of which this "language is the basis of all languages."[13] Slater was adamant that what was discovered would "revolutionise many departments of knowledge"[14] and provided the "knockout blow to animal evolution."[15] He was correct in believing that because he was "not loved by anthropologists,"[16] who he felt were the "authors of modern materialism,"[17] were in his eyes the enemy.

In his fourth and fifth letter Slater was less prone to melancholy and seemed to be quite positive about future prospects, as his research of the Standing Stones continued to expand more horizons. Slater spoke of a renaissance and "awakening of a new interest"[18] in "the wonder of these stones that talk."[19] In a very optimistic frame of mind, he predicted there would be headlines "in the newspapers"[20] reporting "Australia's Link with primordial Man,"[21] and "The Stonehenge of Australia."[22]

Harkening back to his concept of protection through tourism, he lauded this site as "a world discovery,"[23] and declared that "the Mystic Track of Life … is destined to become a magnet for scientists and tourists alike."[24] Continuing in the same positive vein through publicity and paid access, he noted that the current owner "will see the glory of ownership which may prove more profitable than his farm."[25]

Regrettably his buoyant mood was fleeting and by the sixth letter he reminded his colleague once again of whom not to trust and also of what he felt was the sites' legal loophole and saving grace. Unfortunately, as events unfolded both here and abroad, the apparent strength of this tenure eventually became its Achilles heel.

"If you are approached by any museum authorities do not give one of them up no matter how they bluster. They know nothing about them but profess to be the guardians of everything on earth. Fortunately the discovery is on private property and no claim can stand. Nor would anybody be permitted to take possession of them or claim them …"[26]

Boiling Billies at the car park and bus bay

The seventh letter illustrates how Slater constantly fluctuated between utter despair and rattling off proactive ripostes. Knowing secrecy is the weapon of the deceitful and most ruling elites, Slater saw salvation and protection through public interest and commercial incentives as a powerful counter, and set out in his concluding remarks how this could come to fruition.

"Tell XXXX that when we have got the mound properly laid out and the symbols explained he will have to make a charge for entering the ground set aside a place for parking cars and a small area for boiling the billy. If I were drawing up the rules I would permit drivers of public vehicles certainly all buses to enter free only charging for the passengers." [27]

Two letters further on it becomes obvious that the forces of repression and government intransigence were fully mobilised, and the owner of the farm had been formally approached by post.

"I warned you very early in the piece that the anthropologists... would start blustering and making declarations as if they owned the earth. They know nothing about archaeology and consequently are "incompetent" to express an opinion… I would like to get copies of the letters sent to XXXX." [28]

Apparently the pressure had been ramped up considerably and the owner was receiving a series of official "letters." [29] That being the case, Slater's belligerence and disdain may be understandable, but I'm not sure it was the best tactic to adopt in reply. If employing Slater's advice to respond to this action by declaring sarcastically in writing to the anthropologists that "no incompetent person is permitted on it," [30] I can't see how this would create anything other than more grief ahead.

There then seemed to be a brief respite in hostilities because up until the twelfth letter from Slater, there is no mention of plotting from anthropologists, Museum officials or Government agents. This letter opens with new developments and a positive attitude, but as the narrative continues it becomes clear that the new avenue Slater is chasing is a sponsor overseas, because within Australia we suspect he had realised that he'd has lost not only the battle, but perhaps the entire war.

"Are we Downhearted?" [31] MOST DEFINITELY

Slater had made contact in "America where I hope to introduce XXXX XXXX and make an appeal for the diversion of some of those Carnegie and Rockefeller funds." [32] The reason this wasn't done earlier is inferred in an off-hand comment that really shows the local forces stacked up against Slater are in the ascendency. "Are we downhearted? The sun of fortune will shine on us yet." [33] And it seems Slater now hoped that the fiscal sun will rise in America, because it had set in Australia. It would seem that those Slater named as his enemies were directly responsible for his despondency and desperation in seeking overseas funding when every avenue was now closed off in his country of origin.

And so this cynicism and frustration continued throughout the exchange of letters. Finally, in Slater's last letter, we see that his cause is lost and the final step was about to be taken to silence this whole untidy talk of ancient Egyptians in Australia, and of the First Language spoken by modern Original humans. It may well have been viewed as the final solution at the time, but when concealing an ancient truth of such immense importance to global affairs past and present, there are so many loose ends to destroy or cover up.

Of vital importance is Slater's dismay when "your statement about a visit from a Lands Department officer stirred me up a bit."[34] He immediately wrote "to the Minister for Lands"[35] complaining about the actions of people "in the Museum and in the University,"[36] but sensed time was running out, as was his patience. Adopting an unfamiliar tone when instructing his colleague on site, born no doubt out of helplessness and a real sense that the battle with officials and all manner of academics were well and truly lost, he wrote "I suggest - no demand this time - you make a complete chart of the mound." [37] Never before had he been so strident. However, his fears were well grounded, for within months the site and surrounding rock constructions was disc ploughed into the ground and completely destroyed.

Knowing how sympathetic the owner was to what Slater and his colleague were researching, and that he had abstained from ploughing the paddock lest he disturb one shaped or placed rock, the fact he told his son to destroy the site seems at odds with his previous deeds and known sympathies. Of course, a visit from the Ministry of Lands in 1940, when Australia was at war and under martial law, was an interesting development. There could only be one topic under discussion and instruction, the land their ancestors settled in the late 19th century was the only reason this official came to the farm. What was said can never be proven. Nonetheless, the intensity of opposition, threatening letters sent and unlimited powers of acquisition the Australian Government possessed during war-time, could lead one to assume that while the Standing Stones stood, the land was under immediate threat of acquisition. The farmer therefore had no choice. If he didn't destroy the site his land and heritage would be lost.

Put to the Disc-plough

Once the farmer directed his son to disc plough the smaller stones and store the bigger stones in the dairy, the letters stopped and government officials made no further front door visits. Slater was gagged, then officially disappeared without a trace, and everything fell back into place. No more ancient Egyptian mischief was reported in the press and Slater disappeared from all academic records and correspondence.

The case was closed and the coast was cleared of all things Egyptian, and the whole untidy mess remained in stasis for nearly seventy-five years.

With Slater's notes now recovered, more corroborating archaeology has been conducted, and this being a more enlightened and educated climate, one may suspect that the truth can finally be revealed with talk of much earlier official intransigence merely a relic of more repressive times. Alas, nothing has changed and ignorance still reigns. We have also been 'gagged,' threatened by Government officials both by post and telephone over this site, while many of our overseas interviews have been jammed or wiped.

In our final chapter on this long suffering censorship (for the time being), it becomes apparent that academics and government agencies of today are no less proactive or spiteful, and often quite conniving, in suppressing the same, and many new inconvenient chapters of Original history. However, there is one new addition to this mix. Slater had no trouble nominating his enemies, but gave no indication that he was aware of the motives of the many arms of government and academia that were openly conspiring against his research. This time around we can also identify the culprits, but can go the extra step, as we know why they are compelled to maintain the deceit. It is of some use to 'know thy enemy,' what is even more beneficial is to know why thy enemy is manipulating and fabricating.

Armed with the Original truth, aware of who and why, at least the contest is on a 'level playing field.' Knowing that truth and fiction must collide someday, all we have to do is tell the Original truth and patiently wait for that day of reckoning.

Chapter 10

STONES THAT TALK [1]

Frederic Slater believed that the Standing Stones site contained "stones that talk."[2] He was undeniably right but grossly underestimated the volume and variations of these "stones that talk."[3] We knew nothing of rocks like these until a little over three years ago.

Ros Mulder made contact with local bushman extraordinaire Jake Cassar seeking some guidance. Jake realised immediately how important Ros' archaeology was and suggested she contact us as soon as possible. As much as Ros' account of how this amazing relic was found and the list of academics who literally ran away shielding their eyes from this marked rock seemed so compelling, until we could touch the rock and see it for ourselves, we were not prepared to pass any judgement.

I decided it would be both of assistance and in the spirit of sharing if I asked Michael Tellinger [4] and Louise Clark, who were spending a day with us viewing a variety of sites we are researching, if they would also like to examine the rock. We arranged for Ros to meet us at the end of day at an agreed point and approximate time.

During our day on country Michael and Louise were shown pictures of this enigmatic rock and were certainly very keen to inspect. What struck Michael was the delicacy of cut and the similarities to the Blombos Cave Rocks[5] , which was a touch difficult for us to come to grips with as Evan and I had no idea what these rocks were, or that they even existed. A quick glance towards Evans' shrug and raised eyebrows left me none the wiser. Michael spoke about the Blombos stones in such a casual manner, as if such news was well known, and it may well be the case elsewhere, but certainly not by us. I momentarily entertained the idea of bluffing my way through our impasse and feigning familiarity, but such was Michael's enthusiasm and talk of the incredible antiquity of these South African stones, I swallowed my pride and pleaded complete ignorance.

Among his many qualities, Michael is obviously a very patient man, he took us through a 101 introduction of the African stones he has personally seen, and in what is a fascinating extension in timing, they are agreed by mainstream circles to be somewhere between 75-100,000 years old. It is claimed that the engravings on these rocks is the very earliest evidence of Homo sapiens art/communication yet to be found in the world. But in what only added to the possibilities to consider, if relying on these photographs, Michael seemed to think the lines and patterns on this stone could be of a much higher standard.

We met at the end of the day and I can say that what we saw, filmed and touched, and in one case kept, exceeded our expectations. This short introduction is a work in motion and will be followed up after further consultation, but for now this brief description is sufficient. The stone is so unique and sensational and can virtually 'speak for itself.'

Ros' Rock 1

According to Ros, the rock was found in 1990 during excavations when building a new brick home located within two kilometres of the Bambara/Kariong Hieroglyphs. It was found 1 metre beneath the surface. Above and below and in every direction, all the rocks near and far are sandstone and this rock is not part of the local assemblage, as it is neither sedimentary nor sandstone.

One of the many 'experts' Ros showed the rock to, although unwilling to step outside of his own self-imposed 'box' and actually investigate the site and immediate surrounds, did feel that the rock was ironstone[6]. Our resident geological advisor and professor in geology, although limited by only having access to photographs, is adamant it is not ironstone but something even harder. Having held and viewed the rock close up, all we can add is that this stone is extremely hard with small compact grains and would require no less than a chisel of considerable refinement and strength to cut into such a hard surface.

From the very first sighting Ros was aware that the rock didn't belong to the Kariong/Bambara geology, but the markings on three sides is understandably her main focus.

* Figure 35 :
  Ros' Rock No. 1[7]

Whether made of ironstone or something harder will be resolved, that this rock has dozens of fine deep incisions and was positioned a metre beneath the surface until exposure is sufficient. That combination automatically rules out any imported pre-Cook technology, and equally, any form of Original rock, stick and bone tool-kit. The problem Ros faced over the next twenty years wasn't so much that the 'experts' she consulted queried its credentials alleging it to be fake or the outcome of natural processes. They openly acknowledged the markings were due to human hands and sophisticated technology, but everything about this artefact sat outside the realm of acceptable accounts of Original pre-history. Not only was there evidence of tools of the highest refinement in application, but there was also on display a delicate touch and considerable artistic talent. It would be so much easier to walk away, say nothing and maintain current postings and thus remain financially solvent.

The Blombos Rocks, an Inferior Imitation?

When Ros first showed us the marked rock at the rendezvous point, she also presented us with two documents detailing similar finds of this type of marked rock in other parts of the globe.

First up, and there were no surprises here, Ros presented to us some photographs and commentary on the Blombos Rocks. I could now see why Michael made the comparison and who were the novices in this exchange. The markings on the Kariong/Bambara rock were indeed much finer and pleasing to the eye. Artistic merit aside, what is also evident is the softer grain of the Blombos Rocks. Even though we were limited to a photograph, it seems clear that the Kariong/Bambara rock is much harder and that the deeper and finer incisions demand a tool with no less than a hardened iron blade. The problem being, according to all universities and school text-books, until the British Invasion, no such tool was manufactured within this continent. Yet there sat the end product awaiting exposure one metre below the surface, and on its own it rewrites large sections of Original pre-history.

Throughout our evolving education I maintained one concern. If the experts are indeed correct in observing that this rock is an import and foreign to the local geology, if ironstone cannot be found throughout the local tribal estates, its presence in Darkinoong Land is in open defiance to central tenets of Original cultural practises. It is our understanding that sacred sites and artefacts are special because they have a direct physical and intimate connection to that particular tribal estate, nowhere else is acceptable. Of course, it may be as our work is far from complete, that there may be exceptions to this protocol, but at the moment this issue still sits uneasily.

My concerns were allayed when in discussion with Original Custodian, David Fitzgerald. He informed me that there are two small deposits of ironstone nearby protruding out of the sandstone at Umina Beach and Dalley's Point. This made much more sense if the rock was sourced from either location, and during our next trip to the site, comparisons will be made between the engraved rock and both deposits. What can be stated with certainty is that the intricate designs and time given in reverence in creating this sacred object necessitates the existence of an Original technology and sophistication that is so much the norm in this area, and many other locations across the country.

What only accentuates the importance of this rock, irrespective of origin, and an unforgiveable reluctance of those who were shown then cowered, was another article Ros had found while researching. Discovered in China, was a "stunning 30,000-year-old engraved stone artefact,"[8] which was not even half as big and of a less precise line. This important relic had one-tenth of the engravings and was barely scratched into the surface when compared to what was in my hand. It may have been regarded as "stunning"[9] in China, but in Australia with Ros' rock acting as the standard bearer, it is underwhelmingly adequate by comparison and barely rates a mention.

At the same time Ros brought us this amazing marked rock, she also had two cylcon rocks for us to examine. Ros knew that this is a genre Michael Tellinger is very interested in pursuing at every opportunity. One of these cylcons[10] had a particular appeal for Michael and is his story alone. It too is extremely important for different energetic reasons and was bound to be sold on the open market and stored in a private overseas collection, but was now given to Michael. What did resonate once getting a full background briefing from Michael and Ros, was that the Blombos rocks are claimed to mark humanities' first venture into recording art and communication for posterity and could be up to 100,000 years old. If so, where does that place the Kariong/Bambara rock in the great scheme of things? Is it older? Or was it the inspiration behind the Blombos Rocks, which could be merely cruder copies of the original? What tools were used in engraving this rock, we use the plural in this case as there seem to be indications that more than one type of blade was in use?

Once More into the Breach

Although in the preliminary stages the question must be asked, where to next?

To begin with we will issue a challenge to mainstream science that seems permanently detached from Ros' narrative. Every time Ros went through 'official channels' a wall of inertia and denial was all she received, but there was one occasion when the real wisdom and Old Way sensibilities prevailed. Amongst all the official procrastination there was one ray of truth and clarity that Ros never forgot. Ros told us of an Original Elder who stood up when others ran away from the truth and reminded her that not only was the rock the genuine article, but that she was chosen by the Original spiritual guardians of the site and stone to recover, then act as custodian of this precious, and extremely ancient artefact.

We will continue seeking out the counsel of Original Custodians of the Old Ways and any of the few academics remaining with an open mind and disposition, and of course the temptation to examine the site from which this rock was found and look further is another option. But first and foremost, we are obliged to try and cajole and nudge mainstream media into acknowledging that not only does this artefact sit outside the embrace of accepted versions of Australian and global pre-history, but it has to be also recognised that it's presence one metre beneath the surface introduces new paradigms, participants and underlying purposes into this unravelling historical equation. It is a task we approach with trepidation knowing that until now no matter how convincing the archaeology, nothing has changed and official circles are deaf to logic and the Original past.

But if we do fall short as we have before, who is to blame, and how and why did speaking the whole truth and nothing but the Original truth lead to a situation where anyone who dares speak such heresy is treated like an enemy of the state?

Chapter 11

ROS' ROCK 1, THE 'MYSTERY' [1] is OFFICIALLY SOLVED: NOTHING TO DO WITH ABORIGINAL (SIC) PEOPLE." [2]

* **Figure 36:** Ros' Rock No. 1[3]

Of course the claim we are about to make can never be proven and is certainly a subjective call, and one most experts would readily dispute. We believe that Ros' Rock 1 will dramatically reconfigure the foundation stone upon which Australian history is based. However, the academics from the Australian Museum are not so enamoured by our conclusions and see a much simpler and far more comfortable explanation.

Not long after Ros' Rock 1 and the Egyptian tablet were premiered in a public presentation, Ros received a phone call from a resident "academic"[4] speaking on behalf of the Australian Museum. That they even rang her was an interesting opening gambit, as her last name, place of residence or phone number was never written or shared in any media outlet. The representative from the Australian Museum made contact with Ros two weeks after I had rang and also personally approached the museum explaining I was acting on behalf of others and was the only point of contact. What confirmed my suspicions that something a touch devious was afoot, was that this lady* contacted Ros, who was the present holder of the rock, by phone. (*It serves no purpose beyond creating embarrassment in divulging this woman's name, so from this point she will be given an alias, Jane)

Ros' response, that the rock is now with us, was met with a sigh and followed up by a change in tactics in order to re-establish authority. Jane went to great lengths to denigrate our credentials when reminding Ros of the two cardinal academic sins of which we rightly stand accused, in that we were "not academics,"[5] and what only compounds our unworthiness, "they believe in the Pleiades."[6]

Thus clearing away all the scholarly debris, it was time for the officially anointed expert to issue an each-way proclamation. According to the fact-sheet she was reading from, this rock is an African import dropped in the bush before World War 1 by an African tourist or an Australian who had recently been sight-seeing in Africa. Either way, one of them was strolling through the bush near Kariong with rock in hand around 100 years ago and accidentally dropped it then walked off. Believe it or not it now gets trickier and even more convoluted. The academic claims that over the last 100 years, over 1 metre of sandstone eroded and was directly deposited above the rock. She knows nothing of the site from which this rock was extracted, and if she did she would readily concede that this is a geological impossibility and a claim no geologist, not even a 101 student, would propose in any paper or sensible conversation.

Until this point, apart from making ridiculous statements on the phone, no harm was done and what was said could be dismissed as obviously ridiculous and simply ignored with a wry smile and shrug of the shoulders. But it gets decidedly worse, as our academic protagonist began to expand upon her fictional musings on a rock that she has not held and inspected at length, or made any enquiries to the researchers who have written five articles. Jane told Ros that she would be officially informing the Gosford City Council that this engraved rock has nothing to do with Australia, that it "comes from overseas"[7] and our research and sensational findings should be ignored post-haste. Our five papers have the support and contributions of five academics, two with PhDs and another an ex-professor with expertise in geology (and whose reaction, after over an hour holding the rock, will be discussed in this chapter), yet none of that was referenced or acknowledged. No inspection or consultation was needed in Jane's case, but as unforgivable a dereliction in academic duties her actions and words were, she then stepped over the breach into something that many could suggest reeks of patronising racism.

Jane then made a disturbing statement when on the phone to Ros, who confided in me that she found what was said so offensive and "racist"[8], that she was prepared "to go to court-take a lie-detector test."[9] In Jane's opinion, this rock has "nothing to do with Aboriginal (sic) people."[10] End of story, she did not offer the name of one Original person who endorsed that view, as there were none. It was an off the cuff remark meant to quell Ros' objections, but it also went a long way towards revealing some underlying motives and obstacles. To make such an outrageous denial of the truth and origin, that this amazing artefact found beneath the surface of Darkinoong land, which obviously was here well before the British Invasion Fleet dropped anchor, is an import in gob-smacking arrogance. To present such an open-ended statement on behalf of people whom you do not represent, can only be done after extensive consultation with Original Elders and Custodians versed in the Old Ways and local lore such as Aunty Beve and David Fitzgerald.

What happened here is offensive to Original protocol and sensibilities and a public apology should be made forthwith.

So there we have it, now that we have been cavalierly dismissed as non-academic Pleiadian propagandists, all that is left on the negotiating table is the official truth as delivered by the appointed academic. Considering that until the late 1940s Australia was subject to the White Australia Policy, and that particularly applied to all races of a darker complexion of which Africa has a major contributor, the mere notion of a pre-WW1 African tourist casually wandering through the bush near Bambara with such a heavy rock in hand is ridiculous. Why would he bring the rock into bush, and why take it from Africa? How did he manage to sneak into Australia, and being so obviously of the most unacceptable colour and banned from entry, surely he would have been seen before stepping off the boat? The rock weighs over a kilogram and if it was dropped on his foot, his bones would break, and if not, a solid thump on the sandstone floor would be heard. Was he both deaf and African?

There are too many unanswered questions wrapped around a proposal that falls short on every level bar one. They have a back-up theory - a second offering just in case the first is found wanting. They simply reverse the geography, parameters and players and remain faithful to the scenes concocted for their first piece of fiction. In Act 2, Scene 1, an Australian tourist went across to Africa pre-WW1 and picked up the rock while holidaying, then brought it back to Australia and kept it in hand while walking through the same bush and dropped it on the ground, leaving none the wiser. Despite the real fact that there was no surge in tourism from Australia to Africa before and during the first World War, and that the very few that did venture forth were primarily interested in shooting innocent wildlife, and even less of the few had any interest in geology, this is the approved second and final verdict on the rock's history.

We will make no further comment on this rather disappointing response, it is as if they couldn't even be bothered making up a plausible lie and assumed that any old rubbish will suffice, as long as it is delivered by a suitably qualified "academic."[11] But sadly the officials are locked into a series of fictional replies. The "academic"[12] openly conceded the technology evident is too sophisticated and therefore came under the jurisdiction of another continent, and that was her base-line. However, once insisting such technical proficiency was never present in this country before Cook, they are wrong and will never get close to the truth and must continue championing tales of an increasingly inferior quality. The reality is that all of these official denials are background noise and inconsequential, despite the intransigence the Original truths will continue to be revealed.

The Rock has been Identified

The rock is most certainly not local to the area, and is actually a very hard river chert. The photographs taken were a touch deceptive, in that it heightened the colour to such an extent that what seemed to be black was actually brown, and it really isn't even a dark brown chocolate, but more like a milk chocolate. What was interesting is that the very first suggestion Professor X tendered when viewing a photograph was river chert, and the same verdict as to the make of this rock was given within seconds of sighting and holding the rock.

I do remember some of our readers were getting frustrated that we would not be more definite in declaring a geology, but we consistently made the point that we do not have the expertise to be that definite. Until an on-site inspection by a geologist of stature took place, we were not going to budge from our fluctuating 'maybe stance.'

Too many Questions

Professor X spent nearly all our time together with the rock in his hand. It never left him for over an hour. His examination and wonder never ceased, there were things he could see that did not fit into any explanation. This rock is, as he remarked on many occasions, a "mystery."[13]

* **Figure 37:**
Ros' Rock No. 1[14]

In total there were five features discussed that held our attention and triggered questions rarely considered in polite academic circles. The most prominent being the 44 lines engraved into the three faces of the rock. Professor X was adamant that if we went to the closest hardware store and bought a chisel with a steel blade, it would not be able to leave any mark on this rock. If a blade/chisel of incredible delicacy and strength was used, three different widths of incision can be seen. On each face the general direction of engravings/cuts are not coordinated when compared to the other sides. That lack of a commonality in alignment convinced Professor X that there is no chance this is due to natural agents.

In what really had our adviser animated was his discovery of one much fainter line, which he claimed was much older and thus this rock was 'worked' twice. What only added to the intrigue was the evidence of polishing on not only the younger, but older cuts. Professor X gave no date, he wouldn't be that bold yet, but we suspect a solid entry in the five-figure column is a bare minimum date.

What caught us unawares and a touch embarrassed for not seeing it initially, was literally there right in front of our eyes. At some time in the past a hole or depression in this rock was packed with an aggregate of foreign minerals/rocks, then secured back into the rock. Once pointed out, it was obvious that this spherical inset (6 mm by 4 mm) has a much greyer tinge, and that the lip of the original rock can still be felt, along with the gentle depression that sits below the surrounding level of the original rock. Now highlighted, we can see why our guide was so animated. To pack any substance into a hole is not a great feat, nor a technological anomaly, but to find a way to ensure it would adhere in perpetuity to one of the hardest rocks available is something else again, and a fact and exotic feature Professor X returned to throughout our meeting.

The next observation made was ours. It would be impossible not to notice that a portion of the right hand-side of Side 3 is missing. A triangular section of the rock, which we estimate at 7mm wide, 10 mm high and 35 mm long, has been removed. The resulting slope is not smooth and I can identify what seems to be seven separate impact/percussion points, six on the top row and the seventh below the sixth, making that area the widest part of what was chiselled off the rock. We are convinced that the chisel was applied from left to right, and this contribution only expands the ancient tool-kit. The larger blade was not meant to inscribe and create fine points of intersection, but smash and remove. The surface is bumpy and each impact mark is consistent in dimensions, clear and distinct and there was no attempt made to smooth the surface, nor is there evidence of any engraving or pecking. All we can deduce is that this refashioning, thus creating a fifth artificial side, was of importance in passing on another message hidden within the angles, shapes and interface created.

It's for this reason, and many others already discussed, that such is the complexity of factors, synchronicity of alignments and delicacy of the cut, that we are very disposed towards Richard Gabriel and Judith Ann's[15] belief that there is a micro-message that's part of a subtle multi-layered narrative/map/prophecy and esoteric riddle. In that mystical vein, the last point discussed was probably the one that interested Professor X the least. He thought it was possible this was done, but did not seem to place much importance upon why or how.

With that section of rock removed it creates a perfect grip, ready-made, the right-hand thumb sits at the top pointing in the same direction as the three open vertical lines on Side 3. Side 1 sits in the palm and the third finger also has a slight depression to rest upon. So perfect is the balance manufactured with thumb and third finger positioned, the other three fingers can pull away and it makes no difference and adds no discomfort. We believe that this is too deliberate to be accidental and feel it was deliberately made to be held in the right hand with the placement prescribed by the depressions fashioned into the rock. But for what purpose?

It seems to have been made to be pointed, but which side up, or is it both? When you place Side 3 in the palm another depression, which again appears artificial, is the most comfortable place to rest the thumb, and once again another small channel is set at the best angle to accommodate the third finger. With the same balance and digits in attendance, and another three lines from Side 1 pointing in the same direction as the first outstretched finger, the balance feels exactly the same. As before, the other three fingers serve no apparent purpose and bear no weight. Both sides, same grip, and in each case we can see evidence that the positioning of the fingers and thumb was prescribed by the ancients. If the way this sacred rock was held was of such importance, what was coming in and going out? Is this yet another dimension to this rock that is yet to be understood?

That was the upshot of Professor' X's inspection in hand. He resolved one uncertainty in relation to the classification of the rock, but there are still so many questions yet to be answered. He added to the tally of areas to research and openly conceded that this was indeed the genuine article. What we are yet to understand is what this means, it is a "mystery."[16] That word was used by our guide in geology more than once, and we do remember that towards the end of our meeting he shared with us an account of the paper he wrote when sitting for his PhD.

Two Mysteries Still unsolved

This certainly was an unexpected tale of a dichotomy in ancient species taxonomy of which we knew nothing. He wrote a paper on an organism that could not be satisfactorily categorised, it was either a plant or an animal and our adviser wrote his paper advocating his understanding that it was a plant. He confided with us that now he is not so sure, but it was a mystery then and still is. So too, he added in concluding his anecdote, is the rock he now held the equal in mystery to the enigmatic topic of his paper that gained him his doctorate.

As our meeting came to a close Professor X put on his university 'face' and 'hat' and stared directly at Evan, who was taking notes of our conversation and advice given. His parting comments were the slowest delivered and he watched as Evan recorded every word as spoken, making it very clear that this was his summation of events.

"The rock is not ironstone. This rock came from a river and is a well-polished slightly jointed block hard sedimentary rock. The in-filling took place sometime after and I have no idea how the marks were made."[17]

There are so many unknowns, outside of identifying the rock as being chert, nothing is certain. The engravings on the three faces are definitely linked. As to whether they connect into one large map as two of the researchers in our group suspect, or is a combination of map and narrative as we suggest, is yet to be determined. Whether it is a map with applications on Earth or elsewhere is another of the unknowns. Whatever, or if ever - there is an agreed interpretation, there is so much more to unravel. How it was done, and with the assistance of what type of technology is still a long way off, but amongst all the questions yet to be resolved one stands as first among equals. Why is it that officials and academics are absent through apathy? They know the engraved rock exists, we made sure of that by approaching government and private media outlets, a university in Sydney, and of course, the only organisation that did respond on the sly, the Australian Museum.

The answer to this inertia, the jaded defence of the easiest and most reassuring routes, is merely par for the course. Our last proposal in this chapter will certainly gain no converts with the many who refuse to look or engage, but it was observed by others who also are not "academics"[18] when the rock was first shown to the public and deserves consideration. We have already mentioned the presence of two sets of artificial depressions which we feel were formed so that the rock can be held in a prescribed way. As asked earlier in this chapter, what purpose could this holding-pattern serve?

A definitive response is well beyond our abilities, but there are clues and indications. There have been 'reactions' of individuals to this rock that sit well outside the realms of modern-day science and falls into the embrace of what is mistakenly called the 'paranormal.' The mere mention of events and reactions deposited in the 'twilight zone' of mainstream science, for many is the ultimate condemnation. Quite simply, if it is outside the province of test tube, microscope or laboratory, then whatever is alleged will never earn the 'official' tick of approval.

But in this case, the and artefact's new rules are already at play, so why not continue down the same unfamiliar path and embrace the mystical elements of this rock and see what eventuates? The rock is of great spiritual and cultural significance to the Original people, and there are messages engraved into the surface of the rock, and then there is what lays within. From this esoteric vantage point we intend to investigate two areas, one of which we can already answer.

Does this rock contain or relay an energy/power/force? Yes! What is this energy? We have no idea, but with more time and Original guidance …

Chapter 12

"I HAVE NO IDEA HOW THE MARKS WERE MADE"¹

* **Figure 38:** Ros Rock No. 1 Close up²

Amongst all the tragic consequences that evolve out of the Australian Museum's refusal to acknowledge that Ros' Rock 1 is either Australian or of any interest to Original culture or Lore, none is more galling than the illogicality of their proposition that about a hundred years ago either an African tourist, or an Australian just returned from holidaying in Africa, brought the rock across from Africa and accidentally dropped it while walking in the bush near Kariong.

With no option but to concede the technology needed to mark this rock is far too advanced to be part of Jane's understanding of Original history before the Invasion, the spokesperson for the Australian Museum was adamant the carved rock came from "Africa,"³ or somewhere else "overseas."⁴ She is wrong. Knowing it was found in sandstone country near Kariong and even claiming it would take only 100 years for one metre of sandstone to cover the engraved rock on the site it was found on is a geological impossibility.

Irrespective of the faulty premises, for the sake of being balanced in our research let us assume that the rock was found in Africa and brought here 100 years ago and an avalanche fell on top. It still doesn't work, simply because the technology to make the variety of markings, some thick, some delicate and quite a few extremely small, just wasn't in existence anywhere at that time. Australia, Africa or Europe, it makes no difference, as there were no tools or devices that were up to the task on display. And even if there was a cutting-edge machine available during that time that was able to cut, peck and chisel delicate and thick lines, why waste the time, blades and expertise to cut into a common rock, then throw it away? How does such a fruitless economic enterprise cover expenses, and what purpose does it serve?

The location of discovery does not lessen this scientific truth. Even if the rock is an import it makes no difference whatsoever. It breaks the rules no matter where the geography. This blaring scientific truth and imperative was lost in translation by Jane and deserves to be addressed. And in answer to these questions avoided, Professor X provided a measured written response to the rock and the riddle of the engraved lines, peckings, packings and polishing.

The Rock is not ...

"The rock is definitely not ironstone. This rock came from a river and is a well-polished slightly jointed block of hard sedimentary rock. The small infillings took place sometime afterwards (after the initial polishing) and I have no idea how the marks were made. River, and less often beach, pebbles and cobbles can acquire a good polish naturally. This no doubt happens at innumerable places in the world. I am very familiar with natural polish on stones, but of course artificial polish on stones is also possible. The polish on Ros' stone could well be natural but the straight lines on it don't look natural to me."[5]

Professor X has done exactly what the Australian Museum should have done, carefully look, examine, assess all of the six articles we have written and then, after all the information and data available was analysed, has given a considered mid-term verdict. All we are championing here is good science, we have made multiple approaches and offered to liaise with the Australian Museum, and this is what we get!? If they had just ignored us and said nothing, as the other organisations did, it's more of the same and no big deal. But once ringing Ros, saying so many wrong things then threatening to pass these lies on to the Gosford City Council, a line has been crossed, errors have to be corrected and blame must be apportioned.

The two points deserving of immediate attention relate to the polishing and lines. We made note in our previous article that Professor X had identified two distinct stages when polishing occurred. This means that the rock was marked at two different times then placed in the water for many, many, decades until a natural polish began to form, or was it artificially cut then polished twice. That's it, there are no other cards on the table, it has to be one or the other. On at least two occasions the rock was engraved and polished, and knowing the sophistication of the tool-kit required to cut, incise and peck a rock of this hardness is present and accounted for, being able to polish the end-result of this cut and paste is no stretch in technology or logic.

The Blombos Rocks, Lascaux[6] markings, the Calgary Rock[7], and other rocks bearing ancient markings are simply scratchings or engravings into a piece of rock using a crude sharp object, one process from start to finish, end of story. On this rock, which is far harder, we have evidence of no less than four processes, two cuts and two polishes. The agency responsible for the polishing is still a maybe, but certainly leaning towards human intervention.

When it comes to the "infilling,"[8] which happened "after initial polishing,"[9] whatever took place and however this was done, this is an example of non-natural activity. Of a different colour, surrounded by the lipping of the base rock, the skills and expertise required in packing and attaching is again very advanced and so at odds with conventional historical accounts.

The same applies to the "marks"[10] and "straight lines,"[11] which "don't look natural"[12] and could only come about through the application of technology of the highest refinement applying blades of exceptional strength. Forget 1913, that date can be thrown out the window, this is a big ask today, let alone one hundred years ago. In referring to the engraved lines our geological adviser conceded that "I have no idea how the marks were made,"[13] or to put it another way, "the straight lines on it don't look natural to me."[14] Over his many years examining all types of rocks and marks, this rock stands apart simply because what is carved has no parallel or precedent, and in what only adds to the complexity there may well be another contribution to this narrative. The only difference being that this time it was not engraved into the surface, but pecked or incised.

In the Light of the Mid-day sun

Due to a combination of enlightening factors, which included a magnifying glass, the midday sun, clean glasses and some serious staring I was able to substantially add to the tally of peckings on the rock. In particular Side 2, which looks quite innocuous at first glance and until this point in time had never been scanned by a magnifying glass, actually has nineteen new pecks marked on the diagram. There are only two that are not absolutely artificial, but are quite likely due to the impact of a tool. On Side 1 four more were found, which in total adds up to 28 peckings, and there may be more. What this does is add a lot more gravitas to this complex story-board, and yet another level of narrative in this rock.

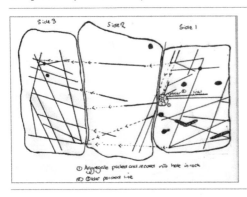

* **Figure 39:**
Ros Rock No. 1 Diagram
(3 Sides)[15]

For myself the biggest surprise was not so much the discovery of which was pecked, but what is two series of very old incisions, one is of three vertical notches in a row and the other four. In our earlier, less well-lit inspections, we assumed these two clusters were each one older thick depression in the surface, which was the result of one strike of the blade. Extremely fine, small, and with the finest margin between each cut, these markings require a blade of a finesse and hardness that is difficult to conceive. Just as important, this is the third technique used in engraving this rock. We have already examined a large variety of engravings and peckings, but these seven marks were incised into the rock, it seems like a blade rock dug in and then flicked out. All other ancient engraved rocks found throughout the world are limited to one type of cutting or engraving, never three.

This rock is wrapped around so many additions to this ever-expanding tool-kit of blades, chisels and hammers, and we have no doubt there is more to come.

A Mid-term Report

However, amongst all the mystery and hints of advanced technology, some signposts have been recognised. At the present stage of proceedings we have identified the presence of 44 engraved lines, 54 points of intersection, 74 shapes, 28 pecks and 7 incisions. We are of the belief that the depth of lines, angles, intersection points, shapes, spaces in between, peckings, incisions, angles of surface, interrelationship between the three sides, in-fillings, prescribed manner of holding the rock and length of each line are but some of the contributing factors that go some way towards creating this multi-dimensional ancient narrative of time, events and space.

What can be declared with certainty is that the lines, pecks, incisions and in-fillings are not natural, that much is definite. When dealing with who, when, why and how, our research is still developing and often promising. However, when it comes to deciphering what this interplay of symbols and markings actually means, whether we can confidently substitute words and numbers and read this as a sequential narrative/map, while there is hope overseas researcher of ancient rock markings, Dr. Derek Cunningham[16], can rise to the occasion and 'crack the code,' but we still harbour substantial doubts. It is our belief that the combination of so many diverse characters and engravings is too cryptic, intelligent and just too hard for the intellect of today's motley crop of *Homo sapiens sapiens*. The inclines, proximity, shapes and so many other factors add to the difficulties in ascribing meaning, and by comparison, makes the decoding of the Rosetta Stone analogous to reading *"The Cat in the Hat."*

In the meantime, even if any interpretation is beyond the reach of mere mortals, there are two immediate concerns that deserve further attention. A closer inspection of the surface through more powerful magnification and a camera-zoom lens may assist, as too is the measurement of every line, shape and space a task of the highest priority. There may be a repetition in number, ratio, proportion or shape within, which is deliberate and adds yet another course to this ancient conversation.

An Inconvenient Truth

Yes this is an extremely inconvenient piece of archaeology that breaks so many rules, in fact nearly all of them, but looking the other way will not make it go away. Our challenge to mainstream outlets like the Australian Museum is simple and justified. Isn't it time that this important part of the Original truth, as inconvenient as it may be, is acknowledged? Or could it be, they just don't care, or maybe they do?

Just like the polish on the rock, there are two answers to select from, and only one can be right.

Chapter 13

CHERT BY CHERT: ROS' ROCK NO.2

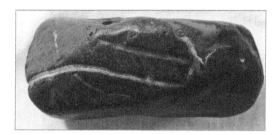

* Figure 40: Ros Rock No. 2 (A Symbol)[1]

Ros' Rock 2 is a deceptive piece of silica, considerably smaller, less ornate and refined. This rock appears to be the lesser sibling of Ros' Rock 1. However, when you look a little deeper, it soon becomes obvious the roles are indeed reversed. This rock has so much more to say, if only we, or any Homo sapiens sapiens residing on this planet, could read between the lines.

Despite the inherent genetic limitations we are beset with, there are some early comparisons made between these two rocks and further observations that can be made that stretch the scope and sophistication of technologies. We believe that these comparisons reinforce our belief there is some sort of symbiotic relationship between these rocks and the right hand and that there were two times, separated by thousands of years, when the engravings on each rock took place. And it is that separation in timing between first and second applications which causes the most contradictory end-product. The final result seems back to front, in that the older, worn lines are more delicate, absolutely straight and the longest on Ros' Rock 2. The second time around with blade on rock it appears cruder, less fastidious in precision and a lot less indistinct. The difference in timing seems much greater than that of Ros' Rock 1.

With five articles written there is no need to revisit past observations and measurements made on Ros' Rock 1. In general terms there is a geometry and patterning on the bigger rock that is deliberate. A repetition of angle and measurement, parallel lines, intersection points, spaces in between and a multitude of shapes resonate to mathematical principles. The peckings on Ros' Rock 1 are about one third the size of those on the smaller rock, and the 28 identified pecks are not clustered, but spread across the rock. Because of their size they are barely visible unless intentionally focusing on the specific site in full sun.

Their contribution to this narrative is intentionally minor, no doubt it is there and has importance, but a minor chapter at best.

On the Second Rock ...

On the second rock, the pecks are bigger and far more numerous, they are restricted to half of one side and, unlike the bigger rock, are the central point of the entire narrative. Even the striking letter A symbol serves a greater purpose in sliding around the edge of the rock underneath the pecked side at the bottom. There is an older engraving and it runs in a perfect diagonal line with a finer cut which begins at the cap of the A and descends around the next two sides before joining the staff of the Figure A at the bottom of the heavily pecked half-side. Such an intersection, the only one apparent on this rock, is of pivotal significance.

Outside of that one convergence, the second rock has nothing in common in setting or script with Ros' Rock 1. The one solitary general point of intersection, as opposed to greater than 70, is a stark contrast. There are no shapes made by intersecting lines on any side, and many lines are of an inferior mathematical quality in manufacture and precision. With the exception of Figure A, which contains an exact width in parallel lines, the same depth, an incredibly steady hand and expertise, and of course the finer, older lines. All that is left is younger, a touch cruder and less committed in the pursuit of exactitude.

As much as the A grabs the eye, the entire narrative revolves around the mass of information encoded on Side 4, and on that face there isn't one 'gun-barrel' straight line, point of intersection or shape to be seen. What we have here is all over the place, as it should be and was in distant times, there is no pattern on these four sides, outside both rocks sharing a clear attempt to relay an interconnection to all sides, they share very little in markings or arrangement.

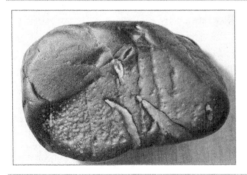

* **Figure 41:**
Ros' Rock No. 2 Side 4 [2]

What is really fascinating is how deceptively complex Side 4 actually is, and equally how cryptic and intelligent is the message encoded. Two large shapes, one an elongated ellipse, the other a fairly straight side, and another is a cross between a tick and boomerang, which are the biggest and thickest lines on either rock. All around, there are close to 200 pecks, the closest to a straight line out of all the younger entries, a few finer older lines, one larger and two smaller semi-circle imprints, five horizontal lines of dashes and dots, some smaller, younger lines and an odd engraving that still retains a piece of the original surface, yet it's surrounded by the now exposed under-surface.

The technological scorecard as tallied after examining what lay on top and beneath the surface of Ros' Rock 1, can certainly be more than doubled. The bigger rock shows evidence of three different widths of cuts and incisions, while on the smaller rock there are five different blade widths on display. The semi-circle imprints are not on the bigger rock and come in two sizes, a diameter of 100 mm or 20 mm. Even though the mere mention of a technique which we suspect is extremely radical and will upset our critics, it looks like there is one shape that was actually punched into the rock which then left an imprint, as opposed to being chiselled or gouged out. The peckings are different and of larger diameters to the smaller pecks on the bigger rock. What only adds to the intrigue and size of the tool-kit needed on the smaller rock, we can identify four different sizing of pecks. The deepest and thickest pecks are most assuredly on the smaller rock.

* **Figure 42**:
Ros' Rock No. 2
Index Finger Depression[3]

As stated in earlier chapters, both rocks were most definitely artificially shaped in a way that can be held in the right hand and in both cases, in a very specific manner. Of course, the second smaller rock has been demonstrably formed to be held with the index finger and this has happened many, many times over an extremely long period of time. The time taken that can account for a depression of this depth that is obviously meant to take the form of the index finger, has to comfortably run into five figures, and perhaps even more.

"The Language we Speak IS NOT ANGLO-SAXON but Just Aboriginal."[4]

The question that now needs to be addressed relates to where in Australia the smaller rock was last held by the index finger, if for no other reason than it's the only part of our research on this rock of which we have been given Original guidance and a location.

Without going into specifics or geography, we can reveal that the smaller rock was found at a location that is within 100 kilometres of the Standing Stones site. From the time Ros rang two hours before the auction for this sacred rock closed, the description was vague in every respect bar one, she made mention of the letter A. My immediate response was to refer to the Standing Stones site, the place where the first language ever spoken was memorialised; a language made of an amazingly diverse combination of characters. When making that comment I had no idea where the artefact was found, but did know that of the 21 letters nominated by Frederic Slater as being part of an Original language that comprised of rock arrangements, angles, hand signs, body parts and animal motifs, he listed A as the first letter of the Original alphabet and of immense importance. According to Slater it is a "language built almost entirely on vowels,"[5] of which the "letters not used are F, Q, S, X, Z."[6] Because the Original language was the inspiration behind all other tongues, Slater openly conceded that "the language we speak is not Anglo-Saxon but just aboriginal (sic)."[7]

The question that arises out of Slaters' research relates to whether this engraving is the first letter of the Original language and of massive historical significance, here in-hand and finger, we have the first letter of the very first alphabet. There is no absolute here, but it is Original, was found in the vicinity of the Standing Stones site, does correspond with the research of the man elected as President of the Australian Archaeological Society who nominated a symbol that looks enough like A to be named A, just as we did. We would suggest that as things stand, the chances are high that this rock was part of that ancient assemblage, which was first desecrated during the 1840's. Even during that disturbance it was noted by those involved in this overwhelming affront to culture, that the rocks were taken off the Standing Stones site by the three Original people who were acting as Custodians. As to whether this rock was one of those hidden, taken from the mound at a later date or used nearby for another purpose, cannot be narrowed down, but the connection to that site and the general area seems highly likely.

CHERT PLUS CHERT EQUALS ...

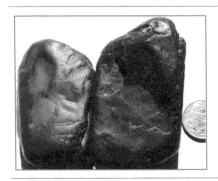

* **Figure 43:**
Ros' Rocks No. 1 and 2[8]

Both rocks are chert and although not of the same dimensions, they share a common general shape. On both rocks, three sides were marked and both seem to indicate a sequence in each narrative. At first glance it may seem that these hundreds of individual engravings constitute the entire message, but perhaps there is more under the surface. These silica rocks are not that different from the silicon chip in chemistry and capacity. What if there is also information stored within awaiting the right vibration in song to unlock ancient secrets?

If our suspicions are confirmed then that mystical doorway, and the key needed to unlock these secrets held within, is the most important legacy that these rocks have bequeathed to modern humanity. It's right in front of us, close enough to touch, and ready to be activated and sung to, if only we knew what words to sing and notes to scale. All we can hope for is that this ancient sacred song is not lost, the rocks are ready and willing to be sung to, and all we're seeking is the one who is able.

My God, what happened then? Our apologies for momentarily straying into the esoteric realms when our brief is to stay on track and convince through the empirical, back to the facts, figures and rock solid archaeology. The rocks are the same shape and make, and serve the same greater purpose. Even though they are separated by more than 700 kilometres, the fact they look similar and are made from the same silicon constituents is indicative of united purpose that may well span the whole continent of Sahul.

There are some geological facts that need to be firmly established before any doubt or verdict is should be cast. The plain geological truth is that no natural processes could striate in this manner. In the simplest terms, glacial striation (which is the only feasible natural process that could leave marks displaying some crude similarities), that can leave a criss-cross patterning. This could happen on one side of a rock, but doesn't keep flowing from side to side, and all the way round. What's on display here looks as though this was placed inside a rotating machine. What is also evident at first glance is the polishing followed by grooving, and in what leaves no room for nature's involvement, a different grain and colour of rock was cemented into some grooves. The infilling is so artificial and evidently equally successful, as it still remains. In what only adds to intrigue and sophistication, the infilling in each grove/depression is different, and every geological rule known or suspected is steadfast in proclaiming that nature doesn't do a variety of artificial in-fills with an adhesive that last thousands of years. Humans, other earlier hominids and beings, those from earlier civilisations, the host of extra-terrestrial visitors, interlopers and residents and any sentient beings that we may have inadvertently omitted, yes they could all do in-fills, but not nature, never.

The processes required, technology applied and the intelligence of the persons involved, breaks every conventional pre-historical mould. To deny this demands that there is contrary evidence, and currently there is none on these rocks, except the stock-standard ploy used when all other defences crumble under the weight of pure science and real geology: it is all a hoax.

There is nothing else left, someone has to stand in front of Ros, face to face, and call her a liar. As with so many pieces of archaeology we are involved in, there is nothing in the cupboard to contend with outside it all being down to mischief and bad people lying. We have heard that same tired old negative mantra when confronted with a crystal skull, the Egyptian jewellery and ancient bone, the Egyptian treaty tablet and so many other artefacts and sites we have shared. The problem is that this time, that urge to perpetrate a hoax has to apply to a second party. Ros discovered the first rock when a backhoe was on-site excavating, but she brought the second rock from another group, so these other people must also be of poor character and deceitful nature.

I say enough of this pathetic character assassination. Accept the truth and fess up. For once stop dismissing and denigrating while seated in a padded chair. Stand up, hold your head high and walk out of the building and into country with us and the truth will be revealed. Else remain seated and committed to an eternal human curse: there are none so blind as those who refuse to see.

Chapter 14

UNITED WE STAND, ROCK BY ROCK

* **Figure 44:** Ros Rock No. 1 and 2 [1]

The reactions to Ros' Rocks 1 and 2 has been heartening even though it has been surrounded by a dismal and somewhat shameful performance. The suggestions and encouragement given by some forward thinking experts has opened up new fields to investigate and there have been invaluable extensions to pursue that are already producing fascinating results. However, in balancing the books, the discrete refusal to look, acknowledge or participate in any overt form with the archaeology we are sharing, is as much a part of the mainstream response as it is an appalling indictment upon those who claim to be professional academics. What has become apparent to us is that many scholars have become timid, thus sacrificing their independent inclinations for a posting or stipend. Alas, the fringe benefits they seek demand obedience and more of the same, such people are bound to repeat and comply yet never be bold.

We know for a fact that these two ancient marked rocks are known of in academic and official circles. Both rocks are the cause of much concern, some hostility, and quite a deal of angst, and possibly even internal doubt. The first rock has been inspected by a geologist of a high-standing, and he will also examine the second rock very soon. Equally, we have extended an invitation to other qualified geologists to examine these rocks with the right to look and touch them. Despite our open approach and offers to share, not one person, agency or expert has accepted the chance to inspect the two rocks that may rewrite huge slabs of global pre-history. We can only assume they have more important archaeology to research and analyse.

Perhaps early settlement buildings, a 300 year-old midden, sunken boats on the west coast or an early settler's rock wall are higher priorities. Obviously early historical remains such as these take precedence over changing world paradigms, and also cause no fuss whatsoever in snuggling seamlessly into the current historical comfort zones.

As far as we can see it comes down to two possibilities when trying to understand why mainstream refuse to look at the rocks or discuss them. They are either fearful of the implications and consequences associated with the rocks, or unconvinced that the two rocks are of archaeological significance. We are prepared to extend the benefit of doubt (even though their track record gives no reason to do so) and work on the premise that the scholars and officials are wavering, but need a little more evidence before being convinced.

Back to Work

To that end we have put together a scientific paper that has five areas of investigation that haven't been addressed, nor mentioned earlier, and with further analysis, new insights or possibilities need to be developed.

We have raised the issue of the in-filling on Ros' Rock 1, with particular focus on two large patches (17 mm by 12 mm and 12 mm by 8 mm). What is of paramount importance is that such a process is supposedly beyond the technological embrace of any tool-kit anywhere until extremely recent times. Found in Australia, and conservatively dated thousands of years before the British invasion, the infilling of different material in two depressions just should not be here. With magnifying glass in hand and the sun shining directly at one angle, something that looks very metallic seems to be glinting. Perhaps not, as it could be a piece of mica, but under certain conditions and positions that metallic-like object appears to have two prominent eyes or circles shining in the sunlight.

The Hot Stamps

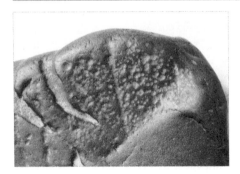

* **Figure 45:**
Ros' Rock No. 2
Imprints[2]

Of less reliance upon any magnification or enhancement, is the existence of three clusters of what we can only call imprinting. All around, the chisel and knife have cut into the surface revealing a consistently creamy under-surface, as both rocks share the same lighter colour beneath. However, what we believe to be the imprinted marks have not broken the surface, it is the same dark brown colour as all of the unbroken sections.

The most dramatic imprint is a semi-circle stamped into Ros' Rock 2, it has a diameter of one centimetre, a flat smooth depression of 25 mm with the sides of the circle smooth and arched. The half-circle is surrounded by two larger strokes of 1 cm by 50 mm and 1 cm by 70 mm and two small pecks below. All five markings have not broken the surface, yet could only come about after considerable pressure was applied by a blade or an extremely hot metal stamp of some type. But if a blade, why is it every other marking, whether cut, chisel or peck, that broke the surface and exposed the lighter under coat?

* **Figure 46**:
Ros' Rock No. 1 Main Imprints[3]

The second set of what appears to be the same imprinting or stamping process is found above the map on Ros' Rock 1. There are many indicators that show this section of rock is artificially imprinted and the end-result of incredibly sophisticated technology. The fact that each of the four vertical lines of the map continue on until meeting a point where the imprint above it changes its path and angle. All four lines mark out the major points on this upper sharp set of lines, which was cut or imprinted with massive force, yet at no stage did this force break the surface. What stretches the boundaries and strengthens the impossibility that these six adjoining lines are due to natural effects, is that the depth of the cut is double that of the semi-circle measuring over 50 mm. That is more than twice the depth of the deepest incision/ engraving on either rock, yet the surface was not disturbed and remains intact, and remains to this day in total opposition to any conventional version of ancient events.

The third collection of imprints is found on Ros' Rock 1 and is the least striking and consists of nine shapes edging around the bottom side of the blank face. There are 5 ellipses, 3 circles and one marking shaped like a cigar, the depressions are shallower (12-5 mm) and could be due to pressure and abrasion during creation or movement. Under normal circumstances, and if on any other rock it would barely rate a mention, but in association with the imprints and variety of other markings, it must be included in the stock-take.

The Enigma of the Older Lines

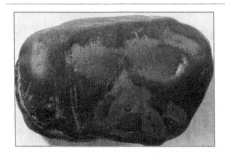

* **Figure 47**:
Ros' Rock No. 2 Faint Lines[4]

Both rocks show clear evidence that the cuts/markings/engravings were made at two different times separated by a very long period of centuries, and more than likely millenniums. What becomes immediately apparent when examining Ros' Rock 2 is that the older lines are incredibly fine and extremely straight. The arrangement is very precise and geometric, while the second younger application is lacking in that mathematical precision and is cruder in style. Whether that means the older civilisation was more advanced is not clear, but is implied.

A closer inspection with higher powered magnification has not only added to the tally of the older finer cuts, but added some unexpected twists and turns. We originally assumed that all the older lines ran 'gun-barrel' straight, we were betrayed by my 62 year old eyes as one line deliberately takes a 10 degree kink and another begins straight and breaks into a curve. It turns out that at one stage many of these lines were spread across all four sides, but unlike Ros' Rock 1 there are virtually no intersecting shapes created through the criss-crossing of lines which is so much a part of the narrative of the bigger rock.

How Many Different Ways.

The most amazing and daunting task is trying to estimate how many different tools, width of blades or points and techniques were used when creating these rock time capsules/testimonials. What keeps dragging us back to what may seem a ridiculous notion, of some sort of ceramic or baking process where the surface was pliable and moist thus able to be cut, pecked, in-filled and shaped, is evidence of what appears to be seven gouge marks on Ros' Rock 1. Placed in two series of four and three gouges, it seems as if the wet surface was dug into and flicked out seven times over, then baked.

Throw in what we suspect to be a series of imprints, four chisel widths and four diameters of pecks, the finely cut lines and two different types of in-fill adhering to one of the hardest rocks available and then wrap it around a time scale of no less than five figures, and start all over again, because there is no alternative. But before doing so, it needs to be appreciated that there is more to this than some clever technological tricks on display.

The numbers certainly do add up, but the equation it is beholding is certainly unfamiliar to many who claim to know about such things.

* **Figure 48**:
  Dr Derek Cunningham's
  Analysis of Ros' Rock No. 1[5]

The map/grid on Ros' Rock 1 seems to be bound to a series of mathematical principles. There are seven horizontal lines and five are 300 mm and two 230 mm in length. So too the four vertical lines obey the same need for repetition with the two longest lines measuring 610 mm and the two smaller lines 430 mm. To suggest this synchronisation is random, whether through unnatural or natural means, is illogical and statistically all but impossible. For any harbouring doubt, the repetition of the angle 33 degrees six times over in this map must refute any notion this is all an amazing coincidence. May we also suggest it is not a coincidence the rock was excavated at Kariong, which is found on the southern latitude of 33 degrees. We believe these measurements were chosen in advance to assist in conveying content and position, but alas, the code is far too cryptic and sublime for the common folk of today to grasp.

On Ros' Rock 2 there is one less imposing example of the same need to repeat, but not so much in length but rather points of intersection. Only recently seen, there is a series of four very faint ancient lines that all cross the longer letter A staff. The four lines intersect in a sequence of 30 mm gaps.

A Message on and Within?

At the present stage of proceedings, in combination we have seen evidence of chiselling, cutting, lines, shapes, intersection points, semi-circles, imprinting, in-filling, ellipses, lines of codes, a long association with the human index finger and mathematical rules. The problem is that none of these activities are supposed to be a part of the Australian landscape until well after the British Invasion.

As to deciphering what all of this ancient assemblage of markings mean; we believe it is doomed to be lost in translation twice over. The symbols, angles, spaces and imprints on the rock are beyond our vision and grasp, and it's possible that many may underestimate the depth of this ancient narrative by not looking deeper within. Both of the rocks are made from silicon which is the basic element of all computer chips, and therefore we can hope that there is much more information yet to be unlocked within. It may be that under the right resonance, through Original songs, yidaki or bull-roarer what is stored within may yet again reclaim its voice and eminence.

What needs to be recognised is that irrespective of our musings and esoteric hypothesis, it doesn't matter either way. The facts are simple; these rocks already rewrite the entire pre-historical narrative. The plot and script alike, everything is now in flux. And in what only adds to the intrigue, these rocks have not yet began to share their deepest secrets.

The Mystery of Two Similar Stones a World Apart: Australian Stone Meets the Bosnian Stone

Figure 49: New Discovery "The bosnian Astronomical Stone"[6]

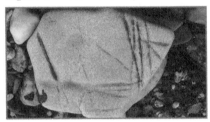 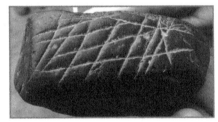

The Bosnian astronomical stones, discovered near Ravne Tunnel Labyrinth in Visoko, Bosnia on January 16, 2015

The Australian astronomical stone, discovered near the Bambara Glyphs in Kariong, NSW, Australia in 1990

We are fully aware that the idea of ancient pyramids in Bosnia is one of the most hotly contested idea in archaeology right now, but owing to the reality of being swamped with a never-ending flow of offers to view and inspect so much Original archaeology, there has been no time to take notice of such idle distractions on the other side of the Earth. In fact we have made a deliberate attempt to keep fully distanced from all talk and research on this controversial topic, if for no other reason than there is more than enough yet to research in Australia. It has never been a matter of taking sides, but simply that we're far too busy.

Our take on the Bosnian site is to let others debate and accuse, there is more than enough grief and derision in this country for any walking down the Original path and we see nothing to gain by looking that far abroad. Moreover, what relevance does any supposed four-sided mound shaped something like a pyramid situated so far away have to do with anything we are investigating in Australia? So ingrained was my ambivalence, that I had not seen a photograph of the site or read one word in support or critique. After all, Bosnia has no archaeology that has any relationship to a Australian or anything Original. Or so we thought. It soon became apparent however, that our narrowly focused disinterest was the first casualty of Jock Doubleday's[7] first email contact.

Both he and Dr. Semir Osmanagich[8] (founder and executive director of the Archaeological Park: Bosnian Pyramid of the Sun Foundation [9]), had taken particular interest in some articles we had written about Ros' Rock 1, and what galvanised their need to know more was one marked rock they had found, and knew from first glance it wasn't natural. Being found so close to, and possibly first taken from within the Bosnian Pyramid, only accentuated their desire to discuss these shared matters engraved into rocks. Relying just on the photographs of this rock with about twenty individual engraved lines into what appears to be a quite hard material is of course well short of what is needed to pass a final judgment, but more than sufficient incentive to proceed further.

However, for this rock to pass muster and be deemed worthy of inclusion somewhere near Ros' Rocks 1 to 5, there are three hurdles to negotiate, and none more daunting than the first and by far the steepest obstacle. A scholar of the highest standing in geological issues who understandably wishes to remain anonymous, is always our first port-of-call whenever a new rock, engraving or artefact appears on the horizon. His scepticism is a vital balance, and on nine out of ten occasions the verdict is in the negative and deemed natural. It is only when he is not sure, where no recognisable natural process or parallel is readily, at hand do we start to wonder if this geological offering is indeed ancient evidence of an advanced technology. When a second look is needed and nothing immediately comes to mind, we then step in, and that is what happened when this rock was scrutinised. The markings do look very deliberate and very reminiscent to those on Ros' Rock 1.

It is the lines engraved and angles deliberately created so long ago on this Bosnian rock which is our major interest. In what was an unexpected turn of events, Dr. Derek Cunningham's measurement of the angles of the Bosnian rock, although incomplete and subject to additions once a better photograph is taken, managed to identify 15 angles.

Even though the Bosnian rock is worn and some lines were not measured and need a higher resolution or personal visit to increase the tally, Dr Derek managed to measure and identify 15 lines. Rising from the horizontal, the angles recorded are: 1, 1, 3, 3, 5.1, 5.1, 5.1, 6.5, 11, 11, 13.66, 13.66, 18.6, 18.6, 30 and 45 degrees. Some angles are not repeated, others are, despite the chance more will be charted this first reading of angles is sufficient to compare against Ros' Rock 1.

* **Figure 50:**
Bosnian Astronomical Stone
Analysis by
Dr Derek Cunningham[10]

Our first comparison is against the angles engraved into Sides 1 and 3 of the Australian rock. It was our hope there would be a sizable match up, but never under any circumstances did we expect a 100% crossover rate. Every angle engraved into the Bosnian rock can also be found on Ros' Rock 1. In what only accentuates this global pattern the five Bosnian angles that were engraved more than once are also repeated in Ros' Rock 1. The chances that both the Bosnian rock and Australian rock share the same angle of inclination 13.66 is surely remarkable, but how much more so is this repetition than just unique co-incidence when considering the fact that the next rock to be compared is located in Calgary and also has an engraved line measuring 13.66 degrees.

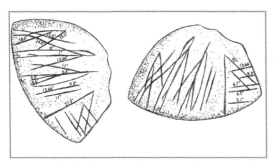

* **Figure 51:**
Calgary Rock - Diagram & Analysis
by Dr Derek Cunningham[11]

But that's not all that shared; ten of the fifteen angles (66%) engraved into the Bosnian rock are also present and already accounted for on the Canadian rock found at Calgary. That figure sits well above our most optimistic expectations when comparing any rock that has only three angles engraved into the Bosnian rock (3, 30 and 45), which were not engraved on the Calgary rock, yet all of these absentees are on the Australian rock. It is almost impossible to put this match down to mere chance or random actions. Such a high rate of match-up is phenomenal, but our task is incomplete and the third part of this trilogy bears testimony to another crossover rate exceeding 90%.

The Calgary rock is also incomplete in measurement, but does have 21 lines with angles supplied (0, 1, 5.1, 6.5, 6.5, 6.7, 9.3, 9.3, 9.3, 11, 11, 13.66, 13.66, 13.66, 15, 18.6, 18.6, 24, 27.3, 33 and 42 degrees). Any comparison made to the two sides of Ros' Rocks 1 will see every angle ticked off except 15 degrees, twenty of the 20 Canadian entries have an Australian counterpart.

When we put all these calculations together, at the simplest level that means 95% of the Canadian angles are also found on the Australian rock. As stunning a result as that number undeniably is, it is eclipsed by not two but one omission of shared degrees off inclination with a 100% match up rate between the Australian and Bosnian rock. In completing this trilogy that spans the planet, the Calgary rock has angles identical to ten of those engraved into the Bosnian rock. In total, these three comparisons culminate in a combined tally of a shared script greater than 87%.

* **Figure 52:**
Dr Derek Cunningham's Analysis of Ros Rock No.1[12]

For any still holding on to the far less likely, but certainly more convenient interpretation that this is all down to random chance, all that is needed is to tally the angles on Side 3 of Ros' Rock 1 and let the maths plot the position. The angle repeated most often is 33 degrees. There are seven different lines where Derek identified that inclination. Surely it cannot be alleged that this is also coincidental? The rock was found at a position 33 degrees south of the Equator, and we believe that setting and latitude is the only reason this angle is the most numerous and prominent on the rock. Knowing that this location was 33 degrees south of the earth's mid-point requires intimate knowledge of the movement of the planet and stars, and extends the knowledge-base of these ancient Original astronomers into yet another unexpected realm.

Conclusion:

It is very difficult not to be absolute in declaring that the lines marked onto three rocks spread around the globe are all part of an ancient global script, that the technology on display is no less than the equal of today, and that there is every chance earlier advanced human civilisations rose and fell. History is more often than not the winner's sanitised version of events, and once spanning back five thousand years everything becomes decidedly murky. Troy was a myth, then it was found, Atlantis is still regarded as a fictional account. Every legend and ancient narrative, including the Old Testament, speaks of giants, but according to the experts of today that too is false and no more than the product of an imaginative mind as evidenced in the quaint tale, *Jack and the Beanstalk.*

We have no doubt there are many who would happily consign these rocks and the angles that bear testimony to a human narrative so unlike the history told today, and into the same academic 'black hole.' Many have already taken this path and refuse to look, engage in conversation or take any action that may lead to further research or acknowledgment into not only Ros' Rock 1 but the dozens of marked sacred rocks that are no less impressive. Despite our open invitation to all scholars to inspect or discuss, not one representative from any university, official agency or any government department has made any attempt to look or write an opposing or supportive paper.

Irrespective of what takes place elsewhere, there are three rocks spread across the planet that resonate to the same inspiration and script. We see Ros' Rock 1 as the 'Rosetta Stone' from which all other ancient marked rocks should be compared against, and before declaring it as authentic stone records of the First Language. The other two rocks exclusively carry a message encoded into angles, which is more than valid and bears witness to one style of communication, but there is so much more than inclinations and lengths involved. Also found on Ros' Rock 1 are up to 28 peckings, of course this pales by comparison to the hundreds of peckings found on Ros' Rock 2, but it still makes a sizable contribution to a cryptic narrative no-one yet can decipher.

The angles, lines, shapes and pecks seem to form the bulk of the messages engraved on Ros' Rock 1, but room must be left aside for the two clusters of imprints, of which Ros' Rock 3 has no less than 25. Of all the imprints yet seen on any of the many marked rocks we have placed in the 'elite category' none are more striking and intricate than the set of nine positioned above the map on Side 3, which we believe to be a star chart.

Even when including all of these types of markings, there are still more elements on display on this very special rock (Ros' Rock 1) that once again draws parallels to the stars above and the renowned Original passion in observing the "great dark shapes"[13] between the stars. The same rules apply on Side 2, which we believe connects the narrative on Side 1 to the map on Side 3, there are five horizontal lines evenly spaced and none are directly connected to either lines or intersection points on Sides 1 or 3. However, although all are separated on both sides by clean silica, if the lines were to continue in both directions all ten end points would connect exactly to the mm to another line or point of intersection. There is not only deliberate intent in this subtle yet cryptic script, but the scribe is a person of exceptional intelligence and skill, having access to tools and technology that may well surpass the best efforts of today.

Using Ros' Rock as the comparative base, both the Bosnian and Canadian rocks scored a better than 90% match. Not once but twice. The chances that this is all due to random and natural forces are infinitesimally low, while the odds that all of these rocks stand united in chronicling an ancient language that spread across the entire globe are ridiculously high. It may have been embellished and revised, but is it possible that the famed 'Tower of Babel' myth speaks of a time when the First Language was spoken by every person, and of the events that led to the abandonment of the universal mother tongue and the confusion that followed?

Again whether we are right is inconsequential, as the numbers stand apart three times over. There is too much that is shared and so little that is unaccompanied.

Connecting the Dots and Lines

There can only be two logical explanations, either the three rocks were marked by a human hand or nature's agents. The less convincing alternative is random and takes place without any plan or intelligent input, the other much stronger possibility is predicated upon the complete revision of the history books and an acceptance that our fundamental understanding of how humanity evolved is seriously under question.

As with all historical debates, the older the setting, the less certainty can be claimed. When claiming human activity on rocks of great antiquity, it becomes even more difficult to be absolute. Having conceded that inherent degree of doubt, we would object in this unique case in declaring that on this occasion there is literally no sensible alternative.

The exceptionally high rate of convergence of angles defies coincidence, the technology employed contradicts every conventional historical narrative and the content engraved could be rightly regarded as the wisdom of the ages, or all of this is just another example of rocks rubbing against rocks. The idea that this just happened three times over at different places without design or control just doesn't make sense, and, as one of the greatest 21st century social commentators (Judge Judy) often opines, "If it doesn't make sense, it must be a lie."

So it comes down to two choices, one that makes sense and the other a lie. We choose the sensible Original truth in proposing that the three marked rocks are examples of different styles of expressing an ancient global language.

Chapter 15

ROS' ROCKS 4 & 5, EQUALS ONE ROCK WITHOUT EQUAL

In some circles, and one of the better records by Rod Stewart, every picture tells a story. In one ancient circle and two very special rocks, every rock tells not one, but many stories. The problem is that these stories are as old as the hills and resonate to a script that is so sophisticated and too intelligent for any mere mortal of today. Despite our shared human deficiencies and ingrained conditioning, we intend to begin in kindergarten and try to make some partial sense of two rocks that break so many rules.

Where to start on this occasion? Wherever we begin and conclude guarantees a task less than half done. Having conceded the reality of many omissions and even more incomplete understandings, it would seem logical to be consistent in how Ros' Rocks 1, 2 and 3 were presented and continue in the same sequence in first examining Ros' Rock 4 then moving on to Ros' Rock 5. Not this time!

The Rock That Changes ...

* **Figure 53:**
Ros' Rock No. 5[1]

The rock we have called Ros' Rock 5 is too intriguing and unlike anything ever seen in this continent, and has to initiate proceedings. The second rock, as impressive as its credentials are, will have to take second billing. Ros' Rock 5 is a six-sided rhombus, every side is rounded off, the five of the sides are incredibly smooth and there is nothing remotely like it in this country.

What really grabs the attention is not the paper smooth faces, but the one side that is slightly uneven and has a distinct depression that we believe was fashioned to accommodate the right-hand thumb. For three quarters of the upward ascent on this slope, it is easy to see how the top surface was pushed away from right to left thus creating a thumb rest. But what to do with the excess rock? Thankfully in this case the residue was not disposed of, but allowed to take its natural course. The resulting crust of unwanted rock runs along seven eighths of the left-hand edge it is obvious to see and measures 6 ½ cm in length and has dripped up to one centimetre down the adjoining side.

* **Figure 54:**
  Ros' Rock No. 5[2]

At the top of this ridge, is a small area that was not pushed away and left untouched, as its role is to pay homage to the stars. It is early days yet, but we have been informed that the ten dots/pecks/circles represent the Navajo Squatting Man star system[3]. Further on we intend to pursue the potential that the four sides that contain clusters of these marks are constellations, but for now our focus is not in what these cream dots and ovals mean. As to whether this rock, which not only belonged to Original Elders but was called the Constellation Rock, was actually indented in a way to replicate the star formations above is a moot point and secondary to a feature that stands above all other rocks. What intrigues is the colour and uniform depth. It seems that past 5 mm in depth the dark brown layer of rock gives way to a colour that is directly opposite, and that uniformity in depth of the top darker crust remains consistent on each side.

How can this be? Undoubtedly this trait has been identified in earlier Ros Rocks, but on this occasion there are more clues to assist. First and foremost is the direction of grain, excluding the widest top edge, all other sides have the grain running up the rock-face horizontally 180 degrees. That is nowhere near natural and for want of a better description it seems as if the top layer of rock, which could be chert[4], was coated or painted onto a different rock of much lighter complexion. As with the lines and imprints, while this semi-liquid upper layer of molten rock began to cool the pecks would have set. What seems to be on show is a technological process that requires an intense accumulation of heat contained within one object/device to bake rocks, very much like a kiln.

Yes this is an incredibly radical suggestion, but it is the culmination of many rocks exhibiting a variety of features that require intense and centralised heat, and a concept we had proposed well before first sighting this rock. What is different this time around is that the form of this rock itself is undeniably artificial, it was shaped into a rhombus then each edge was smoothed off, rounded and baked.

From the very first time we made public our belief that the thin top chert veneer was melted then attached to a base rock of different make, we have roundly castigated in academic circles for our naivety and misplacement of technological expertise.

They are mistaken and have not kept up with the most recent developments in South Africa, which makes it very clear that the "earliest sign"[5] of *Homo sapiens sapiens* problem solving of the highest order is the crude heating of silcrete.[6] Researcher, Dr Patrick Schmidt[7], has collected an abundance of examples of "heat-induced transformations of silcrete."[8]

The South African rocks are much cruder by comparison to the ensemble of marked rocks in Australia, but irrespective of the sophistication of end product and timing, renowned scholar, Dr. Andy I. R. Herries[9], is adamant that "heating silcrete that was the first recognisable act that made us sapiens humans."[10] The central issue is that the heating of silcrete, which is what we see in Australia, is agreed to have taken place in South Africa. Ignoring geography, this seminal act marks our transition into the species we are today. Any example of this ancient process is vitally important and should be regarded as a national treasure.

In Australia, the melting of chert is much more refined and advanced in application, none more so than Ros' Rock 5. There is a much lighter, thicker grained rock lurking beneath the surface of a finer, harder coating of what could be chert. What does become increasingly obvious is that this rock has no parallel or cruder version. It is totally unique, and patently serves no utilitarian function, but does chart the stars, must be held in the right hand and has without doubt other roles.

Walking Down a new Path

Now it gets difficult, because outside the certainty of shaping, heating, marking and fusing two rocks, there is nothing else we can add beyond possibilities and random observations, that at the moment, lead nowhere.

Of the four sides that surround the two larger faces, the upper edge with the thumb-print resting place measures a little over 4 cm across and is the widest of the four edges. What is fascinating is that when rotating the edges to see whether it can also take the weight of the rock and maintain balance, the two adjoining edges to the thicker thumb-rest can also take the weight and create three very different shapes and arrangement of angles.

Of the six sides, five can maintain a steady balance and every alignment creates a different setting, angles and geometry. Knowing Frederic Slater went to great lengths in explaining how shaped rocks convey meanings sourced in the First Language, it would seem logical to propose that such a relationship applies with this rock. Alas, knowing all of this doesn't transform into content, but it does supply some context.

However, the simple acknowledgment that the shaped stones have meaning is only a rudimentary starting point in this case. We have seen hundreds of shaped rocks, very close to the Standing Stones site that are still untouched, but there is not one rock that comes close to this level of refinement.

We cannot be sure whether the rock was already pocked before coating, or that the application of molten rock was not consistent in depth and because of this the thinner areas eroded away and began the localised weathering that grew into these small holes. It is also feasible to suggest the markings were made on the softer rock before the top layer of molten chert was poured. Or perhaps, and this is the most inconvenient option, an extremely sharp and very hard metal point was punched through the fully hardened top chert coat to the softer and lighter coloured rock beneath. We can never be definite, but do have a very strong preference towards the idea that the star points were punched into the amalgam of two fused rocks after cooling.

The only side incapable of balance is less than two cm wide and has six pecks/holes, of which three have tiny sharp points at the centre of the three circles. At least twice as deep as the rest of the base of these circles, it gives the impression that at some stage a sharp metal punch was held on the top surface, then a hammer hit the punch which created this hole. The deepest point will be the tip of punch, and that impact seems to be what took place here. This process is not restricted to one side, the opposite top edge/thumb print has 12 star markers of which six retain the initial sharper and deeper centre point. In what only adds to the intrigue and diversity apparent, it would seem that on the two larger faces there is not one sharp point to be seen.

Digging Deeper

Of course, in each hole whether containing a deeper mid-point or flat and even, the colour revealed beneath is a constant creamy yellow. However, there is one issue still to be resolved, yes there is a layer of creamy rock beneath, but how deep does it run? Could it be just a thin layer of softer rock, which somehow through an unheard of combination of natural forces, created this geological potpourri? This is where Ros Rock 4, the second of the two new rocks we are still trying to understand, comes to the forefront.

* **Figure 55:**
Ros' Rock No. 4[11]

There is one peck measuring 80 mm by 30 mm, which was obviously very deep to begin with and has eroded considerably over the years. So much so, that the hole is now over 1 cm deep, and all the way down this hole the rock remains a constant cream yellow and the inner grains are much larger. There are four other small pecks spread across the three other sides, but it is the bottom edge that catches the eye and reconfirms a dual geological occupancy. There are close to 30 pecks clustered into a very small area measuring 5 cm by 2 cm of which twelve are deeper and have broken the top veneer of chert exposing the second rock. Close to a third of the surface has lost the dark chocolate top layer and is now a lighter colour. All of this only confirms that the processes, technology and high temperatures evident in Ros' Rock 5 was also needed to create this ancient rock artefact.

Ros' Rock 4 resembles a rough rectangular pyramid and has five sides with three widths of lines. The thickest lines are found on the largest and most intricate side. Up until now, all the imprints have been either quite dramatic or less so, but either way each is at least 50 mm or larger, which is much different. There is one cluster at the top and another at the bottom and together there are about 50 small to extremely small imprints. Neither very deep nor easy to see, there is intent and communication taking place, but again it is outside our limited understandings.

Another regular feature discussed earlier and first identified by our resident anonymous geological advisor when examining Ros Rock 1, is that the lines were marked on two different occasions. With these two rocks beginning to surrender a few ancient secrets, we are now less inclined to presume that is the case and more comfortable with the possibility the lines were fainter and thinner when first cut into the molten surface. What alerted us to this far more logical explanation is one thick line on the main side begins to taper slightly as it reaches the edge then continues around the next side with the line's width narrowing even more until barely visible. Knowing the line is unbroken throughout three sides with no disconnect, it is likely the blades were varied as was the pressure applied, much like an artist with brushes in hands.

Our tally of lines on this rock, will ignore the width or vibrancy of mark and treat all as equal, and adds up to a total of around 35. The count of pecks include the majority positioned on the bottom side, and another group of eleven just above the main cluster, which number just over forty in total. What is fascinating is the low percentage of straight lines on this rock. Early on in the piece we tended to dismiss any line that wasn't straight, conceding that the more jagged and erratic the path taken the greater the chance it was natural. We had been spoilt by Ros' Rock 1 which doesn't have one line that is not straight, and is the template from which all marked rocks must be compared. That assumption was called into question once a serious examination of Ros' Rock 3 was undertaken. With the input of this rock, which we claim is in the same category and of equal standing to that of Ros' Rock 4, it has become obvious that the non-straight lines are often, if not nearly always, the result of human hands and tools or devices. All that differs is that each type of line has a different intent and context.

Again in synchronicity with Ros' Rock 3, this rock also has lines that wrap around each side of the rock and nearly all that do not, join a line that does and all serve one purpose, to communicate information and knowledge.

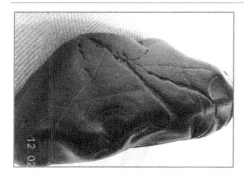

* **Figure 56:**
Ros' Rock No. 3[12]

In concluding the questions yet to be resolved, it seems prudent to balance the scales by focusing on one certainty. In both cases there are two rocks artificially co-joined. The inner base is coarse grained, lighter in colour and nowhere near as hard as the thin crust of chert that coats the foundation stone. The dates of these rocks will obviously vary between hundreds to thousands of years, but is inconsequential as all we need is for one of the hybrids to be over 200 years old. One tick out of one hundred and fifty rocks is sufficient, as the reality is that according to all accepted accounts of pre-Cook Australia, Original people were restricted to a bone, stone, stick and open flame technology. That will not be enough, nowhere near it, there is no possible way that tool-kit will have any impact, or even a mark, on these rocks. The maths just does not add up.

4 + 5 = a new Algorism and Different Equations

We have a total of over one hundred and fifty marked or shaped rocks that we are investigating and none are part of any accepted historical narrative, that is the founding truth upon which every other possibility, opinion and postulation must flow. We have said this before and will continue to do so, it doesn't matter in the least whether our explanations are correct simply because every conventional historical setting is the first casualty of this about-face. Every text, syllabus and lecturer will assure the student that before the British boats dropped anchor in Sydney Harbour the Original people had a stone, bone and stick tool-kit. They are patently wrong and will remain in error unless they re-engage with old perspectives and Original wisdom.

That is why no person or group representing any official agency affiliated with any government, science or academic organisation has made an attempt to look or contact us for details about these marked and shaped rocks. Some are undoubtedly more spectacular than others, but each has a part to play, and it would seem those in control are not in the least bit interested in the script, language or rocks on display. The reason for this refusal to engage with reality and science is simple, from every mainstream perspective the angles, geometry and mathematics just doesn't add up and there is no text to consult. We know for a fact there are many academics who have been alerted to the existence of these rocks and that their responses can be categorised into two reactions, open hostility or a dogged refusal to look, discuss or do anything more than immediately change the subject. Under no conditions will they rely on science. Our rigour, methodology, quality of research or sheer mass of archaeology is not the issue of concern here, it's just the utter inconvenience and the grief it will cause.

What makes it ten times worse is that we are playing by their rules, writing papers fashioned to their setting and sensibilities and offering conclusions that call into question fundamental historical assumptions they cherish. Their response when under attack is to adopt the defensive pose of the ostrich by ramming their heads in the dirt and hoping that the aging hippy and his son, and their disturbing narrative will go away. Relying solely on poor science, theories penned by a quill and ink and a steadfast refusal to look while championing gross historical inaccuracies of monumental proportions is not only an insult to the Original truths, but a stain on their character and an offence to Original Culture and Lore.

Personal damage and bad karma aside, the greatest tragedy of the institutionalised refusal to engage is that by doing so they are robbing the nation and all Australian people of our collective heritage, history and ancestry. These lies cannot be allowed to continue, the earth is not flat, it is not the centre of the universe and humanities' history is not as we are told. We have one piece of advice for those who refuse to budge and get in the way, stand aside and bow your heads in shame because like it or not, the Original truths are coming through and nothing they can do, or not do, will make any difference.

Chapter 16

ROS' ROCK NO.10: THE FIRST HYBRID

This marked rock is yet another sourced from a private collection of sacred rocks that was part of the interaction that took place between Original tribes and Professor A.P. Elkin, Dr Herbert Basedow[1] and other sympathetic researchers between 1926 and 1939. All are genuine products of Original technology and many are extremely old, and we have no doubt that this remarkable rock belongs to the most ancient category. It escorted a marked we have named Thomas' Rock 9.

* **Figure 57:**
  Ros Rock No. 10[2]

Upon first opening the box I was struck by how unlikely a pair these rocks appeared, they are the double bass and soprano of this growing ensemble of marked rocks and opposite in so many respects. Ros' Rock 10 is the heaviest of the series, yet is an intriguing piece of geometry. Each face is consistent in angle of incline and proportion and is obviously artificially formed. The rock was delicately fashioned to be held in a certain way, with slight depressions along one edge provided for each finger and webbing behind the thumb. We believe that the three rectangles and two triangles that make up this shaped rock were made to a set formula, whereas the faint markings and the residual chert overlay is far more indistinct. There has been so much skin rubbing on the chert and it has been going on for so long. What remains at this late stage, at face value are faint lines, gaps, hints, possibilities and a few definites.

* **Figure 58:**
  Thomas' Rock No. 9[3]

Its companion in post and guest from across the waters (Thomas' Rock 9), is the smallest and lightest of all the rocks we have examined. The markings are of the finest precision and clarity without the need to add, subtract or visualise. As small as the rock is, the perfectly flat polished face and engraved lines are undamaged, seemingly protected from the elements. The actual rock itself, once subtracting the undamaged flat section containing the lines, carries no evidence of any interest in the shape itself. The layers beneath make no recognisable form and carry no flat edge or straight line. This rock is, once subtracting the top piece, the most untidy, scrappy member of the collection. Whereas Ros' Rock 10 has the smoothest surface, flattest edges, and an abundance of straight tidy lines, be they ever so worn.

However, it would be a mistake if assuming that it is our intention to separate and dissociate the two rocks, because amongst all the variation what is shared is more than sufficient. Both marked rocks have a top coat of chert, bear evidence of very sophisticated technology, display all manner of markings and lines, and are rightly regarded as sacred. They bear testimony to a shared global language and are a very effective means of preserving information that can remain open for inspection for millions of years.

Skin on Silica

Without a doubt, Ros was adamant in noting that she felt this rock was extra special and not that far behind in stature to that of Ros' Rock 1. When she made such a confident declaration over the phone, I remember thinking at the time that it's a huge call to make. Her reasons for being impressed, in particular is that it is so obviously fashioned to be held in the hand. This wasn't for one second being questioned or ignored, but I just felt we already had so many rocks designed to be held in the right hand. It all sounded a bit like more of yesterday's news, and we have made that point more than once. I just couldn't envisage getting excited by another rock with a groove or depression which was made to accommodate a finger or thumb. I thought we had been there and done that, and were now seeking new horizons.

It didn't get any better upon first arrival, knowing that I was always going to write an article on the American marked rock first, the attention given to this rock was spasmodic and brief. Four fifths of the available space for markings was long gone, most likely rubbed off by skin. There is so little left and so much of what was originally on board lost. This somewhat unexpected phenomena of skin rubbing against chert was first examined on Ros' Rock 2, where one side had been noticeably worn away by the right index finger. However, on this rock the reach of bare skin on silica is far greater. The amount of chert worn away is five to six times greater in area, which is no doubt due to direct contact not with one digit, but five.

Side 1 measures 92 mm in length, of which the remaining upper coat of chert found on the top edge varies between 12 mm to 25 mm. That loss of the top layer approximates to 82% of the original layer of chert being rubbed off through skin friction. The next side measures the same and is almost identical in the amount of 'de-rocking,' with a residual top edge of 12 mm to 28 mm leaving 79% of this side now lacking in the thin upper crust of chert. This is to be expected as the placement of fingers and thumb will see equal amounts of skin and pressure spread across both sides. What adds depth to our suggestion that the chert was slowly rubbed off, is the condition of Side 3, which still has a very thin chert overlay intact with no lighter colour exposed. Being far less worn than the other two sides could be a logical consequence of having very little contact with human skin.

With 80% of the original narrative lost in transit this was a distraction and took a few viewings to negotiate. What soon became apparent is that at each inspection something else became easier to appreciate, as the veils were lifted. Although our progress has been incremental, we have now reached the stage where we can now appreciate why Ros was so convinced, that despite the wear and tear and considerable antiquity, this is an exceptionally important artefact.

Slater's "Shaped Stones"[4] and two Times 180 Degrees

From the moment we first set eyes on this rock, our comparison to the Standing Stones site Frederic Slater was researching (which is literally festooned with shaped rocks down the slope and the flatter paddock below), was an immediate reflex reaction. The most repeated shapes found at that site are the triangle/pyramid and rectangle. Granted the shaped rocks on that site are sandstone, which is much softer than chert, but irrespective of degrees of hardness, the geometry is the same.

* **Figure 59:**
  Ros' Rock No. 10[5]

There are two triangles, one at each end. On one end, which still retains its chert crust, is the larger triangle. The other end has obviously worn quite considerably due to the amount of skin rubbed against the top layer for tens, maybe even hundreds, of thousands of years. The reason we are so confident this is actually what took place is because the numbers and proportions remain utterly constant. The triangle on the unworn side measures 45 mm by 50mm by 65mm, whereas the triangle on the other side, which has been subjected to much more personal handling measures 40mm by 45mm by 60mm. The smaller triangle is exactly 5 mm shorter on every side, which implies that the wear is consistent with the loss of edge and dimensions should also occur at the same rate, which it certainly did.

Again it cannot be a coincidence that the longest line of each rectangular side measures 92 mm. Nor is this a result created through natural forces with the area of the larger triangle being 22.5 square cm and the smaller triangle 18 square cm. That is an exact ratio of 5:4, give or take nothing, and because the numbers do keep adding up as they should, the chances this convergence of mathematics is anything other than calculated, is less than infinitesimal.

Four Fingers and one Thumb

If it wasn't for the considerable wear and two other minor deviations, this would be a perfectly formed piece of geometry. Even in its pristine state it was always almost, but never completely symmetrical. The now smaller end triangle has a smooth flat face, but the same cannot be said for the larger, relatively unrubbed triangle. It bulges slightly and there are three engraved lines, and what could be an index-finger depression near the bottom edge. Apart from this uneven face, which is possibly due to accommodations made to position of the index-finger, everything is in balance and linear, until the final touches were made on two of the three sides that form the three rectangles. On one side there are three evenly spaced undulations that are intended to position three fingers, the index finger sits inside a depression at the bottom of the larger triangle and the thumb runs diagonally across one face with the webbing resting on the centre of the edge, which curves inwards due to the rubbing of skin on rock.

As expected the rock was made to be held in the right hand, which seems to be a hard and fast rule that we are yet to see broken, and of course, this is yet another feature that binds the collection irrespective of location.

Lines, Pecks and so Much More Missing

With 80% of whatever was engraved, pecked or raised as a relief now lost, making any comment in regard to the narrative or context is nigh on impossible. A deterrent for most, but an incentive for us, despite the outages we still believe what remains and vestiges of what could have been is sufficient in providing a general overview.

The pecking can be broken into three categories, two types of 'stand-alone' circles/pecks and a series of pecks that run together and assist in stripping away the chert to create the outlines of no less than four shapes or wide bands.

Until investigating this rock, we had maintained that all pecks took place after the chert had set rock-hard. There are three sizes of pecks/circles and the largest group of six circles (we chose the term circle as there is no way they were pecked) seemed to have been formed before the chert overlay and may have been imprinted first into the rock. Elsewhere there are 15 pin-pricks which were the vanguards for the smaller pecks. For all the smaller pecks, a very fine hard point was punched through the top layer, but the much larger circles show no central puncture point. The smooth even depressions are lacking in a point of impact and are circles, not pecks. Whether this cluster of five circles of varying diameters represent a star system or Dreaming Tracks is an issue still to be resolved, but they are unique in being formed before the chert was applied above, and that alone adds some weight to Ros' high opinion.

The smaller pecks from the stand-alone group are much more in keeping with what is found on other rocks, as nearly all the pecks, no matter how worn, still retain the sharp puncture point. One cluster of seven pecks could well represent the Pleiades, or perhaps another star system.

There are lines of four widths on this rock. The two curved lines on Side 1 which we suspect goes towards creating a serpent 40 mm wide, and once again contradicts another assumption we thought was set in stone. Until now, it was our belief every line was cut into the molten chert or the rock beneath before the chert was attached and hardened. On every other rock we can make a strong case that one of these two techniques was used, but not this time around. The two lines that mark out what we believe to be the edges of a serpent, is made up of dozens, upon dozens of tiny pecks united in one continuous undulation, and this 'peck-line' continues on to Side 2 where the whole top section, excepting two straight lines, has been pecked away after the chert cooled.

As our investigations into Ros' Rocks 10 continues breaking ground and old rules, or forces us into unknown territory, it has become clearer why Ros was so enamoured by this very old worn artefact.

Then we have the 'normal' lines, some straight others curved and all revealing a light creamy brown undercoat. Nowhere near as wide as the pecked lines, they measure 15 mm and 10 mm, of which some taper off to the thinnest 'hair width' fracture, and all of these lines are no different than those found on all the other rocks. As elsewhere, some lines continue on the same trajectory when rounding corners or edges.

Stepping up a Level

In continuing in this tradition of reversals and new additions, from the very beginning apart from the complexity of geometry, the ridging was always the next highest priority. What we see here is very old, but brand new. There is one rectangular ridge fully intact and remnants of another five in various states of disrepair. The almost undamaged relief has two parallel lines and between is a raised rectangular relief of 20 mm width and 5 mm in height, which runs all the way across Side 1, and is another new addition to our ever expanding stock-take of symbols, shapes and sundry markings that make up the First Language. This particular raised rectangle measures 45 mm in length and is plain to see, but until now we have never seen a ridge of such uniformity, precision and geometric conformity on any rock.

Before the critics counter with examples of a bizarre combination of unusual geological agents, it needs to be appreciated that this relief does not stand-alone. There are five others, and one that is moderately worn, but still retains a section of 35 mm by 5 mm with two parallel sides that go towards creating another perfect rectangle.

Rocks can naturally exhibit all manner of ridges and reliefs and the end result could look similar, but nature's work is never perfectly symmetrical, parallel and rectangular without fault. No, this is artificial and leads us to suggest that perhaps the six ridges that remain are but a few of many, and it is possible that ridging like this ran across and down both sides.

Glue on Top???

This is a very tentative entrant and we did vacillate between yes and no as to whether even suggesting that on Side 3 there are two thin trails of an exotic resin-like substance running down the face. A lighter colour and barely 5mm thick, the upper trail measures 7mm in length and the second 9 mm. These strips are of a yellowish colour not seen on this rock and may well be a natural event. However, when placed in context, knowing that this shaped rock has all manner of artificial marks, this deposit deserves no less than serious consideration.

AT ROS' REQUEST

We did look again and again, entirely because of Ros' intuition and lo and behold, she was right and our eyes had betrayed us yet again. It is a shaped stone very much in the tradition of the Standing Stones site, but this hybrid is also a marked rock that was held on many, many occasions, undoubtedly for spiritual reasons. The narrative on this rock uses ridges never seen before, techniques not used elsewhere and what was engraved onto a stone is a piece of geometry that has no known precedent within this continent.

As with every other rock in this series, the rocks have an upper layer of chert, which is a form of silica. Silicon is renowned for its ability to store large amounts of important data. These thin coats of silica display symbols, lines, dots and imprints on the surface that represent something we will have a great deal of trouble decoding.

Despite the enormous difficulties in interpretation all is not lost. We do know that the secret knowledge of these rocks never disappeared. We have no doubt that when the timing is appropriate an Original Custodian of the Old Ways will assist and guide. In the meantime, with over 100 rocks yet to be examined there is more than enough engraved on the outside, let alone what sits within.

Chapter 17

"ALL FOUND TOGETHER..."[1]

A small note written by Ros accompanied a package of "14 marked rocks found at the side of a sand dune that had been weathered away."[2] In her explanation she gave details as to who found the rocks, and in very general terms where, but the most important part of this ancient equation related to the quantity under examination. On every occasion and location, never before has there been a cache of sacred objects in such numbers "all found together,"[3] hidden away and buried in a sand dune until exposed through erosion. The fact that this ensemble is contrasted by differing sizes, styles, scripts and shapes and that none of the individual rocks are merely repeated copies but unique in marking and genre, only adds to the significance of such a huge accumulation of holy objects.

Normally when a larger cluster of rocks is sent by Ros, it's always sourced from a variety of locations. There is one rock, occasionally two, where the impact is muted and the chances of nature's involvement is slim, but possible. This time, even with our 'cynic's hat' firmly wedged whilst standing first in line, there is no room for protest or doubt. All of the rocks were artificially marked and found in situ, exposed long after being intentionally hidden by Original custodians. In every case, bar none, there is rock-solid evidence of cuts, marks, heat and sundry applications that can only come about through technology and science of a level that has to be described as very advanced.

Ros' Rocks 18

In what is the highest benchmark recently set by Ros' Rock 16, this rock (Ros' Rock 18) is its equal in its minimalist approach and empty spaces. Four of the five sides have nothing at face-value to contribute, but the fifth side makes up for these omissions many times over.

* **Figure 60:**
Ros' Rock No. 18[4]

It is a comment and an admission made before, and no doubt will reappear at a time not of our choosing, but on each occasion we are tempted to assume that the scope of expressing information through lines cut into rocks had reached its limits, something like this turns up.

Everything is connected; each line, shape and imprint is part of a bigger picture/ diagram. There is one central line and sixteen other lines and shapes that intersect or merge into this dominant staff. It is very difficult and undeniably subjective when trying to interpret what this very intricate arrangement of lines could represent, but that never concerned us before. The shape created is quite striking and certainly seems to resemble a serpent/dragon, even more so when factoring in the five imprints that do not break the surface. One of those imprints could serve as a second set of limbs, or it could be something else again.

Irrespective of what this diagram represents, never before have we seen 17 lines and shapes formally connected in creating one symbol or statement. To even suggest that this could be due to natural agents is not deserving of a reply. The only task worthy of consideration relates to determining the possible means of production.

The answer to this can be seen in the five imprinted shapes that are spread around this figure. Each small depression still retains the original chert coating, and due to this veneer remaining unbroken, they are less visible. Despite the softer lines and muted effect, they are part of the design and this seems to indicate that the base rock was marked before the molten chert was applied and hardened. It may be that the deeper and wider lines and marks were never covered, or were thinly covered then scratched off, but due to the fact that the five imprints have the shallowest base, we suspect they were always meant to sit in the background, just below the surface.

Undeniably our insistence that molten chert was added at a later date after the base rock was pre-cut, is a formidable hurdle for many experts who haven't kept up with the most recent research coming out of South Africa. However, those five imprints do not stand-alone. There are impressions of six lines found on the adjacent side, but none have broken through the top veneer. All can be seen in good light, each is separate, straight and just as shallow in depth as the five on the most marked side.

We are of the opinion that this rock was shaped to satisfy some very precise ratios. There are three notched areas, one on each side, and in each case some of the original rock was removed from each edge then smoothed off for reasons that do not seem immediately apparent. After all the trouble the artisan went to in shaping, smoothing then chipping into this rock three times over, we felt the least we could do is measure the three lines that connect these gaps on each side which form the outline of a triangle. Whether this happened by coincidence or design, it makes no difference, what does measure up are the three sides of this connecting triangle (12 mm, 21 mm and 24 mm). All lengths are divisible by three, which leads to a ratio of 4:7:8.

The rock is very smooth on each face with rounded edges, and seems to have been polished many times. At first glance it is a small rock measuring at its widest points less than 5 cm by 3 cm, but cut within the chert surface is an intricate diagram requiring skill and sophisticated technology, and skirting around the edges is a theoretical triangle. It is one of many Original sacred marked rocks that heighten the contradictions, admittedly it is quite small and at first sighting somewhat deceptive. So too is another rock found at the same exposed dune that is less than half the size of Ros' Rock 18, but this time around there is no idle space in between. This marked rock is both the smallest we have reported on and the most concentrated in markings and imprints. So intensive and cluttered are the marks, it's nigh on impossible to make an accurate tally, which ends up somewhere near one hundred.

Ros' Rock 19

This rock is so small and so easy to overlook when in the company of other rocks, or if positioned further than a metre from any eye. It is only when under full sunlight assisted by a magnifying glass does the complexity of script and clues as to how this was created become marginally clearer.

* **Figure 61:**
Ros' Rock No. 19[5]

This even smaller rock is heavily pocked with all manner of imprints and a large number of lines. In nearly every respect, it's the complete opposite of the previous rock. There is nothing left that is smooth or even, it is so heavily cut or imprinted that whatever level surface was once in existence, it vanished during the first sitting. And it is that number of separate applications taking place at different times that so intrigues and seems to be very evident on this rock. We suspect that this rock was marked or imprinted on up to four separate occasions.

As with the last rock, but far more numerous, the imprints were engraved/cut into the base rock first, and there is ample evidence of that happening here. There are five lines cut through the chert and deep into the base rock that still retains the very sharp line of the original blade in the middle of the depression, past that point it seems some lines were widened through further cutting beside the line already present. At an even later date the finest lines of all, barely wider than a strand of hair, were cut beside and through the top of these older marks. One such thin line runs down into an older thicker multi-cut line and exits out the top edge, then continues across the next side 'gun-barrel' straight until merging into a large cut shape and raised ridge. We are convinced that line is a more recent addition and obviously was cut after the older thicker incision.

The fringing found on Ros Rock 13, which we felt was part of a topographic map that represented smaller creeks flowing into a central river, is very delicate and requires an extremely steady hand and fine blade. This rock not only picks up on that technique, but blurs the lines. There are three areas where short thin lines like those on Ros' Rock 13 are used, twice as a fringe of sorts and once where these small lines are spread throughout what appears to be a visual depiction of two people, with one holding a spear.

The other two collections are less precise and in one case much less. The smaller and slightly tidier series of small lines run across the front edge of a raised section of rock which has been emphasised by cutting lines down the other two edges of the ridge. Along the front there are eight smaller lines jutting out, two are slightly longer and this gives a slightly irregular feel to the marking.

However, by comparison with the third set of small lines, this is a page out of a geometry text book. There are up to 20 lines in this dishevelled ensemble, all quite small but markedly varied in width and length, and they run down off one straight, diagonal clean line, which is much longer and spans the entire side. They look somewhat like different sized tentacles hanging down from a thicker rod.

The next rock in this ever-increasing tally is certainly much neater and cleaner in line. Although completely unlike the previous rock, Ros' Rock 20 does belong to a genre of shape and setting that has been seen before, and is remarkably similar in appearance, size and manner of line to that of Christine's Rock 17.

* **Figure 62:**
   Christine's Rock No. 17[6]

Ros' Rock 20

We are compelled to begin any investigation of this rock by way of comparing it to Christine's Rock 17. That rock is a touch darker, slightly more polished and has one line that is the cleanest and sharpest yet seen, however, it would be unwise to dismiss this rock as an inferior replica. This rock has not one but six very straight lines, (two of which remain perfectly straight), that circumnavigate all four sides.

* **Figure 63:**
Ros' Rock No. 20[7]

Just like the simpler cleaner version, this rock has horizontal lines, but unlike the earlier rock, this rock also has vertical lines cut into the surface and all are not straight. It seems that there is a mathematical rule at play in this genre. All horizontal lines are straight, while every vertical line is not straight. The two most prominent vertical lines are less geometric and more curved and crooked. There are five other much smaller and fainter vertical lines, but without a doubt the central feature is where the main vertical and horizontal lines intersect in the middle of the rock on Side 1.

On this occasion, we can again only detect one blade and one width of cut, and unlike the last few entries, there is little evidence of imprinting. It is possible that two small shallow imprints were placed on one edge, which we suspect to be the position where the right thumb rested when gripped in the prescribed manner. The roughing up of this edge may have been done to facilitate a better contact between skin and silica. Christine's Rock 17 also has two small worn depressions, and as would be expected, it's the position where the thumb must be placed when held in the right hand.

Those two possible imprints aside, there is nothing else and this leaves open the possibility that the base rock was unmarked and then coated with molten chert. Before the chert hardened it is possible all of these lines were cut, and since that first cutting it would seem there have been no further additions.

Rocks like these which are sparsely marked and bear the same shape seem to form a distinct and frugal category, of which 17 and 20 are part of, but the paucity of lines, maps, imprints and intersection points is a touch limiting and determining any meaning will be a process in need of considerable Original guidance.

Ros' Rock 21

None of the 14 rocks found in the sand dune are particularly large or heavy, and this rock is the biggest of the group. Of the four rocks discussed until now, this rock is probably the oldest. It has a feature shared with Ros' Rock 10 in that the top section of chert remains intact, while the rest of the rock shows signs of heavy wearing possibly through constant contact with the hand. Both rocks have triangular ends and the same polished dark chocolate chert. We are confident that Ros' Rock 10 and 21 belong to a specific group, and that the messages inscribed share many similarities.

* **Figure 64:**
    Ros' Rock No. 21[8]

Of all the rocks in this batch this is the most complex, granted there is a lot of activity on Ros' Rock 19. The lines are small and leave no trail, and it has a much more visual impact, whilst this rock is far more cryptic. There are at least six continuous lines, some very fine, that span all sides of the rock. There are no less than three widths of cut, and very good indications this was the outcome of multiple sittings. Quite a few of the finest lines are cut over the top of older thicker lines, and others are so worn they can barely be seen.

The same attention to precision observed on many other rocks is also on display on what we assume to be the main side. Almost entirely a horizontal narrative slanted towards the diagonal, there is one prominent exception to this general alignment. Positioned on the side with the most markings, this segmented vertical line cuts across the flow, remaining straight from top to bottom. However, that original observation was not given in full sun and with magnifying glass in assistance. With the benefit of better light and magnification, this is indeed one continuous line that varies dramatically in width by a factor of close to 20. This is a task requiring considerable skill, the finest of metal blades and must mean something of significance.

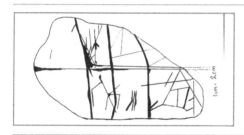

* **Figure 65:**
    Ros' Rock No. 21 Diagram[9]

Beginning just above the top edge, this line cut into chert is at its widest measuring 2 mm and narrows to half that gap over the next 2 cm. At first glance that did seem to be the end of the line, but upon closer inspection there is indeed the thinnest line visible which can be no larger than 0.1mm across that continues for the next 2.7 cm. That hair-width line merges into a thicker line that is one mm in width, 1.5 cm long and once again appears to stop at that point. But no, the same delicate line picks up the same angle and continues on until reaching the edge.

In what only adds to the mathematics and precision involved, under these more enlightening conditions it became apparent that this vertical line was not alone. The side with the largest concentration of symbols and signs measures 6 cm by 4 cm, and this much fainter line begins literally in the central point (3 cm by 2 cm). The second shorter line remains separate by 1mm in maintaining a parallel setting with both lines running down the face a further 3 cm before lipping over the edge and continuing on at the same distance apart.

The complex mathematics, a junior parallel line escorting this line to the far edge, the idea that one continuous line of 6.5 cm can be very thick, then of medium width before becoming extremely thin before merging into a medium sized gap then completing its transformation by shrinking into an almost unseen line can be natural, is impossible at every level. The real issue at play comes down to what tools are required to create such a line that is supposedly far too sophisticated, technical and geometric to be part of any Original tool-kit before Cook. Why go to so much trouble in making one cut into chert? Is the width and depth of cut, along with the length of each gap, yet another part of this rock language?

There is so much more to this rock, and it looks as if our follow up piece will break our self-imposed refusal to focus just on one rock as we have done in the past. This rock is the most imposing and enigmatic of the collection, but for now we will conclude our brief introduction with an unusual convergence that cuts across and brushes against the vertical line of five widths.

This blurred meeting point is very odd and a touch frayed at the edges. Just to the left of the point of intersection between the vertical line and the first main horizontal line, possibly no more than 2 mm away are six separate lines which all meet at one point of convergence. The resulting combined image, no doubt added to by the passing of years, looks very much like an explosion, blasting away beneath the side of the ridge which marks out the point of preservation above or wear below. Whether intentionally highlighting the difference between above and below and that intersection point, or a destination point on a star map is conjecture. Either way, there has to be a good reason to make six lines that meet at the same point.

And that is the real point that needs to be fully appreciated. Finding an exact meaning to all of this information from Ancients, well good luck with that, but there are greener and less spiteful pastures elsewhere. Our brief in research is not to make bold claims about what a script or marking means but identify an intention, intelligence and technology that belongs to this country's past and the Original people's ancestry. As to what the rocks mean, that is a secondary pursuit, first and foremost for these rocks to gain classification and a number they must first tick all three boxes. There has to be evidence of human intention, intelligence and technology that just does not fit into any mainstream account of pre-Cook history of not only in Australia, but as time passes further back, the entire world.

To that end, the vertical line of five widths is utterly intentional and inspired by high intelligence and assisted by a technology and tool-kit that is assumed to be a sole product of the last century. The decision to cut six straight lines and make sure they meet at the same point right next to where the vertical line leaves the ridge and makes contact with the first of many opposing horizontal lines, is also deliberate and an act of unquestionable intelligence.

There are hundreds upon hundreds of cut lines, imprints, shapes and sundry marks on this rock. The number of marks sitting just below the surface runs into three figures, some form clusters or patterns, others individual lines and shapes. Like an earlier rock discussed which sat so comfortably in the hand with the marked face pointing upwards, this rock rests in the hand with a similar feel, and again has the marked face flat and facing the sky. We suspect that the earlier narrative on Ros' Rock 21 was covered and coated, and on two of the sides a brand new story was laid on top. However, the third side is virtually unbroken on the surface, and as a consequence has the largest portion of the imprints. Perhaps this side was deemed to be too important to cover or conceal? All are avenues we will pursue, but for now we still have one rock to examine to satisfy our recent self-imposed five rocks per chapter quota.

Ros' Rock 22

Again if rating these rocks on first impressions this one is scrambling to get a C-. Measuring less than 5 cm in length, with three sides showing very little from a distance, and the side with most of the visible marks small and narrow, there is nothing that overwhelms or grabs the eye.

* **Figure 66:**
Ros' Rock No. 22[10]

As with all, bar the larger rock, the small size is an impediment, but this rock only adds to the anonymity with over 80% of the markings being imprints that do not break the chert surface. What blends into the bland exterior is that very few lines that are visible, do not take 'centre-stage' as they are found near the edge at the top and bottom of one side.

The lines are an assorted crew, with the two thickest (3 mm) are lightly fringed which widens and frays, both being less than 1 cm in length, their impact is minimal. The longest line is relatively straight, one mm in width and 24 mm long. The only other line of note is of the same width and half the length. Outside these not particularly striking markings, there is little else that has broken through the chert overlay, but what is of much more interest sits just beneath the surface.

Until now we have always seen the imprints as one second-tier all-encompassing category, but there are five lines on the main face that add an unexpected nuance and extension that had not been recognised earlier. All five lines have vacillated between being acknowledged as imprints and lines that cut through the veneer and expose the lighter base rock. They aren't deeper than any other imprints, it is just possible that under full sun and magnification that a few lighter grains can be seen. As to whether this was the original intention or the result of weathering is difficult to determine, either way these lines are certainly deep and share sharp edges.

What was of immediate interest relates to how the five lines were created. Two are no different than hundreds we have seen on these rocks, the lines were cut with a sharp blade and as both are not long it seems each was the outcome of one continuous stroke. Both lines are sharp and narrow at the point of entry, widen in the centre and taper to a point as the blade exits, merely more of the same and certainly nothing remarkable on display.

The three lines below were not cut into the base rock or the chert veneer when soft. A technique occasionally seen was used in a way that has no precedent. Pecking is a method used on other rocks, but never to make straight lines. Despite being less precise and much more difficult than one simple stroke, that is the choice made on this rock. The three lines below the two straight cuts are made of five, six and four pecks placed close beside each other in forming lines that are fairly straight, nearly tidy and almost even in width. Each peck mark is still visible under magnification, and this is the only rock where pecks were used to 'punch out' something resembling a straight line. To do this three times over only heightens the significance.

Apart from making the logical assumption that the pecked lines have a meaning that differs from cut lines, nothing can be declared with certainty outside that the markings on the five rocks show similarities and variation, adherence to established patterns and so many features that repeat, yet others that keep extending parameters. The pecked lines are certainly not inferior copies, and does give another insight into the intricacies and cryptic nature of what a line, mark or imprint can be when part of the First Language.

Kangaroo ribs, Eucalyptus Branches and Rocks

As with the four other marked rocks, there is much more to ruminate upon and compare against, and as this is meant to be a very brief introduction of one or two features found on each rock it is sufficient in hopefully dispelling one myth. According to every approved text, lecture, lesson, curriculum and endorsed version of Original history before the British Invasion, their tool-kit consisted of bones, sticks and stones. Nothing else was allowed, there was no metal, machines, melting of rocks, mining or even some crude bows and arrows to lighten the load, it was all very basic with no frills attached. All of the more advanced technologies many cherish and extol the virtues of were never part of the Original landscape until Cook came sailing up the east coast of Australia: that is the official version of events.

So say the books, but these sacred rocks read from a different script that was written into stone long ago, marked and shaped by tools and technology that is modern by today's standards. What we are looking at are two contradicting narratives, one written on paper that can rot in a day, and the other cut into stone, which can outlast the entire lifespan of all hominids on this planet. Make no mistake all five rocks display human intention, human intelligence and show evidence of technology any human of today would agree is advanced.

All five rocks share the same colour, the best description we can offer is a dark chocolate with no variations in grain or other colour, it is so consistent that it's as if they were all painted from the same can of liquid chert. All undercoats are equally consistent, the colour beneath is a light cream grey and within the five base rocks, there is no deviation from that palette.

What this all means, knowing both accounts cannot co-exist, is that one version is false. Paper may cover rock in the child's game, but the reality is that to leave a piece of paper on top of any rock in the hope that will be enough to extinguish or conceal the truth of its existence will see the paper blow, wash or rot away. Despite the short-term inconvenience, the rock will always prevail, and these ancient rocks are genuine in every sense and are ready to reclaim their heritage. The truth is that they are Original artefacts and are much, much older than the two hundred odd years since the British dropped anchors. These sacred rocks were made in Australia by the Original Australians using technology and knowledge that originated in this country.

It comes down to one multiple choice question with two alternatives, *a* or *b*, either the rocks are fake or the official version of Original pre-history is fake.

Chapter 18

STONES THAT "SPEAK WITH THE VOICE OF MALU"[1]

Whenever speaking about the marked rocks at length, inevitably we make mention of the two levels of information encoded into these rocks. Undeniably the most obvious markings sit on the surface, but we are of the opinion that there is something deeper and perhaps sublime that lies within. We strongly suspect there is something far more profound also locked into some of the more sacred rocks, but outside assuming Elders and Custodians knowledgeable in rock language will answer the call either through song, chant or yidaki[2], we had no idea how this secret wisdom is accessed. In fact, beyond assuming that there is more somewhere, we have no specifics or guideposts.

Or should we say had, as that uncertainty may well be deposited in the past tense. Ros Mulder sent us a book through the post written by James Cowan[3] and marked out three pages she felt was of importance. None more so than the first page of Messengers of the Gods she recommended we consider. The very first line my eyes caught on page 52 was difficult to look past and it was, if not heaven-sent, at the very least Ros-sent. With a subtitle on the front cover declaring that "Tribal Elders reveal the ancient wisdom of the Earth,"[4] it was our hope that these revelations included talk of the rocks that can communicate with humans. Once reading that "there are stones on this island that can talk,"[5] we could well understand why Cowan was "astounded by what I heard."[6]

Cowen had spent some time in Torres Islands scaling the esoteric ladder and was so close to the top rung, but what was unexpected was that that final step was entirely up to the talking stones. His guide, Mr. Noa, was a man of high degree, but there was another of greater knowledge in Lore and Old Ways.

"We are not strong anymore. But if you wish, tomorrow I will show you how some of us old fellas stay close to Malu. If you come here before dawn I will take you to visit the Tomog zogo[7]. We will listen to the Si stones. Then maybe you will understand.

"There are stones on this island that can talk?" I asked, astounded by what I heard. Mr. Noa nodded.
"The Si stones are not ordinary stones," he said. "They have a voice.
They speak with the voice of Malu."[8]

Cowan barely slept and made sure he was awake well before dawn. Upon sighting these fabled stones, his first response was tainted by his cultural cargo. He was unable to "detect any formal pattern" [9] and such was assumed to be the extent of disorder, he felt that this place was "much in need of repair and replacement."[10]

Each rock had a shell on top and none seem to be connected in his eyes. Mr Noa saw things differently. "This is a sacred map made of stones. We come here to consult it when we need to know something ... Each stone and shell is a place on Mer[11]. We read it that way." "The *Si* stones, they speak to us about sacred things."[12]

Before the process of consultation with Malu[13] (the central Creation Being) could begin, those seated can only communicate with the stones once certain conditions were met. "It was important to remain perfectly still before the Si stones, almost in a state of trance, and wait for the act of divination to occur."[14] A set prayer is offered, a seated posture is prescribed and the senses are heightened in readiness for the Creation Spirit's guidance, which must never be questioned and always obeyed.

That divine guidance takes on many forms. Sometimes the *Si* stones speak to individuals, and on other occasions an interlocutor is used to deliver a message or insight, and that was the case when Mr. Noa "asked the Tomog *zogo* to say something on my behalf."[15] Not long after Mr Noa, and his colleague Mr. Benny-Father, sought guidance "a Torres Strait pigeon landed on a shell on the far side of the Tomog *zogo* and gazed at us."[16] This omen was the inspiration for a great deal of discussion and a consensus in meaning, which led to Cowan's next meeting.

"What is the pigeon saying?" I asked.
"It's a holy bird," Mr. Noa replied. "He flew in from the west, where you came from.
"He flew in from the west, where you came from. He's telling us how you arrived on Mer by plane. He's also saying that you must must visit and talk to Jack Wailu."[17]

Jack was the keeper of the "old ways,"[18] all the old men and women held him in the highest esteem, as he was "a strong man, a man of *zogo*."[19] Jack and his wife kept apart as they "wanted to live in the old style,"[20] and because of his undoubted wisdom he alone "leads dance ceremonies."[21] This was indeed an auspicious liaison, but even though in the presence of such omens, Cowan still had trouble calming his rational mind. "Let's hope that pigeon knows where he's taking me."[22]

"Don't you worry," Mr. Noa encouraged me. "Tomog zogo never lies. The Si stones know more than we do."[23]
"It's Malu talking," Mr. Benny-Father added. "He knows what's good for you."[24]

So, according to Cowan's associates these stones directly relay the voice of God. Such a claim is somewhat reminiscent of the story behind the Ten Commandments where the Creator used two tablets of stone to relay his teachings and commandments. Both groups are just as absolute about obeying these proclamations in stone without exception or question. Ramindjeri warrior and law-man, Karno, is adamant that the markings on Ros' Rock 1 were made by a Sky-Hero from a distant constellation when landing in Australia, who listed the elemental laws humanity should adopt. The *Si* stones, along with many of the marked rocks, are not historical relics, but still function in a tangible positive way relaying the wisdom of the spirits.

The Many Marked Rock Friends of Malu

Do the *Si* Stones stand-alone? Certainly not, and nor are sacred stones limited to one function. The *Si* stones are not shaped, marked or in any way modified through sophisticated technology. Cowan was decidedly underwhelmed by first appearances, but that soon changed. Upon further questioning Cowan realised his cultural conditioning was an impediment in appreciating the 'big picture.' They represented "our island,"[25] along with every significant site, in every sense "Each stone and shell is a place on Mer."[26]

For the first time in any analysis we have presented on the previous 34 marked rocks in the Ros' Rock's series, we feel it is time to broaden the areas under investigation and look a little deeper into the mystical. Cowan saw and reported absolute evidence substantiating the powers and insights given by these stones, we intend to do likewise and try to find what is also waiting in the shadows within some of the marked and shaped rocks we have been examining.

Fortunately such is the quantity and quality of recent rocks offered to us, there is no need to look back. We can readily identify separate genres of sacred rock from the most recent arrivals that we believe contain both inside, and on the surface, messages from the Gods.

The first of these rocks to be examined appears to be very much another example of more of the same, but although on familiar territory, this rock is so much more than just another marked rock. There is the real possibility that this rock is close to, or the equal of, Ros' Rock 1. Although of the same dark chocolate colour as most of the marked rocks, the make of this rock is unique and unlike any other we have seen. There is no thin top-coat of chert, and nor is the surface as smooth as the other. It's actually the bumpiest of all the rocks examined.

Perhaps this uneven sheet explains why all lines that are vertical or diagonal maintain a consistent straight line, but the horizontal lines are crooked. Not one line that is horizontal can retain the same angle, and this aversion towards the straight is the same on the opposite connecting narrative on Side 3.

It is a very dense and heavy rock, and it seems that what has happened is that three sides were cut into the base rock, and in total that amounts to about 40% of the rock set aside to record information relating to star charts and travelling from distant constellations. Although apparently much older and a touch cruder than Ros' Rock 1, both rocks, along with five others in the series, adhere to a strict regime in setting. This rock also has two opposite sides that contain the entire narrative, a connecting side containing a few linking lines and the last side unmarked and untouched.

We suspect that the top section of Side 1 is incomplete with a small piece missing. There is a collection of irregular percussion bulbs spread across the top section (3 cm by 4 cm), and being the most jagged and multi-angled, it seems safe to assume that the top piece was broken away after heavy localised impact.

What is less open to interpretation is three pyramid incisions. Two are barely visible, but not so the third. It is very prominent, quite deep and extremely precise. Positioned at the intersection point of the two main lines, the geometry and obvious attempt to create a three dimensional pyramid is certainly worthy of further reflection. Measuring 1 cm by 80 mm by 70 mm and at the deepest point 40 mm, any machine of today would be hard pressed cutting finer angles and lines that are the equal of what is on display on this very old rock. The sophistication of technology required is challenging now, and this rock was marked many thousands of years ago. And why carve a pyramid, why not another shape which is easier to engrave? Whatever the reason, it is undeniable that the pyramid is the principle shape in the ancient world and was quite popular in Egypt.

The most crucial difference this rock bears witness to, is that it's a one process product. So many of the chert rocks we have examined have a thin veneer attached to the base rock when molten, or there is evidence of a second and third application of more lines or pecks. Rarely is there an example of one hand and tool at one time only. Moreover, none of the surfaces are as rutted and very few lines are as worn. These features all point towards a considerable antiquity. Not only is this rock older than Ros' Rock 1, but it may be the predecessor of all marked rocks. The star map could be the first charted, and the angles and lines incised are other elements of the very first time a formal style of communication was chronicled into rock on this planet.

As to whether this rock is able to share its holy heritage as the *Si* stones do, we are very inclined to be positive for reasons that will become clearer towards the end of the chapter. Despite the respective strengths of both the *Si* stones and Ros' Rock 1, this marked rock is that it's marked. None of the *Si* stones are artificially marked, stamped, incised, chiselled or pecked. Nor are the two cylcons that we will briefly investigate in the next chapter, are artificially marked. Outside the marginally unusual narrow cylindrical shape of the two rocks, neither rock is remarkable or imposing. Apart from exhibiting a slightly tidier line and more balance than the Si stones, these rocks would be no less unimposing if Cowan sighted them without explanation.

A Box of Rocks in Annagrace's Boot

Formerly under the care of a very interesting lady by the name of Annagrace, she gave us these two rocks, and quite a few other intriguing companion rocks. Now being rudimentarily familiar with the basic premises behind cylcons, the two rocks Annagrace gave us rang a bell that from the first note stirred our interest.

Annagrace joined us on-site with some other people interested in the Kariong hieroglyphs, and at the end of the day insisted we look at her rocks. She did not know what roles any of the rocks she had found performed, but intuitively sensed they were important. We had already received and written about cylcon rocks of the same type, but they did not ring. These rocks make a metallic sound when they make contact with each other. We had heard of rocks like these that claimed to be able to levitate rocks weighing tonnes. Michael Tellinger certainly has genuine cylcon rocks that also ring like a bell[27], but until now we had never personally held such rocks or felt them vibrate.

We saw an opportunity here, granted it is a less than enthusiastically recognised form of scientific measurement, but we knew Richard Clarke was joining us with another group in two days, and is very proficient in dowsing. For those who hold the skills involved in dowsing in a less than favourable light, as we once did, can we suggest they hold judgment until the evidence on the rock platform is carefully considered.

We made contact with Richard at the Kariong glyphs and it was during the time spent resting on the rock platform directly above these enigmatic hieroglyphs, he suggested we try an experiment. To begin with, knowing the power of cylcon rocks is symbiotic and remains dormant until in contact with skin and hand, the first scan was with the dowsing rods untouched. As predicted the rods didn't stir. In the next pass with the two copper rods, I held the cylcons in the wrong fashion pointing down, again the rods were unmoved.

* **Figure 67:**
Cylcons[28]

With the distractions dispensed I held the cylcons as directed by Original Elder Marbuck, pointing slightly upwards. Richard approached with the rods held aloft, and as he got closer the rods spun with considerable force, so much so, one grazed his cheek. A second repeat performance produced an identical result. Emboldened by the reaction and belief that these rocks are indeed special, Richard walked away ten metres and asked me to aim the cylcons. As Marbuck explained the process, the energy generates spirals which that spin around and upwards, as if spinning around the little finger. It condenses as it reaches the fingertip and thus bursts out as a ray rather than a wave, so Richard held the rods above and began a walking line some 10 metres to the side of where I was aiming. They only moved within a 30 cm range, yet this time the rods were ten metres away, positioned at the spot I was pointing.

Not satisfied with this stunning result, Richard walked across to the other edge of the platform, which is at least twenty five metres from where I was stationed. I do remember suggesting he was pushing the limits, nevertheless, Richard persevered and as before began above the line of convergence. And as before it was a very concentrated line of something, but it's really hard quantifying an energy that doesn't have a name or accreditation, all we do know is that the rods spun with as much force as they had ten metres away. There were close to a dozen who were with us and took in all the proceedings, and all assembled, whether a participant or spectator, were taken aback by what we shared.

Yes the device used has no batteries, needles that point at numbers or membership in any laboratory, but all of us saw the expression on Richard's face (and ours) and the impromptu style of methodology and planning. The rods spun when engaged properly and idled when not activated, really the only issue open to debate has nothing to do with the credentials of the rods, but the integrity of the holder. If he is deceitful then this was a sham, but to do so on sacred ground and in the company of good people with honourable intentions requires an extra regression in character. We cannot prove whether or not these metal bars are the real article. What we do know as an absolute fact is that Richard is an honest man who would never offend the spirits or good people.

All Sorts of Shapes

Until now the ever-increasing collection of rocks formed into recognisable geometric shapes has been a novelty that doesn't seem to make sense, and because of this, it's a topic we've avoided. It seems safe to assume any archaeology found in pre-Cook Australia has a purpose. Be it spiritual, utilitarian or some other function, the word decorative or a description lacking in any reason for being there, is supposedly not part of any Original history. Nonetheless, we have a large collection of rocks shaped in a way that achieves nothing except tick a geometric box. Circles, triangles, squares, rectangles, trapezoids, pentagons, a seven-sided pyramid-like object and hearts, are but some of the offerings that is now part of our ensemble.

* **Figure 68:**
Assorted Shaped Rocks[29]

Not for one second are we suggesting that this geometric assortment of shapes is the equal of the *Si* Stones or Ros Rock 1, we have no reason to suspect that they occupy such a lofty station. Our focus is not what it is, but what it isn't, which is that it just doesn't seem to have any contextual setting if relying on accepted accounts of Original pre-history. In each rock presented there is no way another form of stone, stick or bone could create these shaped artefacts. Without a role or tool it would seem anything outside the pragmatic is possible, and with the Original culture being so spiritual in intent and inspiration, to suggest these rocks have an esoteric imprint is not a large stretch in logic, especially since there is no alternative.

The assortment of shaped rocks come from different locations and rock types, nevertheless they share many features. First up, there is no evidence of use-wear, whether through grinding, cutting, ochre staining or fracture points, nothing is on display that indicates these rocks had any functional or artistic purpose. The edges of these rocks are smooth and bevelled, always of the same thickness. All candidates are worthy of further examination, but as this is meant to be a brief overview, we have chosen two from many.

Although not quite a symmetrical pentagon, it does come very close. The rock has five sides and is covered in a red patina. Each side is 180 degrees vertical and is very smooth. The top and bottom is slightly curved, but again extremely smooth. If anything we have always harboured the suspicion that this rock is an artificial conglomerate formed in a mould. It was found in a very remote area and serves no easily identifiable purpose for either non-Original or Original people.

Surrounded by a huge stand of forest, outside gold mining and logging this area has no other commercial interest to serve. As to how this five-sided rock, plus a large collection of other unusual rock artefacts would facilitate mining or logging is not apparent. The same can be said in relation to the accepted Original nomadic hunter-gatherer lifestyle, there is no way this object serves any useful purpose.

So too is a seven-sided construction with some edges still sharp enough to cut skin, there is no way this rock can assist in mining, logging, farming or any other commercial enterprise. Found close to the sea-side in a very sacred site where the only money-making enterprise anywhere nearby was the collection of mud crabs, it's an amazing piece of engraving requiring masonry skills of the highest order. Equally, with the two sides not exposed to the elements so clean and sharp, it is not unreasonable to assume all of the edges were as sharp.

Until enlightened by Uncle Marbuck we have always assigned functional duties to this rock. The technology needed is certainly advanced and it seems to serve no pragmatic concerns, and we had thought that the sophistication in presentation alone was of importance. We were wrong. According to Uncle Marbuck it is a power rock that has to be rubbed in a certain way, and no doubt sung to at the same time. He did give me more details about this rock, but it is enough to know an Original Elder steeped in the Old Ways has endorsed its esoteric credentials.

"Magic Stone"[30]

The same respect should also apply to another rock in our collection, which is the only rock we have received that is claimed to have "magic"[31] powers. Admittedly, we have no way of validating such a claim, but what we are very sensitive to is that no other rock, even the cylcons, has been nominated as being so mystical in complexion. Knowing that this marked rock was part of the ensemble gathered between 1926 and 1939 by people who accompanied Elkin, Basedow, Berndht and Berndht[32] etc. when conducting archaeology and anthropology of a sympathetic nature, the bona fides of this rock do strengthen.

If it wasn't for the very detailed and clear commentary explaining why it is a "magic rock," [33] we would have had some trouble distinguishing from the other power rocks (cylcons). But upon closer inspection some differences do emerge. Most importantly, there is a definite carved thumb position, right hand of course, and as cylcons are to be grasped rather than having a thumb or finger pointing forward, this alone gives some delineation and contrast.

The real issue here is that this written account about a magic rock is the only source available. There is no doubt that the word magic guarantees raised eyebrows and sniggers amongst most of the academic fraternity, but that is the word chosen by the non-Original chronicler. What that magic is and how it comes about, is something that we hope to clarify when in the company of Original Custodians of the Old Ways.

Needles and Pins

Unfortunately, Uncle Marbuck's word and the report of an unnamed source claiming magical powers for a rock taken seventy odd years ago from people who can't read or write will hold little sway with those who set courses and oversee our history and official records. They want more, seeking graphs, instruments, needles that move, this is what moves them and makes their grade.

At a recent workshop we held in Byron Bay, at the end of the last session one of those who attended, Neil Howe, came over to the display of rocks and ran his phone over some of the rocks. Being utterly disconnected with any and everything associated with computers, I took little notice of what he was doing, and maintained that apathy until Neil called me over.

He did make an attempt to explain the intricacies of what the computer chips were measuring, and why the needles moved so dramatically, but all I knew was different rocks gave readings that appeared to mean the rocks were giving off some form of energy. It was, as Neil put it, a "crude measurement of electromagnetic fields and magnetic fields."[34] He used "basic free aps from Apple iTunes,"[35] and he felt this needed a follow up with more precise measurements and sophisticated technology. Neil suggested that this phenomena "warrants further investigation with professional geological measurements,"[36] as there are "a lot of questions to be investigated and answered."[37]

Uncle Marbuck

We would like to close our investigation into the mystical credentials of the marked and magic rocks by referencing the wisdom of a highly respected Original Elder and Custodian of the Old Ways, who spent quite a few hours with some of these rocks in hand.

Uncle Marbuck referred to these rocks as "star rocks"[38] and told me they have been searching for these rocks for the past fifty years. There is no doubt these are the rocks many sought, they are genuine and have an ancient message to share. With that agreed base, the real treasure lay upon and within, and in this area no-one has matched Uncle Marbuck.

Just as it is with the *Si* Stones, Uncle Marbuck was in communion with the Spirits who were talking to him through the ten marked rocks he held and read. It was always one of our briefs to find Original Elders of the highest level and a particular rock that gels - one they can read and bond with. Previously five rocks had already found a custodian, none more so than Ros' Rocks 1 and Ramindjeri Elder and Warrior, Karno. Whether Aunty Vi, Uncle Dr. Noel, Uncle Lewis Walker, Brendan Murray or Uncle Marbuck, in each case and rock, they knew the story and were relaying an ancient narrative. Each Elder locked into one rock, but Uncle Marbuck went one major step forward, he read the entire package.

Moreover, each of Marbuck's reading of another Elder's rock was entirely in synch with their account. There was not one detail Uncle Marbuck relayed that contradicted the earlier reading. He also was given an 'open cheque.' We offered him the choice of any of the rocks not under custodianship and he chose Ros' Rock 28 (which is now called Uncle Marbuck's Rock 28). The rock he chose told of yet another part of an ancient narrative that involves beings from the "stars"[39] and the Original people, but later that night as he slept it had more to say. This time around the vision was more personal and actually had characters from the past and a conclusion that had great relevance to him.

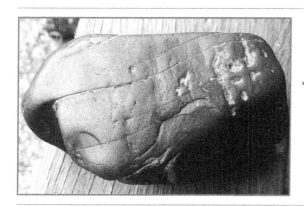

* **Figure 69:**
Marbuck's Rock No. 28[40]

Of course, for those who have never met Uncle Marbuck, making such revolutionary claims may be a challenge for many, and to be honest early on in the piece there were times where I questioned whether what he was sharing was more a matter of saying what I wanted to hear, than relaying the past and thoughts of the spirits. It would be dishonest, and illogical not to harbour doubts. Unlike Karno or Aunty Beve, who we knew for some time and met often, our time with Uncle Marbuck before he passed over was brief and because of this, every now and then I would wonder how could he basically have an open ticket to read every rock with such clarity and vision?

Then about three hours into our time together, all doubts vanished and I surrendered to his counsel. I had no choice and at least had the common-sense to accept the inevitable. He broke his reading of the rocks and asked me about Aunty Beve. Talk of this amazing Original woman came from nowhere, and before I could draw breath to reply, Uncle Marbuck continued this excursion into the unknown by sharing details of something Aunty Beve shared with me, which I had told no-one except my wife. The walls were down and my cynicism checked out for the night. What only adds to the substance of the crossing of sides that night is that what Aunty Beve requested seemed utterly impossible. Even when I relayed this request to a close friend and fellow researcher, Nina Angelo, neither of us could see any light at the end of the tunnel. The instructions seemed impossible.

Within one day it all fell into place and Uncle Marbuck's credentials in such matters was confirmed and cannot be challenged. Just as the *Si* Stones spoke for the Elders of the Torres Strait Island, Mer, so too in the most unlikely of places another set of stones finally found someone worthy of sharing this ancient Lore. These rocks acted as 'royal telephones' and both the spirits and Aunty Beve were on the line. So too Karno, and now Uncle Marbuck is also ready to respond to any who pick up the "star rocks"[41] and dial out. If only we knew how to turn this rock machine on and dial the correct number. Uncle Marbuck had the directory and is no longer on this side, so for now the conversation between silica and skin is on hold and will remain so until another Elder or Custodian of the Original Old Ways fills the breach.

In concluding our presentation on these rocks, we want to take one part of Uncle Marbuck's messages "from afar"[42] to its logical conclusion through two approaches. When opening proceedings, we will as always lead off with an Original testimony, which in this case is a response to a question I asked Uncle Marbuck. Once that base in Original Lore is established, the next chapter will play by white-fella rules in presenting the archaeological and historical evidence in Sahul (Australia and PNG) that validates Uncle Marbuck's divine message delivered via ten marked rocks.

I asked Uncle Marbuck a question I could never reconcile, why did they bother coming here? Humans, well men are the major offenders, are a warlike species, very insular and prone to be fearful. We treat the Earth like a rubbish tip. I just couldn't see what was here amongst all the noisy rabble that attracted so many beings from star systems all over the Cosmos. Or so the story goes, there had to be a motivation to come, and amongst all the stupidity on daily display, the reason they came is lost on me.

His answer was well outside any of my frames of reference, but resonated so deeply I just knew his reply was the missing key, not just in-filling in my gaps, but on a far grander scale. According to Uncle Marbuck, they were drawn to this lonely planet because of our human emotions. The whole gamut from love and compassion through to unbridled violence and greed, this is the lure and enigma that is solely Earthly. Then Uncle Marbuck offered an analogy that fleshed out the details, Dr. Spock from Star Trek. The very first fictional Alien to breach mainstream thinking was a non-Earthly being that assisted, and in his own way, admired the humans from Earth. Among all the traits Spock studied, none were more curious and enticing than examples of love and self-sacrifice that he would witness, then carefully dissect. But no matter how meticulously Spock applied his intellect and rational reasoning, he always just fell short of fully connecting.

Uncle Marbuck told us that emotions are both a blessing and curse, and as it is without parallel elsewhere, our actions on this planet have a far-reaching impact on a Cosmic scale that is well known amongst all Alien groups. This is why they came and keep coming. Karno often spoke of travellers from distant constellations coming to this country, as did Aunty Beve. They all share the same truth, there is not one syllable in disagreement. This Alien presence is an essential part of the Original genesis and global birth-right that we all share.

The rocks speak, and under the right conditions can pass on information just like a computer, which stores data on silicon chips. We do not believe it is coincidence that the chert veneer is a silicate. The only difference between the marked rocks and modern-day computers is that the manufactured item is easy to turn on. The hand-made ancient rock computer also has an on/off switch which both the Elders on Mer and Uncle Marbuck turned on.

Old Way, new way

Then again, we could be wrong, the Elders could be wrong, their Original mythology and oral history could be wrong, and it doesn't matter in the least. We are still well in front. If our explanations as to why there are so many anomalies and archaeological evidence of advanced technology is wrong, it is still much better than absolutely nothing past a deafening silence. Mainstream history and conventional theories of human evolution have no further part to play in the Original version of past events. Everything we have presented is consistent to one truth; the current theories of the way things were is wrong at every level.

It comes down to two ways of seeing things, either Old Way or new way. Only one is right, they cannot sit together. In the Old Way rocks can talk, in the new way such talk is rubbish. In the Old Way of doing things James Cowan has "met others in the world who understand the language of birds."[43] In the new way of thinking, birds have feathers.

The archaeology is in, the Elders have spoken and so have the rocks. Knowing that everything begins in Australia, the only questions remaining no longer relate to where, but who, when and how? In that respect all the Old Way Elders, Dreaming Stories and Original Lore stand united in supplying the first and final answer to all three unknowns: the Pleiades.

Chapter 19

There is a huge backlog of Original sites and artefacts we are investigating that don't fit into any conventional narrative of ancient Australia, and as every day passes the line gets longer. It is no longer a question of debating whether there are so many sites displaying advanced technology in Australia, but more a matter of from where did the inspiration come? If it was from another human civilisation that these complexes and relics were sourced, then why is it that there is no known legend or myth of unknown adventurers sailing to Australia or more importantly, evidence in other countries of the same advanced style of technology?

We do know that quite a few non-Original historians like Graham Walsh[2] prefer the mysterious arrival and rapid departure scenario, relying on two rock paintings he discovered in the Kimberleys. In his scenario an unnamed civilisation sailed to Australia in "totally alien"[3] sailing boats with 23 and 29 people aboard up to 50,000 years ago. Soon after making landfall they left leaving behind a trail of paintings considered too representational and refined to be the work of Original people. The problem is as much as this could explain why so many technological anomalies exist, until the actual location from which these adventurous sailors launched their boats can be supplied, it is a theory steeped in convenience but lacking in geography or facts.

That is not to say there are no Original explanations that could account for the quantity and quality of ancient artefacts exhibiting advanced technology. There are plenty of Dreaming Stories and Elders' testimonies that resonate to the same explanation and off-world ancestry. Such information is prolific, but in mainstream circles it will never be spoken of as being anything other than a quaint misunderstanding or a symbolic embellishment that has been taken too literally. Despite the paternalistic attitude that so typifies the British conquest and invasion mentality, there is a commonality in one Original saying that echoes throughout the continent and will never be silenced: 'as on top, so below.'

The Original custodians of the Old Ways know exactly what this pivotal phrase entails. It is for that reason that the *"Seven Sisters"*[4] Dreaming Story of the arrival of beings from the Pleiades is the only account that spans the country; it belongs to every tribe and excludes none. Ramindjeri Elder, Karno, was adamant if anyone claimed a site to be sacred but not identified by an accompanying star, constellation or planet, it is bogus. If no link to the stars is supplied, he demanded we walk away. Knowing that the Gods are referred to as Sky-heroes who originated in the Pleiades, it would be a grave offence to ignore his advice. As yet, we have not met one Elder or Custodian of the Old Ways who denies a connection to that star system. Equally, to our knowledge we do not know of one non-Original academic who will publically acknowledge a genetic connection between the Original people of this land and beings from any celestial location.

Quite recently the Original Elder entrusted with protecting a very sacred site near Port Hedland, called us across to Western Australia to help in stopping the destruction of a cave called Ganga Maya. With an occupation date of 47,500 years it is one of the oldest occupation sites in Australia, and the mere thought of collapsing the cave through explosions, to excavate iron ore thirty metres away, is outrageous on a good day. What only compounds the offence is that Eddie McPhee was even more concerned for the spiritual welfare of his tribe, as the cave is directly linked to the central star of the Pleiades. If it was destroyed, so too would their Dreaming be lost forever.

Up in the Hills Near Mount Hagan

From the moment we saw Kate Nisbet's photograph of this bizarre elongated skull, delicate facial features and gaping hole in the neck, all we could offer in response was that it looked so Alien-like. No matter how hard we tried to find an alternative hominid model, or put it down to excess through artistic license, we kept coming back to an off-world inspiration. Knowing that it is incredibly ancient, the property of tribal people of Mount Hagan and that it looks nothing like anyone in the country, ever, there are many interesting possibilities to pursue.

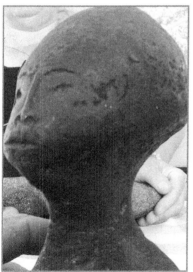

Before walking down a completely different historical path, there is a need to merge Original geography and technology in providing a background sketch of the time and place when this intriguing statue was created. When mainland Australia and Papua-New Guinea was one landmass called Sahul, all tribes were tied eternally to their tribal estate. No other tribe could steal their land as the spirits of this tribal estate were not their makers and could easily dispose of them if trespassing uninvited. The Spirits are in the land and act as eternal guardians of sacred sites and observers of correct protocol when on country. Of particular relevance to the basalt head is the agreed continental avoidance of mining or metallurgy.

* **Figure 70:** PNG Statue[5]

Because of this ancient prohibition throughout this larger continent, it is written in all historical accounts that there was no metal blade in either country until a few hundred years ago. The tool-kit in both countries has always been assumed to be limited to stick, bone and stone. There is no way any of these materials could cut and shape basalt of this hardness. On the other side of the equation, the Elders of the tribe in PNG who gave the artefact away said it is incredibly ancient and came from a time "long before true."[6] What we are confronted with here are two completely different narratives, and there is only room for one.

The rock is igneous, most probably basalt, and the facial features do not resemble any local resident. The very thin nose, delicate mouth and small eyes, are in diametric opposition to the physique of the people of the entire island. A broad nose, wide face and thick lips are the genetic inheritance spread throughout the island, but this being is certainly not part of that ancestry. And nor is the hole in the statue's neck; the circular incision is very clean with uniform sides and a flat 180 degree base. It was cut and excised with great precision and demands no less than a metal blade.

* **Figure 71:**
P.N.G. Stone Artefact[7]

We would hasten to add that if inclined to run with the sheep and accept the 'experts' denial, the basalt head was not the only thing Kate's parents received after spending some time trekking deep into the mountain region. They also gave them a rather unusual flanged circle with six spokes. This strangely shaped object seems so impractical and looks like nothing else seen. But if one was to look further, all the way across to America, there is a sacred Incan stone object used in special ceremonies that looks so close to identical to the PNG artefact it negates any explanation that does not acknowledge a shared heritage.

* **Figure 72:**
Ecuadorian Pre-Columbian Artifacts, Catalogue NO. 2008.34.2-.3.6. Photographed by B. Bernard. courtesy of the Maxwell Museum of Anthropology, University of New Mexico.[8]

The 'UFO Glyphs' and the Mothership

This is not a term we use as it is quite superficial, but is already part of the public setting of the Kariong hieroglyphs. Mainly depicted as semi-circles with legs dangling below, these off-world objects take on a variety of poses. Some seem to be in distress, upside down and apparently plummeting towards the earth, while others are more stable. Until the last full-descent Darkinoong Elder, Aunty Beve, first spoke of the "star beings"[9] and of their mothership "crashing in the still waters of Bambara,"[10] we had taken little interest in the hysteria and rebuttals. To be honest, the whole idea of championing the UFO cause was never an enticing prospect and a topic not mentioned in our first three books.

* **Figure 73:**
UFO Glyph at Bambara[11]

That all changed once Aunty Beve repositioned our agenda. It wasn't long after she opened up a new area to research we came upon what Klaus Dona[12] believes to be the largest engraving of a UFO in the world. The top section of this engraving measures about two metres by four, which is massive by comparison to the much smaller glyphs engraved on the three sandstone walls at Kariong. Ignoring the disparity in size, there is one UFO glyph on the wall that also has a semi-circular capsule and five legs with circles at the end of each leg and looks very similar to the larger engraving.

The smaller glyph is 19 cm at the widest part of the capsule, which has a maximum height of 7.5 cm, with the longest of the five legs 8.4 cm in length. At first glance, and without the benefit of comparison to the larger UFO pecking, there is nothing in this glyph that stands out or grabs the eye. However, after measuring the larger pecking some numbers do add up. The larger semi-circle/capsule is much wider than the 19 cm by a factor of ten and is 190 cm.

Measuring vertically the UFO engraving presents one fundamental difference, in that the Original artist/mason was dealing with an object that is much bigger through having two stories/divisions marked out in the capsule. That being the case, since the craft is doubled in height we decided to remain faithful to that factor. The larger semi-circle is 150 cm in height, the smaller one 7.5 cm, if that is doubled it equals 15 cm and if then multiplied by ten the numbers are the same. The same rule applies for the longest of the five legs which measures 168 cm, when divided by twenty the final figure is identical in length of the longest leg of the UFO wall glyph.

Three comparisons of length once recalibrated by ten or doubling ten, turn out to be the same. Once by accident is feasible, twice by coincidence is highly unlikely and a third match is beyond the reach of anything random, this is intentional and a very clever piece of mathematics at that.

Adding to the connection and context between the two UFO engravings is Aunty Beve's statement regarding the mothership "crashing in the still waters of Bambara"[13] in ancient times. Surely it is no coincidence that the larger UFO engraving actually overlooks these sheltered waters and is less than 100 metres from the shore.

What only adds to the antiquity of this depiction of the mother-craft crashing, is this image was pecked, which is an older technique that was replaced by fully engraved lines.

The Cave of the Golden Boomerang

With the night sky the focus of genuine sites and Original Elders versed in the Old Ways, the underlying inspiration and specific constellation painted in the Cave of the Golden Boomerang is simply another extension of the Original mantra, 'as on top, so below.' It is such a difficult gallery to find, and our chances of ever re-locating this site are less than infinitesimal.

* **Figure 74:**
   Cave of the Golden Boomerang[14]

This sandstone cave and gallery of six figures is over 25 metres in length and 5 metres high. The three main human figures are incredibly representational and without parallel in Australia. Nothing in Australia comes this close, even the famed Bradshaw figures pale by comparison. Many reputed experts, Graham Walsh readily comes to mind, maintain that Original artists were incapable of depicting life-like subjects, the assumption was that this dearth of talent meant that the Bradshaw paintings were painted by an ancient group of people who sailed to, and very soon after departed from, these shores.

That assumption is clearly wrong, because this site is thousands of kilometres south of the Bradshaws / Gwion Gwion[15] and would mean that this hypothetical, small, mysterious small enclave of elite sailors from an unnamed location, were actually spread throughout the entire continent. The three main human figures are about 3 metres high and so representational, with each toe, finger and individual muscle exactly as they should be. The proportions are spot on, as is the body shape and form. The two women have wider hips, the male's hips are markedly narrower and muscular. The only figure in the gallery that runs contrary to this representational style is what appears to be a baby lying in the dirt behind the back heel of the first woman standing. It is as if the baby is neglected, verging on abused, while the adults are oblivious to its existence, involving themselves in something patently mystical. To compound the affront, the baby figure is very rough in artistic execution.

* Figure 75:
Cave of the Golden Boomerang[16]

The 'dreadlocks' were also somewhat unexpected, but it is obvious that the second woman in the 'floating pose' has that type of hair-style flowing in various directions. Both women have belts and some form of cross across the chest. The male is reaching towards the boomerang, as to whether he touches it was never revealed.

The ex-Senior Park Ranger, of which this site once fell under his jurisdiction, assured us that the gallery is at least 5,000 years old. The painting of a Thylacine (Tasmanian Tiger), which is claimed to be have been extinct for the last 5,000 years on the Australian mainland, seems to give a reliable time-frame. He also told us that this was an Original creation story of the beginning of humans, but was unable or unwilling to elaborate past this thumb-nail sketch.

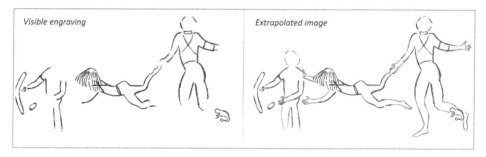

* Figure 76: Cave of the Golden Boomerang Diagram[17]

In what adds to the dimensions, Evan persevered in finally finding out what that one seemingly neglected non-representational symbol meant. It turns out that during a Newcastle University Broadcast[18] the exact same figure, this time engraved into another rock platform was found in the general area, which was posted and thankfully identified as the Pleiades. What is of fundamental importance is that this Pleiadian marker precedes all human figures in the Original story of the creation of humanity.

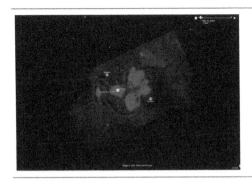

* Figure 77:
Pleiades Engraving[19]

A Rock Platform in the General Area

The Pleiades symbol came from a sacred men's site at the Burragurra Rock Platform which we had been to a little over three years ago, and in what only came about through the Spirit's grace, so too did Frederic Slater in 1937. He was the President of the Australian Archaeological Society and the paper we are referring to was presented at the 1937 Science Congress and was enthusiastically received.[20]

To be honest, we are still confounded by the positive reception. The interpretation Slater presented positively reeks of off-world connections, and goes so far as to mention genetic manipulation. Perhaps many of the scientists assembled misunderstood Slater's repeated descriptions of space-ships landing as launching massive Original canoes? Granted the constant mention of sharing genes between species was ahead of its time and that may well be a fair excuse for those assembled to politely clap when their chosen representative concludes his speech, and be none the wiser while applauding. Irrespective of who did or did not appreciate the depth of his paper, Slater certainly did, and wrote in another paper that the "seed might have been brought from a long distance,"[21] and makes it clear that the Sky-Heroes were not born of this world, so it is obvious he is certainly in tune with the nuances of 'as on top.'

According to Slater and Aunty Beve, this is the place where Baiame / Bhaiame[22] (the Principle Creation Being), his family and the other Sky-Heroes who accompanied him, set foot after their space-craft landed at the near-by Mount Yengo.[23]

* Figure 78:
Mount Yengo[24]

From Baiame's first step onwards it gets extremely genetic and constantly off-world, that is the dominant theme of Slater's paper. The Original name Baiame has his two meanings that are complimentary, to "cut off to build"[25] and in being more anatomically specific, "One Leg Living."[26] Slater reported that the principle Sky-Hero "cut off his own leg for the purpose of making a living man."[27] Quite literally Baiame "brought life into the world."[28] And if unsure of from where this essential gift came, Slater is positive "He brought life from on high."[29]

Even the one-foot footprint (Mundowa[30]) Baiame leaves behind on the ground eventually acts like a boomerang in returning to the sender. "The disappearance of the Mundowa footprints is also explained in the story written on the rocks. He brought living things from on high and then stepped back into the high regions from whence he came."[31] Make no mistake, this "high region"[32] does not refer to Mount Kosciuszko, the journeys of Baiame's wife leave us in no doubt that the distant location is somewhere "from afar"[33] in another solar system. It is for that reason the Creation Gods' female equivalent and wife, "Mulla Mulla[34]... (whose name was not allowed to be mentioned outside the sacred circle) ... was lifted down alive from a high place, and so, instead of being made on earth, she came from the sky above, where Bhaiame dwells. There were eight children, four sons and four daughters."[35]

One of Baiame's sons found no joy on this distant planet and had no intention of being Earth-bound any longer. The "nameless one"[36] left without warning and his brother tracked him. Boobardy[37] "followed the footprint until he saw his comrade walking ahead and called out to him, ... "Come back my friend. But the nameless one ... pointed to the setting sun and said, ... "Not I; I go that way ... But the unknown figure went on until he came to a tree huge in girth and so tall that the foliage mingled with the clouds."[38]

Boobardy knew his brother would not listen and gave up the chase, "looking backward he saw that the tree had vanished in a cloud of smoke. This beautiful tree is now the Southern Cross."[39] If that is not a graphic literal description of a rocket launching, then what is? In summarising the case for the legacy bestowed upon humanity's genetic code, Slater noted that "He who brought life into the world, set down man and woman and gave them the sacred means of propagating life."[40]

In concluding this examination of the ancient coalition of inter-galactic species and the Original people, and of the incredible potential and gift that awaits if we can activate the ancient genetic code dormant within, we will close this article by quoting from the greatest Original Elder we have met face-to-face and spirit-to-spirit, Ramindjeri Elder, Karno Walker.

When asked by researcher Ros Mulder about the ancient times when Ros Rock 1 was made, which we believe to be the most important single artefact the Pleiadians bequeathed humanity, Karno replied that it needed "a lot of time and labour. You have to understand it was made in times when humans had more DNA."[41] Or, as Slater put it, "Man (life) came to Earth as man with his senses (seven of them) and was established in truth."[42]

Conclusion: WHAT WILL COME TO PASS?

Six books completed and the truth of the matter is that we have barely scratched the surface. There is more archaeology ahead than has been discussed thus far, and at the moment we are barely one-third of the way through our stock-take of sites and artefacts. Such is the influx of archaeology at our disposal that, we've had to prioritise locations and relics that are of the highest significance as our primary concern.

Amongst the litany of supposed errors and indiscretions of which we are accused, quite a few of our critics seem to think we are fixated on three sites of interest and that's all there is. Undeniably the Standing Stones site and Ros' Rocks series stand united at the forefront, with the Kariong sites comfortably secure in third place. There is no doubt that these three Original sites/marked rocks are of immense importance, but that does not lessen the considerable impact and implications of dozens of other Original sites/artefacts that we are also investigating.

IN THE NEXT BOOK ...

Every site and relic ever so briefly listed below which will appear in our next book, shares one defining trait, they do not fit into any conventional historical narrative of pre-Cook Original life and history.

In a sliding scale of weight, beginning at the top end of the scale, ancient rock constructions/walls with individual rocks weighing tonnes, can be found at Trina's Site, Klaus Dona's Walls and Emu's Nest. Slightly less imposing in individual weight, but more spectacular in the precision and artistry of cut, shaped and marked rocks located at the Gympie Pyramid/Healing Table, the ten metre shaft behind the Kariong hieroglyphs, two Far North Coast sites, the enigmatic cray-fish rock and a sickness site that reeks of utter destruction in the Blue Mountains and two amazing astronomical walls in the Snowy Mountains, ask questions no mainstream academic can begin to answer. At the lightest end of the scales, as of today there are over 150 sacred Original marked rocks with a vast array of sophisticated forms of technology applied to select from, and there is room in our next book for another half a dozen rocks to be examined and analysed.

Still rock-bound, the next category was not cut through advanced tools, rather it is far more stationary and captive to simpler stone technologies. The engraving of an ankh, some Egyptian hieroglyphs separate from those at the Kariong walls, an ocean-going boat, the largest star chart in Australia, another star chart commemorating the first arrival of Egyptian royalty at around 2,500 BC and the Bulgandry complex; are all examples of Original rock on rock technology and may appear to be simply 'par for the course.' The reality is that what is on display is a case of both yes and no. It is not the way these sites were created, but the subject matter that both supplements the many examples of higher order technology, and goes some distance towards identifying extremely ancient sources, inspirations and techniques.

Even more rock-attached, and despite the best attempts of white-fella technology to desecrate and destroy through a bulldozer running directly over an engraved eight-armed compass with each arm of the same width and depth, this engraving is certainly not the outcome of any rock on rock technology. According to a local professor, anything less than a laser beam in a laboratory is a huge ask.

Throw in another healing table reserved solely for women, what is possibly a formal treaty between the Original people of Sydney and ancient Egyptians, what could be an extremely legitimate and very intricate crystal skull and the femur bone and metal jewellery of the son of an Egyptian Pharaoh, and in total these upcoming additions ask the same questions once again and stand in direct opposition of what has become today's historical truths.

The Unpardonable Academic Gaffe

With both purposes served, in providing quantity and scope to the archaeology soon to be discussed, which has no 'mainstream home,' and none too a subtle sales pitch for our seventh instalment, it seems an appropriate time to share with the reader that pivotal moment where and when we crossed the line in the sand when making our first public statement about an off-world contact. Once stepping into the cosmic side of global history and assisted evolution it gets very bumpy, as every academic institution has an unwritten no-go UFO clause with the same penalty for every offender: public ridicule and employment elsewhere.

In our last chapter we made mention of the larger UFO pecking being positioned close to the shores of the Bambara Waters. What was never discussed is the orchestrated outrage and posted denials denigrating our credentials and ridiculing our suggestion that this engraving is of a Pleiadian Mothership.

Within a month of the publication of our article, a You Tube video was posted disputing our claims and countered with a denial that it was an extra-terrestrial craft of any type, but merely a simple engraving of a whale. A local historian, a bevy of academics from Sydney University and long-term critic of our existence and right to breathe. had assembled a defence of the same site supplemented by a white-fella's official account in the 1890's. An educated gentlemen with the surname Campbell, was employed by the Government to compile an approved compendium of Original sites and artefacts in the Gosford area. With pen and paper at the ready Campbell sought out the advice of a local Original man as to what this particular engraving was. The casual response to a non-initiated, non-Original person working for the Government (those directly responsible for the theft of tribal lands and culture) was that it is a "whale."[1] Without a cut, ceremony, tribal affiliation or permission to enter sacred land any reply offered to an uninitiated Government representative could be presented as the simplest meaning given to children, or an attempt to mislead or confuse. Alternately, he may have told the truth and broken an elemental Tribal law in revealing any insight or information to a person with no right to even be there.

Apparently, according to Government reports and academics, this Original person did indeed break the Law and offended the Guardian Spirits in sharing any information with a person he barely knew. Despite the strident critiques and carping of others who joined the conga-line of sarcasm, we refused to ignore the contradiction and the recurring fact that we had seen many whale engravings in the immediate area and none had looked remotely like this odd concoction of shapes, internal lines and double stories.

Not long after the video release of the officially sanctioned final word on the whale site, Original Elder Gerry (last name withheld as he is recently passed on) rang and nonchalantly asked me about all the fuss and what our stance was. I wasn't sure if he was ringing to join in the condemnations or offer support, nevertheless we held fast to our belief this was a representation of some type of extra-terrestrial craft. As did Gerry! Not only did he encourage us to persevere, he alerted us to a very old publication that would finally resolve what this engraving was and its connection to 'as on top, so below.'

Once David Uniapon's[2] name was spoken of as the author and supporting source, I didn't really need to look any further. If an Elder of this pedigree was used by Gerry as a positive referee, that whale is a UFO. Uniapon is the only Original person whose image can be found on any Australian note. His face is on the back of the $50 note, because of his stature, wisdom and the volume of unpatented inventions which include the helicopter, electric shears and a wide variety of devices. Such is range and quality of his work, Wikipedia refers to him as Australia's Leonardo Da Vinci.[3]

Gerry drew our attention to one specific chapter Uniapon wrote called "Wondangar Goon Na Ghun (Whale and Starfish),"[4] which he believed gave more detail to this off-world intervention. As expected he did not lead us astray, and nor did "Koala"[5] who was regarded as the leader and "astronomer"[6] who guided this fleet of assorted "Beings"[7] who each spoke in "strange languages"[8] and bore little physical resemblance to each other. So great were the differences in distant origins and mother-tongues, Koala decided to create a common "sign"[9] language and thus improve communication. For close to a year after landing[10] (as opposed to docking or reaching shore if in a canoe on water), all of these diverse beings stayed close to the point of first arrival, before slowly moving outwards to meet and interact with the Original humans already present and accounted for.

This ancient Dreaming Story relayed by such a venerable Original authority makes it clear that the whale's totem comes from the stars and that engraving specifically addresses that cross-over relationship. This Original truth certainly emboldened our spirit and resolve to hold fast. Two days after Gerry rang, another Original Elder of high esteem, Aunty Minnie Mace, also phoned and just like Gerry went straight to the heart of the matter in asking if we intended to maintain that the engraving is a Mothership. She was just as forthcoming in demanding we unconditionally accept Gerry's confirmation of a Pleiadian mothership as the final word.

So there we have it, out of all the fuss and acrimony there are three Original Elders, of which two I have spoken to directly, who insist this mistaken whale symbolises an Alien spacecraft of considerable dimensions. In seeking an animal totem associated with massive size travelling large distances, is there any animal better suited to the task of being huge and travelling long distances? As has been our approach on every occasion, we follow in the footsteps of Original Elders and Sky-Heroes, and if Baiames' last engraved footstep always leads to another journey into the stars, then that is the route we must follow.

A Win/Win Situation

And the best part about our methodology through the division of this research into two totally separate parts, is that even if it turns out that we are mistaken in ascribing humanities' ascension to non-Earthly intervention, it matters not in the least. Since the beginning, it has always been the same first step in highlighting all the technological and cultural inconsistencies that do not fit into any mainstream historical account of pre-Cook Australia. Once that base is set in stone, only then can we indulge in why, how and when.

It could be what we are examining is the result of a much earlier non-Original civilisation that was allowed to prosper then fell, perhaps a much larger hominid, somewhat in the vein of the Nephilim[11] was responsible for or, which is our preferred option, are the remains of an earlier advanced Original civilisation which saw the errors of their ways and turned to nature? At this stage of proceedings there is no absolute certainty, all that can be stated without fear of contradiction is that the artefacts and sites are genuinely Original.

It doesn't matter if we are wrong in our interpretations or the second part of our research is totally mistaken or partially flawed, simply because the archaeological evidence is constantly at odds with every mainstream understanding of Australian and global world history. All we can be sure of is that the current model is lacking in every location and none more so than ancient Australia.

Whether the latest research on mtDNA, Y Chromosomes, skull morphology or the eleven sites in Australia that are older than the supposed entry date of African mariners, none of the recent science coming out of Australia agrees with any conventional understanding of the evolution and spread of *Homo sapiens sapiens*. Why that happened, who or what was responsible is still to be established, but what is definite is that the old historical narrative is fraying at the seams and needs a complete rewrite.

As to whether our version of ancient events is fictional, non-fiction or a hybrid of both is still to be seen, but what if we are right? How is it that it all began with such promise, and ended up stuck in the middle of neither? What if our 'fictional' musings are actually the truth? What if our heritage does not sit inside a cave, but the Cosmos?

Once Upon a Time

A long, long time ago in a distant galaxy one massive Space-ship set off on a journey that would resonate throughout the Cosmos and change the destiny of one species of hominid residing in remote planet that had two redeeming features, it was full of water and gold. At first glance there was nothing special about any of the hominids or primates already present on this exceptionally beautiful planet.

However amongst this not so impressive gene bank, there was one hominid living in Australia that showed promise. The travellers from afar had no intention of visiting and every reason to stay, but would only do so if they were accepted by those already on country. This is the crucial difference in a tale peculiar to Australia alone, it was the Pleiadians who came to this southern continent, at other locations beings from other constellations made the same journey but their motives were nowhere as altruistic. What set this extra-terrestrial intervention in the affairs and genetics of the Original people apart, was that this had to be a compact between equals.

It must be pointed out that the actual arrival of this Pleiadian mothership was quite literally a catastrophe. Thainghetti / Dunghutti[12] Elder Uncle Rueben Kelly was aware that "our legends tell us that we came to this planet on a space ship made of energy. When it hit this atmosphere, it turned to crystal."[13] As to whether this rapid transformation upset the internal dynamics of their craft or through deceit and a surprise attack is not clear, but Aunty Beve was adamant that the stricken crystal Pleiadian mothership crashed "in the still waters of Bambara."[14]

The sheer scale of this calamity is reason enough to engrave the crucial turning point in humanity's ancestry into rock somewhere nearby. And it is for that reason the Kariong hieroglyphs are so close by and have up to 8 UFOs much smaller engravings, of which two are upside down and in distress. Could it be these smaller craft were escape vessels/pods that were ejected when under attack/malfunction? Irrespective of why the main ship was destroyed, most of what was thought appropriate and needed at journey's end was lost in the crash. Although not destitute in comforts from home, it would take some considerable time to make up for the conveniences destroyed and loss of life suffered during this misfortune/act of treachery.

Knowing that this was always a partnership of equals and the hybridising of genetics was the desired outcome between both parties, it calls into question what the long-term goals were. To begin with, we suspect that the Pleiadians always knew that the heat, extremes of climate and gravity would never suit their weaker bodies if exposed unshielded from such hardships. Beneath the surface they could survive in the shadows and live apart, but to thrive and prosper they had to become a part of the Original people and walk upon the earth as brothers and sisters. To facilitate that bond, a few genetic adjustments were agreed to and from that point on the survivors of the initial crash of the Pleiadian mothership had a continent, people, home and culture in which to reincarnate.

On other continents other beings came to Earth but with far less honour in their hearts. Driven by their egos and need for gold they manipulated the genetic make-up of the local hominid residents in manufacturing a master/slave relationship. A wholesale genetic pacification was needed to cultivate a compliant labourer who obeyed upon command.

In Australia a different union was encoded into the genes with nobler aims and a long-term plans. As Adam confided to his son Seth that Eve "taught me a word of knowledge of the eternal God. And we resembled the great eternal angels, for we were higher than the God who created us and the powers with him."[15] (*Apocalypse of Adam*) According to Original Elders and Dreaming Stories the "god who created us,"[16] was Pleiadian. However, as Eve advised Adam, they may have resembled their creators, but they had also had the potential and genetic coding to be "higher"[17] than their "god."[18]

This was why the Pleiadians "came to Earth,"[19] knowing that the genetic merging of the best of both worlds was Heaven-sent. Way back in the beginning this began as a union of the precepts of the Original Dreaming supplemented by the good intentions and genetic artistry of the Pleiadians. And there we have it, from this mixed assemblage drawn from throughout the Cosmos a genetic dichotomy of unparalleled proportions was both a blessing and a curse. The *Homo sapiens sapiens* of today is a genetic hybrid of the innate need to conform and be led by the nose, and the mystical urge to set off on your own 'walkabout.'

Unlike other places, in Australia both species learnt from each other, but behind the accommodations the power and spirituality of the land was always in control. Nevertheless, the Pleiadian Sky-Heroes did bring knowledge of technologies, buildings and sundry devices that were unknown in this land. Their use took place with consent and involved technology still beyond present-day capacities, and because of this cities and constructions did flourish. Then all of this 'progress' came to a sudden halt.

At a variety of sites there is evidence, some seemingly without any chance of natural forces being responsible, that is saturated in massive heat, death and broken remains of what once was. It may well be that some earlier civilisations were consumed by massive tsunamis, but on this occasion something far more sinister was at play. We strongly suspect that phenomenally advanced weaponry was used to destroy and kill.

At some stage in the distant past during the ebb and flow of empires and mighty cities and fortresses throughout the planet, the Original people of Greater Australia (Sahul) made a continental decision to cease and desist. Whether that happened before, after or because of widespread use of weapons of such destruction is unknown. Nevertheless, a clean cut from this recurring source of turmoil was made and all cities, trappings, clothing and advanced technologies were banished from that point on, until Cook.

The Original/Pleiadian genetic bond was a mixed blessing in that the technology brought "from afar"[20] never found balance with the Earth, but their arrival and coalition was the salvation needed in other continents where the genetic limitations imposed from above had blinded them to the same truth Eve taught Adam. That was step two in the master-plan, establish this liberating mitochondrial base in Australia, then set sail to distant locations and meet, greet and spread their seed and the Original truths. With enlightenment and good intentions as the modus-operandi, this Original lifestyle was totally in harmony with nature and the Spirits of the Land. Once Original/Pleiadian genes and teachings were established throughout the planet, this blessing opened up new senses and visions concealed by genetic design. The liberation and genetic mixing abroad gave choices and insights that led to a world-wide decision to join the Original example and live a nomadic lifestyle where the Spirits and nature set the agenda.

The planet was cleansed by the Original Dreaming. Whether acting as a Sky-Hero or a Villain made no difference in the mid-run, each time technology was allowed to dictate events and contest against the Land, calamity ensued and people suffered. With Original emissaries and genes now established throughout the globe, direct rulership through these beings from distant constellations came to a close. The Dreaming reigned supreme and until the appearance of money, the plough and personal ownership by an elite few, the world was at peace with spiritual concerns paramount.

Then this harmony once again unravelled as men and money ruled and women were marginalised. The Original people began to retreat, and from about 7,000 years ago severed all relations with others and went home. But the borders were never closed and invitations never rescinded. The ancient Egyptians, Phoenicians, Chinese, Vikings, Spanish, Portuguese, Celts and many others maintained direct contact with their esoteric masters and sailed to this continent. They came in pilgrimage as novices, merely students seeking the greatest prize there ever was, the meaning of life and joy of death.

All who came stayed for varying times, the Egyptians for over four thousand years, the Spanish barely a decade, it all depended on motives and protocol. In each case, offence was caused and those who came from afar were asked to leave and not to return, and they did as directed. There is only one instance where that directive was ignored, the British Invasion Fleet refused to raise anchor and set sail back to Britain. Once refusing to vacate the Original premises, the suffering and injustice started (and still continues) when that illegal invasion began.

That is our take on what happened and could be it factual, fictional or a mix of the two. It is a diverse conglomeration of Original Elder's accounts, Dreaming stories, archaeological evidence, intuition, filling in the dots and extensive research, with a dash of channelling from another to top off the mix. We have no doubt that this version of antiquity will be received with the customary scorn and condescension we are so accustomed to, but it makes no difference either way. All of this is after the event, as the accepted version of ancient proceedings has been dispensed with and thus disqualifies any rebuttal given by critics found wrong in every earlier instance. The defenders of orthodox history now live in far too many glass-houses to even think of picking up one pebble.

A Mid-Semester report

There is no doubt that there is no African connection to Original people in Australia through mtDNA, Y Chromosomes or skull morphology; that is undeniable. Nor can the antiquity and significance of the Standing Stones site be questioned, and the same can be said about our huge collection of Original marked rocks. Between those rocks and a hard place the authenticity is proven. The large spread of science we have assembled denies any African entry, and the archaeology on country contradicts everything assumed about pre-Cook Original history. And in reaching back to the very beginning of humanity, the ancient statue that came from a time "long before true"[21] introduces a personal face and distant place far off in the stars.

Despite the archaeology presented and the abundance of sites/ artefacts to be discussed in our next book, the official reactions span the full gamut of negativity. Condescension is a stock response, hostility tinged with a steadfast refusal to look or discuss is also a popular stance. Even if some aspect of our research is begrudgingly acknowledged, there is still plenty of room to attack our character, craving for notoriety and greedy motivations.

Whether that hostility remains or intensifies is merely background noise and irrelevant to the task at hand. Our role, from the time I (Steven) was given ceremony by the Ramindjeri under Karno's guidance, is to prosecute the whole truth and nothing but the Original truth. It is to the spirits of the land and Original custodians of the Old Ways we are accountable. Same for all of us. We are judged on the worth and truthfulness of every word uttered, and when telling any Original story, integrity is everything.

This is but one small chapter in a story that began here, ended here and will begin again here. All we have to do is to read from and between these same lines and become part of this rebirth.

OTHER BOOKS:

Shunned: The Hidden History Of Australia's Originals

"In their startling new book, Steven and Evan Strong challenge the Out-of-Africa theory, looking at the strong DNA and archaeological evidence that Australia is where modern human beings – Homo sapiens sapiens – derived.

The Original Australians (referred to by some as Aboriginals), like so many indigenous peoples, have been stripped of their heritage by an aggressive European colonizing power while has re-written the history books, largely as an exercise in justifying exploitation, suppression, cultural genocide at best and in a number of cases, actual racial extinction as with the mainland Tasmanians. Partially to justify these crimes, and partially through a cultural blindness, the original Australians were perceived as, and portrayed as, the most 'backward' and 'primitive' of people. Yet, as the Strong's show, Original Australians had a rich culture which may have sown the first seeds of spirituality in the world. They had the technology to make international seafaring voyages and have left traces in the Americas and possibly, Japan, Southern India, Egypt and elsewhere. They practiced brain surgery, invented the first hand tools and had knowledge of penicillin.

Shunned brings together thirty years of intensive research in consultation with Elders in the Original Australian community who have shared their knowledge and wisdom with the authors to an extent few people outside their community have been privileged to experience.

This ground-breaking book is essential reading for anybody who wants to know where the human race came from and perhaps where they should be going..." (Jan Scherpenhuizen- Our Editor/ Literary Agent Possible Press Publisher)

EBook:
http://www.amazon.com/dp/B00G2C21TS

Paperback:
http://www.amazon.com/Shunned-Steven-Strong/dp/0980813581/ref=tmm_pap_ swatch_0?_encoding=UTF8&qid=&sr=

Ancient Aliens in Australia:
Pleiadian Origins of Humanity (with Bruce & Daniella Fenton)

In this remarkable book, supported by numerous photos and images, we are introduced to the incredible physical evidence for a lost civilisation in Australia that held advanced knowledge and high technology. A civilisation that seems to proclaim for itself an out of this world origin – in the direction of the seven sisters of the Pleiades constellation. This lost race of progenitors may well be the true ancestors of modern Homo sapiens, the mysterious unknown third race included in our DNA alongside that of Neanderthals and Denisovans.

The evidence is supplied for you examination.

This is not just a sharing of physical research relating to an ancient alien contact event, it is far more. It is also the record of an incredible modern contact event, a series of spontaneous shamanic journeys into altered states of consciousness, these have supplied a wealth of information about the Pleiadian beings themselves and their intimate connection with the authors. Allow yourself to be taken through time and into other dimensions of reality to gain an understanding of one of our galaxies most advanced ancient species. This direct contact has already led to the ruins of two other lost civilisations being brought to the awareness of the authors, the Pleiadians continue to seed a path of discovery about the true history of ancient humanity. Read with an open mind and much wisdom can be gained here.

Are you ready to finally reclaim the lost knowledge of your true origins? Are you ready to meet the ancient aliens of Australia?

EBook:
http://www.amazon.com/Ancient-Aliens-Australia-Pleiadian-Humanity-ebook/dp/B00EXFNNO8/

Paperback:
http://www.amazon.com/Ancient-Aliens-Australia-Pleiadian-Humanity/dp/149236536X/ref=tmm_pap_swatch_0?_encoding=UTF8&qid=&sr=

Forgotten Origin

Forgotten Origin is the third in a series of books dedicated to the first Homo sapiens: the Australian Aboriginal people. Steven Strong and Evan Strong continue in their investigation into the global impact of Aboriginal people sailing from, never to, Australia no less than 50,000 years ago, paying particular attention to the shared principles found within many Gnostic scriptures and the Dreaming. As radical as this theory may appear, the rigor applied, whether through mtDNA, Y Chromosomes, skull morphology or historical accounts, and the religious ancestry upon which this hidden history is founded, demands serious consideration. This is not their story. Steven Strong and Evan Strong make no claim to speak on behalf of anyone. They do, however, have the right to relay that which Aboriginal culture-custodians insist is true. The First Australians are unique, and in no way descended from Africans or any other race. Forgotten Origin is merely another reminder of this hidden truth.

THROUGH AMAZON:

http://www.amazon.com/Forgotten-Origin-Steven-Strong/dp/0761853340/ref=sr_1_6?s=books&ie=UTF8&qid=1452742697&sr=1-6

Book and eBook also available through University Press of America (Publisher):

https://rowman.com/ISBN/9780761853343

Mary Magdalene's Dreaming:
A Comparison of Aboriginal Wisdom and Gnostic Scriptures

In Mary Magdalene's Dreaming Steven Strong and Evan Strong continue their esoteric journey tracing the origins of religion that they began their first book, *Constructing A New World Map*. Strong and Strong examine the Gnostic Scriptures detailing the words and deeds of Mary and Jesus recently found at Nag Hammadi. They were, as Jesus stated in the Gospel of Thomas, custodians of a secret tradition. Jesus insisted he is but the caretaker of a "bubbling spring that I have tended". The authors further assert their belief that this "bubbling spring" is identical to the "secret place" aboriginal elder, Bill Neidjie, urges all to discover and it is their contention that a closer inspection of the ancient mystical spring Jesus and Mary accessed is evident in many Gnostic texts. The secret knowledge Mary and Jesus preached, stripped of cultural and geographic differences, is undoubtedly the purest replication of the Dreaming since the first mariners were banished from Australia.

THROUGH AMAZON:

http://www.amazon.com/Mary-Magdalenes-Dreaming-Comparison-Aboriginal dp/0761842802/ref=sr_1_4?s=books&ie=UTF8&qid=1452742697&sr=1-4

Also available through University Press of America (Publisher):

https://rowman.com/ISBN/9780761842804

Constructing a New World Map

The first book in the trilogy. Nearly 50,000 years ago Australian Aboriginals set sail seeking new horizons. As they arrived on distant shores, they brought with them beliefs and a lifestyle unknown elsewhere. Their legacy was a mixed blessing. Although founding the basis of modern culture and cooperative living, they also exported knowledge of one errant practice.

These mariners did not volunteer to leave Australia, they were banished for selecting an agricultural practice that offended the Ancestral Spirits and the land. Living in the first Garden of Eden, as it was with Cain and Abel who chose to farm the land and animals, they were exiled for breaking a sacred covenant with the Dreaming. Common sense would dismiss these radical claims, but findings made at Aboriginal sites, ancient graves, and cave walls, along with new advances in genetics, have created circumstances that require the construction of a new world map.

Recent discovery of Gnostic texts at Nag Hammadi, particularly scriptures devoted to Mary and Jesus, reveal the ancient mystical tradition that began in the Dreaming was the inspiration behind their teachings. The message, preached by both the Dreaming, and Mary and Jesus is as relevant and important today as it was 50,000 years ago.

THROUGH AMAZON:

http://www.amazon.com/Constructing-New-World-Steven-Strong/dp/0761840818/ref=sr_1_5?s=books&ie=UTF8&qid=1452742697&sr=1-5

Also available through University Press of America (Publisher):

https://rowman.com/ISBN/9780761840817

Bibliography:

Barcelona, Universtitat De. "Heat Treatment of Silcrete. Patrick Schmidt: Synopsis." (2015: 3rd Nov.),
     http://www.ub.edu/ubtv/en/video/heat-treatment-of-silcrete-patrick-schmidt.
Beve, Aunty. 2014.
Bonner, Rick. "Ufos and the Oval Office: What the President Knows, and Doesn't."no. May 23 (2012),
     http://www.examiner.com/article/ufos-and-the-oval-office-what-the-president-knows-and-
     doesn-t.
Brynes, Dr John G. 2016.
Burenhult, Goran. "Illustrated History of Mankind." Hamburg, Germany: Weltbild Verlag, 2000.
Butler, Kevin, Kate Cameron, and Bob Pervical. *The Myth of Terra Nullius: Invasion and Resistance - the
     Early Years*. North Sydney, NSW, Australia: The Board of Studies NSW, 1995.
Cairns, Hugh, and Bill Yidumbuma. *Dark Sparklers*. 2nd ed. Merimbula, Australia: H.C. Cairnes, 2004.
"Came from Africa to Australia Our Blacks' Ancestors." *The Mail (Adelaide)* (1937 23rd Oct.),
     http://nla.gov.au/nla.news-article55070946.
Campbell, W.D. "Aboriginal Carvings of Port Jackson and Broken Bay." In *Memoirs of the Geological
     Survey of New South Wales: Enthological Series no. 1*. Sydney: Department of Mines and
     Agriculture, 1898.
Cowan, James. *Messengers of the Gods: Tribal Elders Reveal the Ancient Wisdom of the Earth*. Milsons
     Point, NSW: Vintage Books, 1993.
Cunningham, Dr. Derek. "Bosnian Astronomical Stone Analysis by Dr Derek Cunningham." Jock
     Doubleday (Photographer), 2015.
———. "Calgary Stone Analysis by Dr Derek Cunningham (Diagram)." 2014.
———. "Dr Derek Cunningham's Analysis of Ros' Rock No. 1." Evan Strong (Photographer), 2014.
"David Unaipon." https://en.wikipedia.org/wiki/David_Unaipon.
Di Gravio (Interviewee), Gionna, Carol Duncan (Presenter), and Jeanette McMahon (Producer). "The
     Antiquities of the Wollombi District." *News from Cultural Collections, UON Library at the
     University of Newcastle Australia* (2009),
     https://uoncc.wordpress.com/category/aborigines/aboriginal-rock-art/.
Doubleday, Jock. "Comparision of Ros' Rock No. 1 and Bosnian Astronomical Stone." Jock Doubleday,
     Evan Strong (Photographer) 2015.
"Dr.Sci Sam Semir Osmanagich, Phd.". http://www.semirosmanagic.com/en/.
Dutchen, Stephanie. "Genetic Studies Link Indigenous Peoples in the Amazon and Australasia." Phys.org,
     http://phys.org/news/2015-07-genetic-link-indigenous-peoples-amazon.html.
Flood, Josephine. *Archaeology of the Dreamtime: The Story of Prehistoric Australia and Its People*. 6th
     ed. Marleston, Australia: J.B. Publishing, 2004.
———. *The Original Australians: Story of the Aboriginal People*. Crows Nest, Australia: Allen and Unwin,
     2006.
———. *Rock Art of the Dreamtime: Images of Ancient Australia*. Sydney, Australia: Angus and Robertson,
     1997.
Gander, Kashmira "Former Canadian Defence Secretary Paul Hellyer Calls on Governments to Reveal Ufo
     Information." *Independant* (2015 [20th April]),
     http://www.independent.co.uk/news/world/americas/former-canadian-defence-secretary-
     paul-hellyer-calls-on-governments-to-reveal-ufo-information-10190024.html.
"Genetics Home Reference: Y Chromosomes." (2010), http://ghr.nlm.nih.gov/chromosome/Y.
Geology.com. "Chert: What Is Chert, How Does It Form and What Is It Used For."
     http://geology.com/rocks/chert.shtml.
Gibbons, Ann. "DNA from Neandertal Relative May Shake up Human Family Tree." *Science: Latest News*
     (2015 [11th Sept.]), http://news.sciencemag.org/archaeology/2015/09/dna-neandertal-relative-
     may-shake-human-family-tree.
"Halotypes / Haplotypes." (2013), http://www.nature.com/scitable/definition/haplotype-haplotypes-
     142.
Herman, Douglas. "Were Us Astronauts Ordered Not to Report Ufos & Aliens?" *rense.com* (2006),
     http://www.rense.com/general70/rep.htm.
Herries, Dr Andy I.R. "Hot Rocks, Shells and Red Earth - the Origins of Modern Human Behaviour in South
     Africa." Paper presented at the The Castlereagh Talks: Some talks about the past, Upper

Castlereagh, 2009: 5th Sept.

Howe, Neil. 2015.

https://www.youtube.com/watch?v=LLRsWdVNKes. "Egyptians in Australia Part 2 - Steven Strong." In
     Egyptians in Australia, 45:02. Australia: You Tube, 2012.

https://www.youtube.com/watch?v=uX2P8utjk3A. "Michael Tellinger - Stones That Ring Like Bells." In
     Michael Tellinger - Uncovering the Truth, edited by Michael Tellinger, 4:26. South Africa: You
     Tube, 2010.

Jamison, Tressa. "The Australian Aboriginal People: Dating the Colonization of Australia." (2004),
     http://www.biology.iastate.edu/InternationalTrips/1Australia/04papers/TressaAborigOrign.htm

Jane. 2014.

Jarmbi'je. 2014.

Jones, Tim. "100,000 Year-Old Incised Orchre Found at Blombos Cave." *Anthropology.net: Beyond bones
     and stones* (2009: 12th June), http://anthropology.net/2009/06/12/100000-year-old-incised-
     ochre-found-at-blombos-cave/.

Karno. 2015.

Klyosov, Anatole A., and Igor L. Rozhanskii. "Re-Examining the "out of Africa" Theory and the Origin of
     Europeoids (Caucasoids) in Light of DNA Genealogy." *Advances in Anthropology* 2, no. 2 (2012):
     80-86.

Lawlor, Robert. *Voices of the First Day: Awakening in the Aboriginal Dreamtime*. Rochester, Vt.: Inner
     Traditions International, Ltd., 1991.

MacRae, George W., trans., and Douglas M. Parrott ed. "The Apocalypse of Adam (V,5)." In *The Nag
     Hammadi Library in English*, edited by James M. Robinson, Pp. 279-86. New York, N.Y.:
     HarperSanFrancisco, 1990.

Marbuck, Uncle. 2015.

Maryboy, Dr Nancy D. *A Guide to Navajo Astronomy*, A Collection of Curricula for the Starlab Navajo
     Skies Cyclinder. Bluff, Utah USA: Indigenous Earth Institute, 2004.

Maxwell Museum of Anthropology, Bernard B. (Photographer), and Karl Schwerin (Donator).
     "Ecuadorian Pre-Columbian Artifacts." In *Catalogue No. 2008.34.2-.3 and .6*. University of New
     Mexico: Maxwell Museum of Anthropology.

"Moyjil Point Richie." Warrnambool City Council, http://www.moyjil.com.au/.

Mulder, Ros. "Marked Rocks Note." 2015.

———. 2014.

Nesbit, Kate. 2014.

Oppenheimer, Stephen. "74,000 Years Ago: The Mount Toba Volcanic Super-Eruption."
     http://www.bradshawfoundation.com/journey/toba2.html.

Paez, Natalie Jacqueline. "Marked and Shaped Rocks." Third Eye Society (Photographer), 2015.

Patterson, Richard. "Coarse Grain Sandstone Rock." (Photographer), 2013.

———. "Sandstone "Shaped Stone"." (Photographer), 2013.

———. "Smaller Mound / Burial Site." (Photographer), 2013.

———. "Standing Stones." Computer Image, 2015.

———. "Standing Stones: Looking South East." Computer Image, 2015.

Prostak, Sergio. "Engraved Stone Dating Back 30,000 Years Found in China." *Sci-News.com* (2012),
     http://www.sci-news.com/archaeology/article00755.html.

Schaef, Anne Wilson. *Native Wisdom for White Minds: Daily Reflections Inspired by the Native Peoples of
     the Now World*. Milsons Point, Australia: Random House Australia Pty Ltd, 1995.

Skoglund, Pontus, Swapan Mallick, Maria Catira Bortolini, Niru Chennagiri, Tabita Hunemeier, Maria
     Luiza Petzl-Erler, Francisco Mauro Salzano, Nick Patterson, and David Reich. "Genetic Evidence
     for Two Founding Populations of the Americas." *Nature* 525, no. 7567 (2015): 104-08.

Slater, Frederic. "Aboriginal Rock Carving: To the Editor of the Herald." *The Sydney Morning Herald*
     (1937), http://nla.gov.au/nla.news-article17302881.

———. "Personal Letters - Correndspondances - Notes." In *2013*, edited by Richard Patterson, No. 1-19
     & Original: 53-61: Achaeological and Educational Research Society, 1939.

———. "Section F: Ii) Intrepretation of the Drawing at Burraguura and Yango." In *Australasian and New
     Zealand Association of the Advancement of Science*. Auckland, New Zealand, 1937 (14th Jan.).

Smith, David, and Ros Mulder. 2015.

Steen-McIntyre, Dr Virginia "The Collapse of Standard Paradigm New World Prehistory." *Pleistocene*

Coalition News 3, no. 6 (2011 Nov-Dec): 18-20.

Strong, Evan. "Assorted Marked and Shaped Rocks." (Photographer), 2015.

———. "Australia as Sahul (Map)." 2016.

———. "Cave of the Golden Boomerang." (Photographer), 2011.

———. "Kariong - Bambara Glyphs." (Photographer), 2013.

———. "Mount Yengo." (Photographer), 2014.

———. "New Marked Rocks and Cyclons." (Photographer), 2016.

———. "New View of the Ancient Americas [Adapted] (Map)." 2016.

———. "Out of Africa Theory of Human Migration (Map)." 2016.

———. "Possible Migration Routes from Sahul to the Americas (Map)." 2016.

———. "Pryamid Rock 1." (Photographer), 2012.

———. "Pryamid Rock 2." (Photographer), 2013.

———. "Ros' Rock No. 1." (Photographer), 2014.

———. "Ros' Rocks No. 1 and 2." (Photographer), 2014.

———. "Shaped Sandstone Rock 1." (Photographer), 2013.

———. "Shaped Sandstone Rock 2." (Photographer), 2013.

———. "Site Locations of Anomalous Dates (Map)." 2016.

———. "Table 1: Eleven Sites with Anomolous Dates." 2015.

———. "Test Trench." (Photographer), 2013.

———. "Ufo Glyph at Bambara." (Photographer), 2013.

Strong, Evan, and Erica Schmerbeck. "Diagram: Haplogroup Tree of Y Chromosomes." 2015.

———. "Diagram: Out of Australia Theory - the Spread in the Pacific." 2015.

Strong, Steven. "Cave of the Golden Boomerang (Diagram)." 2012.

———. "Diagram: Test Trench." 2013.

———. "Emu's Nest Jetty (Diagram)." 2013.

———. "Emu's Nest Rocks." (Photographer), 2013.

———. "Map 1 of Western Slope of Bigger Slope." 2013.

———. "Map 2: Smaller Mound and Scatter of Sandstone Rocks." 2013.

———. "Map 3: Gps Placement of Sandstone Rocks." 2013.

———. "P.N.G. Statue and Rock Artefact." (Photographer), 2014.

———. "Ros' Rock No. 1: 3 Sides (Diagram)." 2014.

———. "Ros' Rock No. 21 (Diagram)." 2015.

Strong, Steven, and Evan Strong. *Shunned: The Hidden History of the Original Australians*. Sydney, N.S.W., Australia: Possible Press, 2013.

Strong, Steven, Evan Strong, and Karno (Surame with held). "From the Begining with Karno (Surname Withheld) Ramindjeri Spokesperson." 2014, http://forgottenorigin.com/from-the-beginning-article-by-steven-evan-strong-with-karno-walker-ramindjeri-spokesperson.

Strong, Steven, Karno (Surname Withheld), and Frederic Slater. "Mix of Karno's and Slater's Symbols (Diagram)." Complied by Steven Strong, 2015, 1939 and 2013.

Unaipon, David. *Legendary Tales of the Australian Aborigines*. Edited by Stephen Muecke and Adam Shoemaker. Carlton South, Victoria: The Miegunyah Press: Melbourne University Press, 2001.

Wade, Nicholas. "Australian Aborigine Hair Tells a Story of Human Migration." *The New York Times* (2011 [22nd Sept]), http://www.nytimes.com/2011/09/23/science/23aborigines.html?_r=0.

Webre, Alfred Lambremont. *Exopolitics: Poltics, Government and Law in the Universe*. Vancouver, B.C. Canada: Universe Books, 2005.

Wilson, Allan C., and Rebecca L. Cann. "The Recent African Genesis of Humans: Genetic Studies Reveal That an African Woman of 200,000 Years Ago Was Our Common Ancestor." *Scientific American* 266, no. 4 (April 1992): 68-73.

Windschuttle, Keith, and Tim Gillin. "The Extinction of the Australian Pygmies." *Quadrant*,no. June 2002 (2005), http://www.quadrant.org.au/blogs/history-wars/2002/06/the-extinction-of-the-australian-pygmies.

Winkler, Michael. "Rock Star of the Kimberley." *The Age* (20 Sept. 2004), http://www.theage.com.au/articles/2004/09/17/1095394002333.html?from=storyrhs.

Wood, Samarah. "Marked and Shaped Rocks." (Photographer), 2014.

X, Professor. 2014.

Endnotes

REFERENCES & NOTES:

General Overall Notes

* All Map Templates from dmap.com http://www.d-maps.com/.
* Surnames of deceased Australia Original Elders, Custodians and peoples are with-held to observe protocols of respect and culture.
* Other names have been changed to ensure the security and safety of some of our sources.

INTRODUCTION:

[1] Steven Strong and Evan Strong, *Shunned: The Hidden History of the Original Australians* (Sydney, N.S.W., Australia: Possible Press, 2013).

[2] Frederic Slater, "Personal Letters - Correndspondances - Notes," in *2013*, ed. Richard Patterson (Achaeological and Educational Research Society, 1939). no. 2.

[3] Ibid. no. 2.

[4] Ibid. no. 2.

[5] Kevin Butler, Kate Cameron, and Bob Pervical, *The Myth of Terra Nullius: Invasion and Resistance - the Early Years* (North Sydney, NSW, Australia: The Board of Studies NSW, 1995). 34.

[6] Sky Heroes: Creation Spirits who descended from the sky above. They were instrumental in the creation of humanity in Australia.

[7] Evan Strong, "Australia as Sahul (Map)," (2016).

[8] Sahul: refers to the combined and joined landmass of: the continent of Australia, Papua New Guinea and Tasmania. Pleistocene-era when the sea levels were 150m lower than present times.

[9] Clever-fella: An Original male advanced in spiritual matters; an Elder who has acquired some form of supernatural power.

[10] Wee-un: An Original female in equivalent to a Clever-fella in respect, stature and powers.

Chapter 1: Australian Aboriginal Hair Tells two Stories of Human Migration, but Only one is Correct

[1] Nicholas Wade, "Australian Aborigine Hair Tells a Story of Human Migration," *The New York Times*(2011 [22nd Sept]), http://www.nytimes.com/2011/09/23/science/23aborigines.html?_r=0.

[2] Ibid.

[3] Ibid.

[4] Ibid.

[5] Ibid.

[6] Ibid.

[7] Ibid.

[8] Evan Strong, "Table 1: Eleven Sites with Anomolous Dates," (2015).

[9] ———, "Site Locations of Anomalous Dates (Map)," (2016).

[10] Jim Bowler: (Professor) a geologist and geo-morphologist (Australian National University and now University of Melbourne).

[11] "Moyjil Point Richie," Warrnambool City Council, http://www.moyjil.com.au/.

[12] Ibid.

[13] Alan Thorne: (Professor) He was one of Australia's leading academics (Archaeology, Biology, Human Anatomy) from A.N.U. (Australian National University). Alan Thorne has been extensively involved in numerous discoveries at Lake Mungo and Kow Swamp. He co-wrote a paper on W.L.H.3., suggesting the male

individual carried a unique genetic strain that calls into question the "Out of Africa" theory. He was a leading proponent of Multiregional Hypothesis of Evolution Theory/ Regional Continuity Theory .

[14] "Moyjil Point Richie."

[15] Gurdup/Gurdip *Singh*: (Dr) From A.N.U. (Australian National University) he was the first scholar to present evidence that indicated Aboriginal presence at Lake George around 120,000 years ago.

[16] Josephine Flood, *Archaeology of the Dreamtime: The Story of Prehistoric Australia and Its People*, 6th ed. (Marleston, Australia: J.B. Publishing, 2004). 3.

[17] Michael Morwood: (Professor) Archaeologist best known for discovery of *Homo* floresiensis (the hobbit-like hominids recently discovered on the island of Flores in Indonesia).

[18] Josephine Flood: (Dr) archaeologist, author, lecturer from A.N.U., award winner and Australian Heritage Commission Assistant Director from 1979–91. Her book "*Archaeology of the Dreamtime*" is Australia's bestselling book on archaeology.

[19] mtDNA: DNA found in the Mitochondria (portion of cell which generated energy). Human mtDNA are clones passed on by the mother with little genetic difference from generation to generation. This type of DNA consists of 37 genes and 16,568 base pairs.

[20] Strong and Strong, *Shunned*.

[21] Josephine Flood, *The Original Australians: Story of the Aboriginal People* (Crows Nest, Australia: Allen and Unwin, 2006). 175.

[22] Keith Windschuttle and Tim Gillin, "The Extinction of the Australian Pygmies," *Quadrant*, no. June 2002 (2005), http://www.quadrant.org.au/blogs/history-wars/2002/06/the-extinction-of-the-australian-pygmies.

[23] Tressa Jamison, "The Australian Aboriginal People: Dating the Colonization of Australia,"(2004), http://www.biology.iastate.edu/InternationalTrips/1Australia/04papers/TressaAborigOrign.htm.

[24] Ibid.

[25] Y chromosomes: "The Y chromosome is one of the two sex chromosomes in humans (the other is the X chromosome). The sex chromosomes form one of the 23 pairs of human chromosomes in each cell. The Y chromosome spans more than 59 million building blocks of DNA (base pairs) and represents almost 2 percent of the total DNA in cells." From: "Genetics Home Reference: Y Chromosomes," (2010), http://ghr.nlm.nih.gov/chromosome/Y.

[26] Anatole Klyosov: (Dr) of physical chemistry, biomedical science, industrial biochemistry and DNA computer Statics and mathematics.

[27] Anatole A. Klyosov and Igor L. Rozhanskii, "Re-Examining the "out of Africa" Theory and the Origin of Europeoids (Caucasoids) in Light of DNA Genealogy," *Advances in Anthropology* 2, no. 2 (2012). 80.

[28] Ibid. 83.

[29] Subclades: a subgroup of a Haplogroup (has similar Haplotypes, genetic population group that shares a common ancestor).

[30] Klyosov and Rozhanskii, "Re-Examining the "out of Africa" Theory and the Origin of Europeoids (Caucasoids) in Light of DNA Genealogy." 83.

[31] Ibid. 82.

[32] Erica Schmerbeck & Evan Strong, "Diagram Haplogroup Tree of Y Chromosome," (2015) Based on Klyosov & Rozhanskii's research

[33] Klyosov and Rozhanskii, "Re-Examining the "out of Africa" Theory and the Origin of Europeoids (Caucasoids) in Light of DNA Genealogy."

[34] Ibid. 80.

[35] "A haplotype is a group of genes within an organism that was inherited together from a single parent. The word "haplotype" is derived from the word "haploid," which describes cells with only one set of chromosomes, and from the word "genotype," which refers to the genetic makeup of an organism. A haplotype can describe a pair of genes inherited together from one parent on one chromosome, or it can describe all of the genes on a chromosome that were inherited together from a single parent. This group of genes was inherited together because of genetic linkage, or the phenomenon by which genes that are close to each other on the same chromosome are often inherited together. In addition, the term "haplotype" can also refer to the inheritance of a cluster of single nucleotide polymorphisms (SNPs), which are variations at single positions in the DNA sequence among individuals.""Halotypes / Haplotypes," (2013), http://www.nature.com/scitable/definition/haplotype haplotypes 142.

[36] Jamison, "The Australian Aboriginal People: Dating the Colonization of Australia."

[37] Ibid.

[38] Ibid.

[39] Wade, "Australian Aborigine Hair Tells a Story of Human Migration."

[40] Ibid.

[41] Flood, *The Original Australians: Story of the Aboriginal People.* 175.

[42] Ibid.

[43] Ibid.

[44] Ibid.

[45] Ibid.

[46] Windschuttle and Gillin, "The Extinction of the Australian Pygmies."

[47] Wade, "Australian Aborigine Hair Tells a Story of Human Migration."

[48] Ibid.

[49] Ibid.

[50] Allan C. Wilson: (Professor) biochemist from University of California and a pioneer in molecular approach to evolution. Wilson created the hypothetical molecular clock which led to the erroneous, and conceded as false through further research conducted by Wilson, belief all modern humans are related to one African woman born between 150–200,000 years ago.

[51] Rebecca L. Cann: (Professor) geneticist in Cell and molecular biology in University of Hawaii. Made the breakthrough in mtDNA variations and evolution – Eve,(see Allan Wilson's entry above).

[52] Allan C. Wilson and Rebecca L. Cann, "The Recent African Genesis of Humans: Genetic Studies Reveal That an African Woman of 200,000 Years Ago Was Our Common Ancestor," *Scientific American* 266, no. 4 (April 1992).

[53] Wade, "Australian Aborigine Hair Tells a Story of Human Migration." 68.

[54] Ibid.

[55] Ibid.

[56] Ibid.

[57] Ibid.

[58] Evan Strong, "Out of Africa Theory of Human Migration (Map)," (2016). Original from: Goran Burenhult, "Illustrated History of Mankind," (Hamburg, Germany: Weltbild Verlag, 2000).

[59] " Toba Lake in northern Sumatra is the world's largest active volcanic caldera. The volcanic eruption that resulted in Lake Toba (100 x 30 km) 74,000 years ago, is known to have been by far the biggest eruption of the last 2 million years. This mega-bang caused a prolonged world-wide nuclear winter and released ash in a huge plume .... In our story the Toba eruption is the most accurately dated, dramatic, and unambiguous event before the last ice age." Stephen Oppenheimer, "74,000 Years Ago: The Mount Toba Volcanic Super-Eruption," http://www.bradshawfoundation.com/journey/toba2.html.

[60] Flood, *The Original Australians: Story of the Aboriginal People.* 173.

[61] Wade, "Australian Aborigine Hair Tells a Story of Human Migration."

[62] Ibid.

[63] Robert Lawlor, *Voices of the First Day: Awakening in the Aboriginal Dreamtime* (Rochester, Vt.: Inner Traditions International, Ltd., 1991). Back Cover.

Chapter 2: The Final Nail In The Coffin

[1] Stephanie Dutchen, "Genetic Studies Link Indigenous Peoples in the Amazon and Australasia," Phys.org, http://phys.org/news/2015-07-genetic-link-indigenous-peoples-amazon.html.

[2] David Reich: (Professor) Geneticist Harvard Medical School.

[3] Dutchen, "Genetic Studies Link Indigenous Peoples in the Amazon and Australasia."

[4] Ibid.

[5] Ibid.

[6] Ibid.

[7] Ibid.

[8] Ibid.

[9] Pontus Skoglund et al., "Genetic Evidence for Two Founding Populations of the Americas," *Nature* 525, no. 7567 (2015). 104.

[10] Dutchen, "Genetic Studies Link Indigenous Peoples in the Amazon and Australasia."

[11] Skoglund et al., "Genetic Evidence for Two Founding Populations of the Americas." 104.

[12] Dr Walter Neves: (Assoc. Professor) Anthropologists, archaeologist and biologist from University of Sao Paulo (Brazil), best known for morphology work on hominid remains from South America.

[13] Skoglund et al., "Genetic Evidence for Two Founding Populations of the Americas." 107.

[14] Pontus Skogland: (Dr) evolutionary geneticist from Harvard Medical School and Uppsala University in Sweden.

[15] Dutchen, "Genetic Studies Link Indigenous Peoples in the Amazon and Australasia."

[16] Evan Strong, "New View of the Ancient Americas [Adapted] (Map)," (2016). Original from: Dr Virginia Steen-McIntyre, "The Collapse of Standard Paradigm New World Prehistory," Pleistocene Coalition News 3, no. 6 (2011 Nov–Dec). Fig. 1.

[17] pre–Clovis: (>15,000 years) refers to sites, remains etc in the Americas.

[18] Dr Virginia Steen-McIntyre: Tephrochronologist: (volcanic ash specialist) known for the Hueyatlaco Valsequillo site dating controversy.

[19] Lake Valsequillo: An enigmatic area that has produced some quite sensational archaeological dates. Near Puebla in Mexico, their dates push back the date way back of Homo Sapiens being in the Americas eg 250,000 (BP).

[20] Strong and Strong, Shunned.

[21] Ann Gibbons, "DNA from Neandertal Relative May Shake up Human Family Tree," Science: Latest News 11th Sept.(2015 [11th Sept.]), http://news.sciencemag.org/archaeology/2015/09/dna-neandertal-relative-may-shake-human-family-tree.

[22] Chris Stringer: (Professor) Palaeoanthropology and Human Origins and Research Leader at The Natural History Museum of London.

[23] Denisovans: (Denisova Hominin) Originally their remains were found in Altai Mountains in Siberia, Russia, however they ranged from this area to southeast Asia and over into Western Europe eg Spain. 3–5% of Australia Original and Melanesians DNA come from Denisovans.

[24] Red Deer Cave People: relatively around till recent times 11,500 (BP), however still considered a separate Hominid species with a mixture of archaic and modern features, their remains are found in China.

[25] Gibbons, "DNA from Neandertal Relative May Shake up Human Family Tree."

[26] Ibid.

[27] Ibid.

[28] Ibid.

[29] Ibid.

[30] Ibid.

[31] Ibid.

[32] Ibid.

[33] Ibid.

[34] Ibid.

[35] Ibid.

[36] Erica Schmerbeck & Evan Strong, "Possible Migrations Routes From Sahul to the America's (Map)", (2016).

[37] ———, "Diagram: Out of Australia Theory - the Spread in the Pacific," (2015).

Chapter 3: The Standing Stones– the Most Important Site in Australia, Perhaps the World

[1] Richard Patterson, "Standing Stones," (Computer Image, 2015).

[2] Slater, "Personal Letters – Correndspondances – Notes." no. 5.

[3] Ibid. no. 2.

[4] Ibid. no. 2.

[5] Ibid. no. 8.

[6] "Came from Africa to Australia Our Blacks' Ancestors," The Mail (Adelaide) Saturday 23rd October(1937 23rd Oct.), http://nla.gov.au/nla.news-article55070946. 6 (n).

[7] Frederic Slater, "Aboriginal Rock Carving: To the Editor of the Herald," The Sydney Morning Herald 23rd Jan.(1937), http://nla.gov.au/nla.news-article17302881. 14 (n).

[8] Eliza Hamilton Dunlop: (1796 –1880) ethnographer of Australian Original folk-lore, language, poetry and songs. Also a respected poet /lyric writer and an Australian Original welfare activist.

[9] "Came from Africa to Australia Our Blacks' Ancestors."

[10] Ibid.

[11] Slater, "Personal Letters – Correndspondances – Notes." no. 12.

[12] Ibid. no. 8.

[13] Ibid. no. 12.

[14] Ibid. no. 12.

[18] Ibid. no. 15.

[19] Ibid. no. 7.

[20] Ibid. no. 11.

[21] Ibid. no. 11.

[22] Ibid. no. 11.

[23] Ibid. no. 19.

[24] Ibid. no. 19.

[25] Ibid. no. 11.

[26] Ibid. no. 6.

[27] Ibid. no. 11.

[28] Ibid. no. 11.

[29] Richard Patterson, "Smaller Mound / Burial Site," ((Photographer), 2013).

[30] Slater, "Personal Letters - Correndspondances - Notes." no. 2.

[31] Ibid. no. 8.

[32] Ibid. no. 8.

[33] Ibid. no. 8.

[34] Richard Patterson, "Standing Stones: Looking South East," (Computer Image, 2015).

[35] Slater, "Personal Letters - Correndspondances - Notes." no. 2.

[36] Ibid. no. 2.

[37] Ibid. no. 1.

[38] Ibid. no. 2.

[39] Ibid. no. 3.

[40] Ibid. no. 6.

[41] Ibid. no. 2.

[42] Frederic Slater, "Section F: Ii) Intrepretation of the Drawing at Burraguura and Yango," in *Australasian and New Zealand Association of the Advancement of Science* (Auckland, New Zealand1937 (14th Jan.)). 14.

[43] Slater, "Personal Letters - Correndspondances - Notes." no. 19.

[44] Githabul: Australian Original Tribe (a part of the Bundalung*[sic] Language Confederation) and land estate in Northern NSW and Queensland incorporating the area with the towns of Woodenbong and Urbenville.

[45] Steven Strong, Karno (Surname Withheld), and Frederic Slater, "Mix of Karno's and Slater's Symbols (Diagram)," (Complied by Steven Strong, 2015, 1939 and 2013).

[46] Ramindjeri: Australian Original Tribe and Lands incorporating Karta (Kangaroo Island), Victor Harbour Encounter Bay area, to Adelaide and River Torrens within South Australia.

[47] Southern Law Confederation: "Ramindjeri spokesperson Karno (dec. surname withheld) has spoken on many occasions in some detail about the Southern Law network that has been in existence for hundreds of thousands of years. According to Karno this web of tribes runs 300 kilometres inland from the coast, beginning up near the Kimberleys (WA), the area of influence extends all around the Australian coastline down to South Australia, Victoria and all the way up the east coast until reaching Cape York. By landmass it would make up about one quarter of the Australian continent, and by Old Way sensibilities and norms it is still in existence and will continue functioning as a binding agent for all tribal estates under its jurisdiction." Steven Strong, Evan Strong, and Karno (Surame with held), "From the Begining with Karno (Surname Withheld) Ramindjeri Spokesperson," 2014, http://forgottenorigin.com/from-the-beginning-article-by-steven-evan-strong-with-karno-walker-ramindjeri-spokesperson.

[48] Slater, "Personal Letters - Correndspondances - Notes." no. 4.

[49] Ibid. no. 5.

[50] Ibid. no. 8.

Chapter 4:   Australia's Stonehenge Resurrected: Original Elders and Custodians on Site

[1] Ibid. no. 3

[2] Ibid. no. 8.

Dreaming.

[4] Jarmbi'je, 2014. Personal Communication.

[5] Ibid.

[6] Kadaitcha: (or Kurdaitcha/ kurdaitcha/ Cadiche man) is a sorcerer and ritual executioner from Central Australia eg Arrernte people. Punishment may involve death after 'singing' the victim, sometimes a secret object is used to amplify and relay his powers into the body of the lawbreaker e.g. bone, quartz stone.

[7] Jarmbi'je.

[8] Slater, "Personal Letters – Correndspondances – Notes." no. 15.

[9] Ibid. no. 15.

Chapter 5: Australia's Stonehenge may Rewrite World History

[1] Ibid. no. 4.

[2] Ibid. no. 3.

[3] Ibid. no. 3.

[4] Ibid. no. 2.

[5] Ibid. no. 9.

[6] Ibid. no. 2.

[7] Ibid. no. 12.

[8] Ibid. no. 3.

[9] Ibid. no. 3.

[10] Ibid. no. 3.

[11] Ibid. no. 3.

[12] Steven Strong, "Map 1 of Western Slope of Bigger Slope," (2013).

[13] ———, "Map 2: Smaller Mound and Scatter of Sandstone Rocks," (2013).

[14] Slater, "Personal Letters – Correndspondances – Notes." no. 3.

[15] Ibid. no. 3.

[16] Ibid. no. 3.

[17] Ibid. no. 3.

[18] Ibid. no. 3.

[19] Ibid. no. 3.

[20] Ibid. no. 3.

[21] Richard Patterson, "Sandstone "Shaped Stone"," ((Photographer), 2013).

[22] Evan Strong, "Shaped Sandstone Rock 1," ((Photographer), 2013).

[23] ———, "Shaped Sandstone Rock 2," ((Photographer), 2013).

[24] Slater, "Personal Letters – Correndspondances – Notes." no. 3.

[25] Ibid. no. 9.

[26] Steven Strong, "Diagram: Test Trench," (2013).

[27] Evan Strong, "Test Trench," ((Photographer), 2013).

[28] Slater, "Personal Letters – Correndspondances – Notes." no. 15.

[29] Ibid. no. 15.

[30] Ibid. no. 2.

[31] Steven Strong, "Map 3: Gps Placement of Sandstone Rocks," (2013).

[32] Richard Patterson, "Coarse Grain Sandstone Rock," ((Photographer), 2013).

[33] Slater, "Personal Letters – Correndspondances – Notes." no. 5.

[34] Ibid. no. 2.

[35] Ibid. no. 1.

[36] https://www.youtube.com/watch?v=LLRsWdVNKes, "Egyptians in Australia Part 2 – Steven Strong," in Egyptians in Australia (Australia: You Tube, 2012).

[37] Robert Bednarik: (Professor) cognitive archaeologist, prehistorian, prolific writer and rock art specialist.

[38] Josephine Flood, Rock Art of the Dreamtime: Images of Ancient Australia (Sydney, Australia: Angus and Robertson, 1997). 178.

[39] Ibid.

[40] Ibid.

[43] Slater, "Personal Letters – Correndspondances – Notes." no. 7

[44] Ibid. no. 7.

[45] Evan Strong, "Pryamid Rock 1," ((Photographer), 2012).

[46] ———, "Pryamid Rock 2," ((Photographer), 2013).

[47] Slater, "Personal Letters – Correndspondances – Notes." no. 12.

[48] Ibid. no. 15.

[49] Ibid. no. 5

[50] Ibid. no. 8.

[51] Jarmbi'je.

[52] Slater, "Personal Letters – Correndspondances – Notes." 61.

[53] Ibid. no. 8

[54] Ibid. no. 1.

[55] Ibid. no. 4.

[56] Ibid. no. 8.

Chapter 6: The Australian Mother Tongue

[1] Ibid. no. 2.

[2] Ibid. no. 2.

[3] https://www.youtube.com/watch?v=LLRsWdVNKes, "Egyptians in Australia Part 2 – Steven Strong."

[4] Flood, *Rock Art of the Dreamtime*. 178.

[5] Ibid. 178.

[6] Slater, "Personal Letters – Correndspondances – Notes." no. 7.

[7] Ibid. no. 7.

[8] Ibid. no. 12.

[9] Ibid. no. 15.

[10] Ibid. no. 5.

[11] Ibid. no. 8.

[12] Jarmbi'je.

[13] Slater, "Personal Letters – Correndspondances – Notes." no. 8.

[14] Ibid. no. 8.

[15] Ibid. no. 1.

[16] Ibid. no. 4.

[17] Ibid. no. 8.

Chapter 7: On the Boat Again

[1] Steven Strong, "Emu's Nest Rocks," ((Photographer), 2013).

[2] Ibid.

[3] ———, "Emu's Nest Jetty (Diagram)," (2013).

[4] Slater, "Personal Letters – Correndspondances – Notes." no. 8 and 52.

[5] Strong, "Emu's Nest Rocks."

[6] Ibid.

[7] Ibid.

[8] Ibid.

[9] Ibid.

[10] Slater, "Personal Letters – Correndspondances – Notes." no. 8 and 52.

[11] Strong, "Emu's Nest Jetty (Diagram)."

[12] Slater, "Personal Letters – Correndspondances – Notes." no. 12.

[13] Samarah Wood, "Marked and Shaped Rocks," ((Photographer), 2014).

Chapter 8: The Sacred Language of Rocks ·- Fact or Fiction

[1] Slater, "Personal Letters – Correndspondances – Notes." no. 15.

[2] Ibid. no. 3.

[3] Ibid. no. 11.

[4] Ibid. no. 7.

[5] Ibid. o. 16.

[6] Darkinjoong: (Darkinjung) Australian Original Tribe and Lands comprising the Central Coast area of N.S.W. including Gosford, Wyong and the Wollombi.

[7] https://www.youtube.com/watch?v=LLRsWdVNKes, "Egyptians in Australia Part 2 - Steven Strong."

[8] Evan Strong, "Kariong - Bambara Glyphs," ((Photographer), 2013).

[9] Slater, "Personal Letters - Correndspondances - Notes." no. 2.

[10] Ibid. no. 12.

[11] Ibid. no. 14.

[12] Ibid. no. 14.

[13] Ibid. no. 5.

[14] Ibid. no. 2.

[15] Ibid. no. 1.

[16] Ibid. no. 1.

[17] Ibid. no. 2.

[18] Ibid. no. 3.

[19] Ibid. no. 2.

[20] Ibid. no. 2.

[21] Ibid. no. 8.

[22] Ibid. no. 8.

[23] Ibid. no. 2.

[24] Ibid. no. 10.

[25] Ibid. no. 2.

[26] Ibid. no. 19.

[27] ———, "Section F: Ii) Intrepretation of the Drawing at Burraguura and Yango." 14.

[28] ———, "Personal Letters - Correndspondances - Notes." no. 5.

[29] Ibid. no. 5.

[30] Ibid. no. 2

[31] Ibid. no. 1.

[32] Ibid. no. 6.

[33] Ibid. no. 19.

[34] Ibid. no. 6.

[35] Ibid. no. 19.

[36] Ibid. no. 2 and 6.

[37] Ibid. no. 5 and 19.

[38] Ibid. no. 19.

[39] Ibid. no. 1.

[40] Ibid. no. 2.

[41] Ibid. no. 6.

[42] Douglas Herman, "Were Us Astronauts Ordered Not to Report Ufos & Aliens?," rense.com(2006), http://www.rense.com/general70/rep.htm.

[43] Alfred Lambremont Webre, Exopolitics: Poltics, Government and Law in the Universe (Vancouver, B.C. Canada: Universe Books, 2005). 118.

[44] Rick Bonner, "Ufos and the Oval Office: What the President Knows, and Doesn't," no. May 23 (2012), http://www.examiner.com/article/ufos-and-the-oval-office-what-the-president-knows-and-doesn-t.

[45] Ibid.

[46] Ibid.

[47] Kashmira Gander, "Former Canadian Defence Secretary Paul Hellyer Calls on Governments to Reveal Ufo Information," Independant(2015 [20th April]), http://www.independent.co.uk/news/world/americas/former-canadian-defence-secretary-paul-hellyer-calls-on-governments-to-reveal-ufo-information-10190024.html.

[48] Ibid.

Chapter 9: Comspiracy: the Man who was, Then Wasn't

[4] ———, "Aboriginal Rock Carving: To the Editor of the Herald." 14.

[5] Ibid.

[6] Ibid.

[7] ———, "Personal Letters - Correndspondances - Notes." no. 1.

[8] ———, "Aboriginal Rock Carving: To the Editor of the Herald." 14.

[9] Ibid.

[10] Ibid.

[11] ———, "Personal Letters - Correndspondances - Notes." no. 1.

[12] Ibid. no. 2.

[13] Ibid. no. 2.

[14] Ibid. no. 2.

[15] Ibid. no. 2.

[16] Ibid. no. 4.

[17] Ibid. no. 4.

[18] Ibid. no. 4.

[19] Ibid. no. 4.

[20] Ibid. no. 4.

[21] Ibid. no. 4.

[22] Ibid. no. 4.

[23] Ibid. no. 5.

[24] Ibid. no. 5.

[25] Ibid. no. 5.

[26] Ibid. no. 6.

[27] Ibid. no. 7.

[28] Ibid. no. 9.

[29] Ibid. no. 9.

[30] Ibid. no. 9.

[31] Ibid. no. 12.

[32] Ibid. no. 12.

[33] Ibid. no. 12.

[34] Ibid. no. 19.

[35] Ibid. no. 19.

[36] Ibid. no. 19.

[37] Ibid. no. 12.

Chapter 10:" Stones that talk"

[1] Ibid. no. 4.

[2] Ibid. no. 4.

[3] Ibid. no. 4.

[4] Michael Tellinger: researcher, historian, writer, scientist and politician of Ubuntu Party in South Africa (Presidential candidate). See http://michaeltellinger.com/

[5] Blombos Cave Rocks: refers to incised patterns and designs that are on chunks and pieces of iron ore stone ochre, they have been dated from 75,000 to 100,00 years (BP). Blombos Cave is in South Africa about 300km east of Cape Town near the coast. For more Info: Tim Jones, "100,000 Year-Old Incised Orchre Found at Blombos Cave," *Anthropology.net: Beyond bones and stones* 12 June(2009: 12th June), http://anthropology.net/2009/06/12/100000-year-old-incised-ochre-found-at-blombos-cave/.

[6] Ironstone: a sedimentary rock bearing a large portion of iron, ore is extracting from this.

[7] Evan Strong, "Ros' Rock No. 1," ((Photographer), 2014).

[8] Sergio Prostak, "Engraved Stone Dating Back 30,000 Years Found in China," *Sci-News.com* Dec. 1st(2012), http://www.sci-news.com/archaeology/article00755.html.

[9] Ibid.

[10] Cyclons: stone implement/tool that is cylindrical- conical in its shape/appearance.

Chapter 11: Ros' Rock 1, the "Mystery" is Officially Solved: "Nothing to do with Aboriginal (sic) People."

[1] Professor X, 2014. Personal Communication. To Steven & Evan Strong. (Name withheld).

[2] Jane, 2014. Personal Communication. To Ros Mulder. (Name withheld replace with Jane).

[3] Wood, "Marked and Shaped Rocks."

[4] Jane.

[5] Ibid.

[6] Ibid.

[7] Ibid.

[8] Ros Mulder, 2014. Personal Communication. To Steven & Evan Strong.

[9] Ibid.

[10] Jane.

[11] Ibid.

[12] Ibid.

[13] X.

[14] Wood, "Marked and Shaped Rocks."

[15] Richard Gabriel and Judith Ann: researchers especially of photos and author of *Echoes of the Chamber*. See http://www.richardgabriel.info/.

[16] X.

[17] Ibid.

[18] Jane.

Chapter 12: " I have no Idea how the marks were made"

[1] X.

[2] Wood, "Marked and Shaped Rocks."

[3] Jane.

[4] Ibid.

[5] X.

[6] Lascaux: UNESCO World Heritage site of Paleolithic cave paintings mainly of animals dated up tp 20,000 years ago and is located in southwestern France.

[7] Calgary Rock: see Figure 51 and Dr. Derek Cunningham, "Calgary Stone Analysis by Dr Derek Cunningham (Diagram)," (2014).

[8] X.

[9] Ibid.

[10] Ibid.

[11] Ibid.

[12] Ibid.

[13] Ibid.

[14] Ibid.

[15] Steven Strong, "Ros' Rock No. 1: 3 Sides (Diagram)," (2014).

[16] Dr Derek Cunningham: Published author – researcher ("*Long Journey 400,000 years of Stone Age Science*"). Dr Derek combines archaeology, astronomy, cartography and language-scripts in his research see: http://www.midnightsciencejournal.com/.

Chapter 13: Chert by Chert: Ros' Rock No. 2

[1] Wood, "Marked and Shaped Rocks."

[2] Ibid.

[3] Ibid.

[4] Slater, "Personal Letters – Correndspondances – Notes." no. 8.

[5] Ibid. 52.

[6] Ibid. 52.

[7] Ibid. no. 8.

[8] Evan Strong, "Ros' Rocks No. 1 and 2," ((Photographer), 2014).

Chapter 14: United we Stand, Rock By Rock

[1] ———, "Assorted Marked and Shaped Rocks," ((Photographer), 2015).

[2] Wood, "Marked and Shaped Rocks."

[3] Ibid.

[4] Ibid.

[5] Dr. Derek Cunningham, "Dr Derek Cunningham's Analysis of Ros' Rock No. 1," (Evan Strong (Photographer), 2014).

[6] Jock Doubleday, "Comparision of Ros' Rock No. 1 and Bosnian Astronomical Stone," (Jock Doubleday, Evan Strong (Photographer) 2015).

[7] Jock Doubleday: Videographer and Acting Public Relations Director for Archaeological Park: Bosnian Pyramid of the Sun Foundation see http://anamericaninbosnia.blogspot.com.au/

[8] Semir Sam Osmanagich: (Dr) "is Bosnian-born Houston (USA) resident author, researcher and businessman. He discovered an ancient pyramid complex in Visoko, Bosnia-Herzegovina consisting, to date, of ten artificial structures: the Bosnian Pyramid of the Sun, the Bosnian Pyramid of the Moon, the Bosnian Pyramid of Love, the Bosnian Pyramid of the Dragon, the Temple of Mother Earth, Vratnica Tumulus, Dolovi Tumulus, Ginje Tumulus, KTK Tunnel, and Ravne Tunnel Labyrinth. He has established non-profit and non-government "Archaeological Park: Bosnian Pyramid of the Sun" Foundation to pursue the excavation and geo-archaeological work. He teaches at the American University in Bosnia-Herzegovina as Anthropology professor, in particular Bosnian megalithic sites." From: "Dr.Sci Sam Semir Osmanagich, Phd.," http://www.semirosmanagic.com/en/.

[9] http://piramidasunca.ba/eng/home-en.html?view=featured

[10] Dr. Derek Cunningham, "Bosnian Astronomical Stone Analysis by Dr Derek Cunningham," (Jock Doubleday (Photographer), 2015).

[11] Cunningham, "Calgary Stone Analysis by Dr Derek Cunningham (Diagram)."

[12] ———, "Dr Derek Cunningham's Analysis of Ros' Rock No. 1."

[13] Hugh Cairns and Bill Yidumbuma, *Dark Sparklers*, 2nd ed. (Merimbula, Australia: H.C. Cairnes, 2004). 42.

Chapter15: Ros' Rock 4 and 5, Equals one Rock Without Equal

[1] Strong, "Assorted Marked and Shaped Rocks."

[2] Ibid.

[3] Navajo Squatting Man Constellation: *Hastin Sik'ai'ii* (Man with Firm stance with Legs Ajar) Located in Corvus. and " the constellation is representive of solidarity, strength and the continuity of cycles. At the same time it stands for the parting of the seasons between summer and winter." From Dr Nancy D. Maryboy, *A Guide to Navajo Astronomy*, A Collection of Curricula for the Starlab Navajo Skies Cyclinder (Bluff, Utah USA: Indigenous Earth Institute, 2004). 11.

[4] Chert: "is a microcrystalline or cryptocrystalline sedimentary rock material composed of silicon dioxide (SiO2). It occurs as nodules, concretionary masses and as layered deposits. Chert breaks with a conchoidal fracture, often producing very sharp edges. Early people took advantage of how chert breaks and used it to fashion cutting tools and weapons." From Geology.com, "Chert: What Is Chert, How Does It Form and What Is It Used For," http://geology.com/rocks/chert.shtml.

[5] Dr John G. Brynes, 2016. Personal Communication via email: Silcrete Information.

[6] Silcrete: " is a tool stone of good quality; it was extensively used for knapping at various periods in Southern Africa, Western Europe and Australia ... stone knappers did not content themselves with the naturally available silcrete types but began to transform their properties by heat treatment". From Universtitat De Barcelona, "Heat Treatment of Silcrete. Patrick Schmidt: Synopsis," 3rd Nov.(2015: 3rd Nov.), http://www.ub.edu/ubtv/en/video/heat-treatment-of-silcrete-patrick-schmidt.

[7] Patrick Schmidt: (Dr) University Tuebingen (Germany), specialties archeology, geology and mineralogy.

[8] Barcelona, "Heat Treatment of Silcrete. Patrick Schmidt: Synopsis."

[9] Dr. Andy I. R. Herries: (assoc. Professor) Archaeophysics and Palaeoscience La Trobe University (Melbourne, Australia).

[10] Dr Andy I.R. Herries, "Hot Rocks, Shells and Red Earth – the Origins of Modern Human Behaviour in South Africa" (paper presented at the The Castlereagh Talks: Some talks about the past, Upper Castlereagh, 2009: 5th Sept.).

[11] Strong, "Assorted Marked and Shaped Rocks."
[12] Ibid.

Chapter 16: Ros' Rock 10: the First Hybrid

[1] Herbert Basedow:(Dr) anthropologist, geologist, medical practitioner and politician. Basedow complied Original languages, life and customs, was a prolific photographer and a campaigner for Original rights. For more information see: http://adb.anu.edu.au/biography/basedow-herbert-5151
[2] Strong, "Assorted Marked and Shaped Rocks."
[3] Ibid.
[4] Slater, "Personal Letters - Correndspondances - Notes." no. 12.
[5] Natalie Jacqueline Paez, "Marked and Shaped Rocks," (Third Eye Society (Photographer), 2015).

Chapter 17: "All Found Together..."

[1] Ros Mulder, "Marked Rocks Note," (2015).
[2] Ibid.
[3] Ibid.
[4] Paez, "Marked and Shaped Rocks."
[5] Ibid.
[6] Evan Strong, "New Marked Rocks and Cyclons," ((Photographer), 2016).
[7] Paez, "Marked and Shaped Rocks."
[8] Ibid.
[9] Steven Strong, "Ros' Rock No. 21 (Diagram)," (2015).
[10] Paez, "Marked and Shaped Rocks."

Chapter 18: Stones That "speak with the voice of Malu"

[1] James Cowan, Messengers of the Gods: Tribal Elders Reveal the Ancient Wisdom of the Earth (Milsons Point, NSW: Vintage Books, 1993). 52.
[2] Yidaki: Original name for the Australia Original musical instrument the Didgeridoo.
[3] James Cowan: Internationally acclaimed writer and literary award winner.
[4] Cowan, Messengers of the Gods: Tribal Elders Reveal the Ancient Wisdom of the Earth. Front Cover.
[5] Ibid. 52.
[6] Ibid.
[7] Tomog Zogo: oracle/ divination shrine.
[8] Cowan, Messengers of the Gods: Tribal Elders Reveal the Ancient Wisdom of the Earth. 52.
[9] Ibid. 54.
[10] Ibid.
[11] Mer: (Murijingalong or Murray Island) found in the Torres Strait Islands and populated by the Australia Original Meriam People.
[12] Cowan, Messengers of the Gods: Tribal Elders Reveal the Ancient Wisdom of the Earth. 54.
[13] Malu: the God of Mer Island and one of the four northern creation brothers that settled in the Central and Eastern portions of the Torres Strait Islands.
[14] Cowan, Messengers of the Gods: Tribal Elders Reveal the Ancient Wisdom of the Earth. 54.
[15] Ibid. 55.
[16] Ibid.
[17] Ibid. 56.
[18] Ibid.
[19] Ibid.
[20] Ibid.
[21] Ibid.
[22] Ibid.
[23] Ibid.
[24] Ibid. 57.

[25] Ibid. 54.
[26] Ibid.
[27] https://www.youtube.com/watch?v=uX2P8utjk3A, "Michael Tellinger – Stones That Ring Like Bells," in *Michael Tellinger – Uncovering the Truth*, ed. Michael Tellinger (South Africa: You Tube, 2010).
[28] Strong, "New Marked Rocks and Cyclons."
[29] Ibid.
[30] David Smith and Ros Mulder, 2015. Marked Rocks Note (Magic).
[31] Ibid.
[32] Berndt and Berndt: (Married research team) Ronald Murray Berndt (Professor) writer, social anthropologist and advocate of Original rights, recognition and people. Catherine Helen Berndt (Dr) anthropologist, monograph publisher and art collector.
[33] Smith and Mulder.
[34] Neil Howe, 2015. Personal Communication.
[35] Ibid.
[36] Ibid.
[37] Ibid.
[38] Uncle Marbuck, 2015. Personal Communication: Analysis of Marked Rocks.
[39] Ibid.
[40] Strong, "Assorted Marked and Shaped Rocks."
[41] Marbuck.
[42] Slater, "Personal Letters – Correndspondances – Notes." no. 19.
[43] Cowan, *Messengers of the Gods: Tribal Elders Reveal the Ancient Wisdom of the Earth.* 96.

Chapter 19: " Long Before True"

[1] Kate Nesbit, 2014. Personal Communication.
[2] Graham Walsh: photographer, author and technical officer for NPWS (National Parks and Wildlife Service), expert on Original rock art and figure of some controversy.
[3] Michael Winkler, "Rock Star of the Kimberley," *The Age*(20 Sept. 2004), http://www.theage.com.au/articles/2004/09/17/1095394002333.html?from=storyrhs.
[4] Seven Sisters: A Dreaming Story that is spread throughout all Tribal estates in Australia. There is very little variation in the narrative and it is agreed that the Seven Sisters represent the Pleiades and some form of contact between these beings and the Original people occured.
[5] Steven Strong, "P.N.G. Statue and Rock Artefact," ((Photographer), 2014).
[6] Nesbit.
[7] Strong, "P.N.G. Statue and Rock Artefact."
[8] Ecuadorian Pre-Columbian Artifacts, Catalogue No. 2008.34.2-.3 and .6. Photograph by B. Bernard. Courtesy of the Maxwell Museum of Anthropology, University of New Mexico.
[9] Aunty Beve, 2014. Personal Communication.
[10] Ibid.
[11] Evan Strong, "Ufo Glyph at Bambara," ((Photographer), 2013).
[12] Klaus Dona: spiritual archaeologist/researcher and art exhibition curator for the Habsburg Museum in Vienna.
[13] Beve.
[14] Evan Strong, "Cave of the Golden Boomerang," ((Photographer), 2011).
[15] Bradshaws (Gwion Gwion): refers to controversial paintings of a certain style (human figures with ornaments and accessories) found within the Kimberley region of north-western Australia.
[16] Strong, "Cave of the Golden Boomerang."
[17] Steven Strong, "Cave of the Golden Boomerang (Diagram)," (2012).
[18] Gionna Di Gravio (Interviewee), Carol Duncan (Presenter), and Jeanette McMahon (Producer), "The Antiquities of the Wollombi District," *News from Cultural Collections, UON Library at the University of Newcastle Australia* 16th Feb(2009), https://uoncc.wordpress.com/category/aborigines/aboriginal-rock-art/. Monday 16th Feb.
[19] Ibid.
[20] Slater, "Aboriginal Rock Carving: To the Editor of the Herald." 14.
[21] ———, "Personal Letters – Correndspondances – Notes." no. 6.

[22] Biamie/ Baiame / Bhaiame: Sky Father/All Father came from the skies to create the lands, give laws and culture etc then returned to the skies. The creator Sky-Hero for many Original Nations of south-eastern NSW.

[23] Mount Yengo: 668m in height, in lower hunter valley NSW. Of paramount spiritual significance as this is where Baiame, after creating everything, returned to the skies by stepping on this spot the top of the mountain was flattened.

[24] Evan Strong, "Mount Yengo," ((Photographer), 2014).

[25] Slater, "Section F: Ii) Intrepretation of the Drawing at Burraguura and Yango."12.

[26] Ibid. 13.

[27] Ibid. 13.

[28] Ibid. 13.

[29] Ibid. 12.

[30] Mundowa: " spirit pads.... He who came from on high brought life into the world." From ———, "Personal Letters - Correndspondances - Notes." no. 19. The footprint of a single leg- being Bhaiame's.

[31] ———, "Section F: Ii) Intrepretation of the Drawing at Burraguura and Yango." 12.

[32] Ibid. 12.

[33] ———, "Personal Letters - Correndspondances - Notes." no. 6.

[34] Mulla Mulla: consort/wife of Baiame.

[35] Slater, "Section F: Ii) Intrepretation of the Drawing at Burraguura and Yango." 13.

[36] Ibid. 12.

[37] Boobardy: one of two men, that were made by Baiame, means Father.

[38] Slater, "Section F: Ii) Intrepretation of the Drawing at Burraguura and Yango." 11-12.

[39] Ibid. 12.

[40] Ibid. 14.

[41] Karno, 2015. Personal Communication. (Surname Withheld).

[42] Slater, "Personal Letters - Correndspondances - Notes." no. 6.

Conclusion: What Will Come To Pass?

[1] W.D. Campbell, "Aboriginal Carvings of Port Jackson and Broken Bay," in *Memoirs of the Geological Survey of New South Wales: Enthological Series no. 1* (Sydney: Department of Mines and Agriculture, 1898). 68 and Plate 27: Fig 6.

[2] David Unaipon: (David Ngunaitponi) preacher, writer, ballistics expert, Original rights campaigner and inventor (shearing machine, centrifugal motor, multi-radial wheel, perpetual motion and helicopter).

[3] "David Unaipon," https://en.wikipedia.org/wiki/David_Unaipon.

[4] David Unaipon, *Legendary Tales of the Australian Aborigines*, ed. Stephen Muecke and Adam Shoemaker (Carlton South, Victoria: The Miegunyah Press: Melbourne University Press, 2001). 189-209.

[5] Ibid. 189.

[6] Ibid.

[7] Ibid.

[8] Ibid.

[9] Ibid.

[10] Ibid.

[11] Nephilim: the giant offspring of The Watchers (Grigori- Fallen Angels) and human women, also described as being around in the pre-flood times and being powerful and well known.

[12] Dunghutti: Australian Original Nation from the mid-north coast area of NSW incorporating Kempsey, Macleay River valley and Oxley Wild River areas.

[13] Anne Wilson Schaef, *Native Wisdom for White Minds: Daily Reflections Inspired by the Native Peoples of the Now World* (Milsons Point, Australia: Random House Australia Pty Ltd, 1995). June 10.

[14] Beve.

[15] George W. MacRae, trans. and Douglas M. Parrott ed., "The Apocalypse of Adam (V,5)," in *The Nag Hammadi Library in English*, ed. James M. Robinson (New York, N.Y.: HarperSanFrancisco, 1990). 279 (Verse 64).

[16] Ibid.

[17] Ibid.

[18] Ibid.

[19] Slater, "Personal Letters - Correndspondances - Notes." no. 2 and 6.

[20] Ibid. no. 19.

[21] Nesbit.

Index